THE UNITED-INDEPENDENT COMPENSATORY CODE/SYSTEM/CONCEPT

A TEXTBOOK/WORKBOOK
FOR THOUGHT, SPEECH, AND/OR ACTION,
FOR VICTIMS OF *RACISM
[*WHITE SUPREMACY]

"If you do not understand White Supremacy (Racism) —— what it is, and how it works —— everything else that you understand, will only confuse you."

Neely Fuller Jr. [1971]

PRODUCED: 1957 - 1980

CONTENTS
AND
GENERAL SUBJECT INDEX

NOTE: To expedite production, this textbook-workbook is presented in basic-draft manuscript form [typed].

This Contents and General Subject Index includes a limited listing of topics. **There is no end-of-book index.** All material in this work is closely inter-related. Some material presented in one place may **appear** to contradict, or not coincide with, material presented in another place. A substantial number of suggestions presented in one place, may appear in another place. Some viewpoints expressed in one area of activity, may be repeated in another area of activity.

It is best for a person to read this work thoughtfully, and carefully, **and to read it, at least once, in it's entirety.** By so doing, the reader of this work can better understand the **overall purpose** for the production of this book, as well as develop a more detailed understanding of how to **best use** the concepts presented. Also, it is important that the "Compensatory-Functional Definitions" section of this work should be referred to often. Each definition of each word, or term, [should] be understood, and thought of as to how each one can best be used to reveal truth, promote justice, promote correctness, and/or compensate for the effects of Racism [eliminate Racism].

Contents And General Subject Index

<u>Contents And General Subject Index [Continued]</u>

Contents And General Subject Index [Continued]

Contents And General Subject Index [Continued]

Contents And General Subject Index [Continued]

Contents And General Subject Index [Continued]

Contents And General Subject Index [Continued]

Contents And General Subject Index [Continued]

Contents And General Subject Index [Continued]

Contents And General Subject Index [Continued]

THE PURPOSE OF THIS BOOK

- To present material, in book form, which can be used as a basic guide for those individual non-white persons who are the Victims of Racism (Victims of White Supremacy), and who may wish to think, speak, and/or act to eliminate Racism (White Supremacy), and do so, not as a "formalized group", but as **individual persons.**

  [This means that an individual non-white person who is the **victim** of Racism can pick, choose, and support through **individual** thought, speech, and/or action, **only** those parts of the book which he or she, as an **individual person** "sees fit" to support, through his or her individual thought, speech, and/or action].

- To present material, in book form, which can be used as a **start** for a "complete" code of thought, speech, and/or action for Victims of Racism [non-white people], which when promoted by an effective number of **individual** Victims of Racism, will result in a "collective" **effect** against Racism.

- To present material, in book form, which may serve as a basic guide and/or general format for the **making of other books** which can serve as a compliment, and/or supplement, to the "codified", and/or systematic concept of eliminating Racism (White Supremacy) through the thought, speech, and/or action of **individual persons,** by their **own will,** at a time and place of their **own choosing.**

- To help any and all persons to know and/or understand truth, and to use truth in such manner as to produce justice and correctness at all times, in all places, in all areas of activity.

- To explain the necessity of eliminating functional Racism **before** attempting to make any other major changes in the socio-material activities of the people of the known universe, and to function as a general guide toward doing so.

  This is **not** a book to be used to promote dislike or hatred for white people.

  This is **not** a book to be used to encourage animosity toward white people or to promote a dislike for white people because of their "whiteness", and/or because they appear to be "White" to the eye/mind of the onlooker.

This is not a book to be used to embarrass, belittle, nit-pick, poke fun at, or otherwise show "disrespect" for **any** people, be they "White", "Black", "Brown", "Red", "Yellow", Blond", "Brunette", etc.

This book is not designed to be used to **basically oppose** any people **except** those persons racially classified as "White"--and **only** those persons so classified, who are responsible for establishing, maintaining, expanding, and/or refining the practice of White Supremacy (Racism), in any one or more areas of activity, including economics, education, entertainment, labor, law, politics, religion, sex, and/or war.

This book, when correctly used, will help to promote thought, speech, and/or action, specifically designed to help reveal truth, promote justice, **and** promote correctness.

The **ultimate** purpose of this book and/or any of it's parts, is to help to produce "**peace**".

■ HOW TO USE THIS BOOK ■

1. **Think** seriously about everything that you read herein.

2. **Speak,** and/or **act, ONLY** in support of those observations and/or acts that **you** believe will help most to do the following:

- Reveal truth.
- Produce justice.
- Produce correctness.

■ STATEMENT OF INTENT ■

To the best of my knowledge and understanding, the basic-initial requirement for establishing justice among the people of the known universe is to [first], eliminate the practice of Racism (White Supremacy).

All persons in the known universe, both "skilled" and "unskilled" who have attempted to establish justice, and/or who have attempted to eliminate Racism, have, so far failed.

Therefore, as a Victim of Racism, and as one who is both subject to, and a participant in, the overall support of injustice, I intend to use what knowledge and understanding that has been given me, to help develop the correct procedures for eliminating racism, and producing justice.

-Neely Fuller Jr. (1/0)
July 23, 1982

INTRODUCTORY NOTES

AND

GENERAL WRITINGS RELATIVE TO

RACISM AND THE LAW OF COMPENSATION

Racism: A Basic Perspective

The matter sometimes referred to as the "race problem", is the **basic-initial** "unfinished business" among the people of the known universe.

Therefore it is not possible to **effectively** speak and/or act to eliminate **any** major problem that involves people without **first** eliminating the problem of racism, in every area of activity, including economics, education, entertainment, labor, law, politics, religion, sex, and war.

In order to do this, it is necessary for victims of racism [non-white people], in effective numbers, to know and understand who the racists are, how they function, and for what **ultimate** purpose.

The victims of racism must also know and understand how the power of the racists (to practice racism) can be nullified and/or eliminated, by victims of racism, speaking and/or acting as **individual persons.**

Racism: Some Initial Questions

Why race?

What makes racism so important as a problem?

Are there not other problems among the people of the world that are much greater?

What about the problems of unemployment, housing, food shortages, health care, robbery, and laziness?

What about tribalism and sexism?

What about the confusion that exists in the area of religion?

What about capitalism, and communism, and drugs, and alcohol, and ignorance, and pollution, and lying politicians?

Why race?

Is it not narrow-minded to see racism as the major evil? Did not other evils exist long before the practice of racism?

What about the problems of distrust, and greed, and envy, and murder, among **non**-white people as well as white?

What about economics? Why not see to it that everyone is adequately fed and housed **first?**

Why not work to establish a system that guarantees that **every** person will be comfortable and protected--regardless of color, or non-color?

Why not reach for a greater goal? Why not eliminate the problems of distrust, greed, envy, and murder among **all** people?

Why single out the "race" issue as being more important than any of the other problems that continue to plague the people of the known universe?

Why continue to be bogged down in endless squabbles about conflict between white people and black people?

Why not eliminate the other major problems, and, by doing so, through that process, dismantle the "need" for people to practice racism?

Why not have the **smartest** people of goodwill, regardless of color, or sex, or age, come together and solve the **real** problems of the world instead of wasting time with what is really an artificial barrier?

Racism: Some Initial Answers

Two Facts:

(1) The **white** people of the known universe, are collectively, the smartest, **and** the most capable, of **all** people, and,

(2) The **white supremacists** (racists) are the smartest, and the most capable of **all** the white people.

Of all the people of the known universe--both white and non-white--those white people who practice racism (white supremacy) have the **greatest ability** to use truth, and to use it in such manner as to produce justice and correctness, in all places, in all areas of activity, in the shortest period of time.

The white people who practice racism know that they could, if they **chose** to do so, produce justice and correctness among the people of the known universe. They are smart enough to do this. They also know, however, that in the **process** of producing justice and correctness, they would also eliminate white supremacy (racism). Knowing this, they have chosen **not** to produce justice and correctness. They prefer to continue to practice white supremacy, though they fully understand that in order to practice white supremacy they must do so by promoting **falsehood, non-justice,** and **incorrectness.** They apparently have judged that white supremacy is better than revealing truth. They apparently believe that the value of white supremacy is at least as "valuable" as the practice of justice and correctness. To them, the promotion of white supremacy **has proven** to be, in many respects, "better" than justice, and "better" than correctness.

The white supremacists (racists) have a **total** need to be, and to feel, supreme over **all** non-white people, at **all** times. This supremacy is what they value most, though they know that it can only be maintained by promoting falsehood, non-justice, and incorrectness. Through the skilled use of deceit, direct violence, and/or the threat of direct or indirect violence, the masters of racism (white supremacists) have chosen to continue this practice for no apparent basic reason than to be "proud" of themselves for causing others to be fearful of them, and/or to be dependent upon them. Such a relationship is non-just and incorrect. This is not the way that [any] people should relate to each other.

Those white people who practice white supremacy should stop doing so. They should strive to become **wise** instead of being satisfied with being "smart". The knowledge and understanding that they possess is a **gift**. That gift should not be wasted on what is fundamentally an ego-producing enterprise. It is incorrect to squander the gift of knowledge and understanding on the promotion of racism. All knowledge and all understanding should be used to produce a universe in which no people--white or non-white--abuse each other. The basic duty of each and every person in the known universe is to find truth, and to use truth in such manner as to produce justice, and correctness, at **all** times, in **all** places, in **all** areas of activity.

In practice, there is no other way for any person in the known universe to "justify" his or her existence.

Explanation of the Law of Compensation:

Question: What is meant by the term "compensation"?

Compensation is a law.
Compensation is a law of "nature".
Compensation is a law of existence.
Compensation is a law of mathematics.
Compensation is the **"law of laws".**

Every **thought** is a compensatory thought.
Every **word** is a compensatory word.
Every **act** is a compensatory act.

A person compensates for his or her lack of ability by relying on the ability of other persons or things.

A "people" compensate for their "weakness" by depending on the "strength" of other people, or things.

One who tills the soil is compensated by the fruit of the soil.

A microscope compensates for the limitations of the eye. So does candle light.. So does electric light.

Light compensates for dark, and dark compensates for light. Heat compensates for cold, and cold compensates for heat. Sound compensates for silence, and silence compensates for sound. Existence compensates for non-existence, and non-existence compensates for existence. "Death" compensates for "life", and "life" compensates for "death".

A flying machine compensates for a person's physical inability to fly.

Writing is a compensatory process used to make up for limitations in knowledge and/or memory.

A **school** is a compensatory process through which compensatory thoughts, words, and/or deeds are transferred between persons, plants, animals, etc.

"Religion" is a compensatory **system.**

Production of off-spring is a compensatory **act.**

Money is a compensatory **tool.**

To eat is to compensate.
To sleep is to compensate.
To walk is to compensate.
To talk is to compensate.
To breathe is to compensate.
To cry is to compensate.
To ride is to compensate.
To work is to compensate.
To play is to compensate.

There is no such thing as "**over**-compensation".
There is no such thing as "**under**-compenation".
There is no such thing as "**partial**-compensation".
There is no such thing as "**degrees** of compensation".

Compensation either **is** [compensation] or it **isn't** [compensation].

The law of compensation is applicable to all that is in the known universe.

__Special Note__:

It is important to know and understand that the word "compensation" is, at best, a word that can be used to describe a ["compensatory"] condition that does exist, and/or a [compensatory"] "desire" for a condition that does not exist, and/or has never existed.

The use of the word "compensation", may or may not, sometimes, promote contradiction and/or confusion.

For that reason, both the word and the "concept" of "compensation", should, like all other words and "concepts", be used to reveal truth, **and** produce **justice** and **correctness.**

<u>Explanation of Racism as Related to the Law of Compensation:</u>

Question: How does the law of compensation relate to Racism?

Within the vastness of a phenomenon commonly known as "space", there exists a phenomenon commonly known as the "universe".

Within the "Universe" there exists numerous bodies of massed materials of various sizes and shapes which are situated at various "distances" in their relationship to each other. Upon, and/or within some of these massed materials exist things which have been commonly referred to as "plant life" and "animal life".

Some of this "animal life" is commonly referred to as "human beings", and/or, "people".

None of these "people" are **exactly alike** in the way that they **are.**

None of these people are **exactly alike** in the way that they **think.**

None of these people are **exactly alike** in the way that they **appear** to other people. Because none of these people are exactly alike in the way that they are, none are exactly alike in the way that they think, and none are exactly alike in the way that they appear to other people, some of the people, sometimes "treat" some of the other people in a "different" way. The difference in treatment between people is always a result based on a difference in thinking that exists among people. The difference in the thinking of some people sometimes causes differences in the treatment of other people, based on the difference in the thoughts of people as regards the "size", "shape", "height", "weight", "color", "complexion", "general presentation", "general state of being", of people and/or **parts** of people or persons. Ofttimes some people are treated in an unjust manner, by other people, on the basis of "color", and/or, on the basis of factors which some people regard as being "associated" with "color", and/or an "idea" of color.

When people are treated "unjustly", they are deprived of, and/or denied access to, something of "value" to which they are entitled.

When people are deprived of, and/or denied access to something of value to which they are entitled, it is correct for them to **ask for that to which they are entitled.**

When people **ask** for that to which they are entitled, and are **refused,** they are then entitled to compensation.

When people ask for compensation from **others**, and are refused that compensation, they must then acquire compensation for **themselves** through their own efforts.

When people seek to acquire compensation for themselves through their own efforts, they must establish a **"Compensatory System"** to use as a basic guide for thought, speech and/or action.

When people form, and function through, a "Compensatory System" they should base that system on some form of compensatory "Code" which is especially designed to help serve the "needs" of people according to their "Status" and/or "Classification".

Most people of the known universe "classify" themselves as being **individual persons.**

Most people of the known universe "classify" themselves, and/or **are** classified by **other** people, as being members of a "Group", and/or as members of a combination of interrelated and/or associated "Groups", on a basis of "Language", Customs", "Religion and/or Philosophy", Economics", "Color", etc.

Some people of the known universe **have classified themselves** on the basis of the "Non-Color" ("White"). These people call themselves "White People" and/or "Caucasian".

Some people of the known universe **have been classified** on the basis of the "Color(s)" ("Non-White"). These people are generally referred to as being "Black", "Brown", "Red", and "Yellow" and/or collectively, as being "Non-White People".

Other people of the known universe may, or may not be, or may, or may not, **have been** classified by other labels.

Those people of the known universe who have classified themselves as "White" people and/or "Caucasian", and/or as members of the White Race, and who are in **need** of compensation, are, should be, or have been, provided with compensatory "Codes" which are designed to serve the "Needs" of "White" and/or "Caucasian" people. Those people of the known universe who have been classified as "non-white" people, and who are in need of compensation, are, should be, or have been, provided with compensatory "Codes" which are designed to serve the "needs" of "non-white" people.

Any "other" people of the known universe who may be classified by other labels, and are in need of compensation, should be provided with compensatory "codes" which are designed to serve the "needs" of those "other" people who are classified according to those "other" labels.

The "needs" of **all** people are best served when their thought, speech, and action is promoted through the adoption of correct [compensatory] "codes".

No "code", however, should be used to promote falsehood, non-justice, or incorrectness. All "codes" should help to produce justice and correctness.

<u>Some Questions and Answers Relative to "Racial" Compensation</u>

What is the "statute of limitations" on justice?

> There is no "statute of limitations" on justice.
> No matter when, or where, **non**-justice exists,
> it should be immediately replaced with justice.

How does the Law of Compensation relate to "color"?

> All color, "shades" of color, or absence of color, is "neutral".
>
> There is no such thing as a so-called "right" color or "wrong" color.
>
> All known color, "shades" of color, or absence of color, have a correct claim to existence.
>
> It is **incorrect** to either "hate" or "love" color, "shades" of color, or absence of color.
>
> The action toward, and/or re-action to, color, "shades" of color, or absence of color, by people, is always determined by the way people "see" themselves in relation to all people, places, things, etc.
>
> To **recognize** and/or **acknowledge** the differences in "color", "shades" of color, or absence of color, in the appearance, and/or in the essence of people, animals, plants, etc., is **correct.**
>
> To treat people, animals, plants, etc., **unjustly,** and/or **incorrectly,** by utilizing factors "associated with" differences of color, shades of color, or absence of color, is to contribute to one of the major reasons for the absence of "peace" in the known universe.

General Notes Relative to Racism and the Law of Compensation

If a **system** produces injustice, then the **rules** that maintain the system are **incorrect,** even though these **same** rules, if used to maintain a **just** system, would be correct rules.

White Supremacy (Racism) is an incorrect system, that promotes injustice. Any person who willfully helps to establish, maintain, expand, and/or refine a condition of White Supremacy, and/or, who does, does not, at all times, strive to speak and/or act against this condition, is a **criminal**, and/or an **agent** of criminals.

All "comforts" that come to any white person as a direct or indirect result of the practice of White Supremacy (Racism) are "comforts" **unjustly received.**

All persons [white] who directly or indirectly practice White Supremacy are **equal to each other** in that practice. This is true because each individual act of Racism is interrelated with all other acts of Racism. This means that all white persons who practice Racism in **any** form, are equally as guilty as those white persons who practice Racism in **all forms.** Racist Man and Racist Woman, by functioning as the White Nation (White Supremacists, collectively) and by acting to maintain, expand, and/or refine the existence of Racism, have, more than any other creatures in the known universe, "violated" the "natural" Law of Compensation. By doing so, they have deliberately forced and/or directed all other creatures--particularly non-white people--to do the same.

Facts About the United-Independent Compensatory Code/System/Concept

The term "United-Independent Compensatory Code/System/Concept" refers to the **basic** means **through** which the people of the known universe, as **individual persons**, think, speak, and/or act, in order to compensate for those things which they, as **individual persons**, judge to be **missing**, that they have judged to be of value.

When pertinent to those people of the known universe who are the Victims of Racism (Victims of White Supremacy), each of the words used in the term, mean the following:

- The word "United", as used here, means that the Victims of Racism who choose to be "United", are "United" in regards to their **thoughts** as to the **need** to resist, and/or elimiate Racism (White Supremacy).

- The word "Independent", as used here, means that each and every **individual** Victim of Racism is, at all times, in all places, in all areas of activity, "Independent" in regards to his or her **choice of methods** used to resist and/or eliminate Racism (White Supremacy). This means that **no person**, white or non-white, has the just and **correct** "Authority" to **force**, and/or **command**, any Victim of Racism, to adopt **any** means of speaking and/or acting against Racism (White Supremacy) other than the means that the **individual** Victim chooses for him, or her, **self.**

- The word "Compensatory", as used here, means to "make-up" for that which is **missing**--namely, the revelation of truth, and the use of truth, in such manner as to promote justice and correctness.

  Justice and correctness is missing among the people of the known universe because the people of the known universe are dominated by, and/or tolerant of, the Racists (White Supremacists). It is the Racists who, in order to maintain the practice of Racism (White Supremacy), have produced the greatest and most effective system for promoting falsehood, non-justice, and incorrectness in the known universe.

- The word "Code", as used here, means that each individual Victim of Racism speaks and/or acts to help **eliminate Racism** by utilizing selections from a "list" of **suggestions**, or from a "combined" list of suggestions designed to help an individual Victim of Racism accomplish that purpose.

- The word "System", as used here, means that each individual Victim of Racism speaks and/or acts to help eliminate Racism (White Supremacy) as an **individual person** according to that part of a "pattern" of certain forms of speech and/or action "suggested" in a kind of "listing" [Code] from which any or all Victims of Racism can pick and choose as they see fit.

  When many Victims of Racism (Victims of White Supremacy) pick and choose to speak and/or act against Racism from the same general "pattern" and/or "Code", at a time and place of their choice as individuals, a "system" of speech and action becomes "self-developing".

- The word "Concept", as used here, means that the entire "United-Independent Compensatory Code/System" is no more than a "Concept", or idea, during **any** period when no person in the known universe is speaking and/or acting to use **truth** in a manner that helps to produce **justice** and **correctness.**

In sum, the overall term "United-Independent Compensatory Code/System/Concept means:

> Any number of individual persons, who are Victims of Racism (Victims of White Supremacy), who are in the **process** of thinking, speaking, and/or acting **effectively** against Racism (White Supremacy), according to what they, as **individual persons,** pick and choose from a general "Code", "outline", and/or "suggestion list", for thought, speech, and/or action, that is especially designed for the purpose of helping an **individual person** to think, speak, and/or act against Racism. The "Code", "outline", and/or "suggestion list" must be designed, and used, for the purpose of not only eliminating Racism, but to do so through the process of using **truth** in such manner as to simulataneously **promote justice** and/or **correctness.**
>
> All speech, and/or action, must be at a time, and place, and in the areas of activity, of the individual Victim's **own choice.**

Some Other Titles for the United-Independent Compensatory Code/ System/Concept Are As Follows:

- The Code.
- The Compensatory Code.
- The Compensatory Code/System/Concept.
- The Compensatory Counter-Racist Code.
- The Compensatory Counter-Racist System.
- The Compensatory System.
- The United-Independent Compensatory Code.

Any person, **while** speaking and/or acting in effective opposition to Racism (White Supremacy) is a "producer", a "promoter", and/or a "supporter" of the United-Independent Compensatory Code/System/ Concept. Also, any person **while** speaking and/or acting in a manner that helps to promote justice or correctness, is a "producer", a "promoter", and/or a "supporter" of the United-Independent Compensatory Code/System/Concept.

The United-Independent Compensatory Code/System/Concept "Works" In the Following Manner:

- **Ideas** for speaking and/or acting to eliminate Racism and for producing justice and correctness are "listed" as they come to mind.

- The "list" of ideas are arranged into an order, or "code", of thought, speech, and/or action that is designed to be used by an **individual person.**

- The **individual person** uses "parts" of the "code" that he or she judges to be "best-suited" for promoting justice and correctness, and eliminating Racism. The **individual person** does this by his or her **own will**, at a time and place of his or her **own choosing**, in any **one** or **more** "listed" areas of activity, namely: economics, education, entertainment, labor, law, politics, religion, sex, and war.

- The **individual person** may, or may not, add "refinement" to the "code" by making his or her own additions or modifications to it.

  The basic "guides" used by supporters of the United-Independent Compensatory Code/System/Concept are: any and all sources of knowledge and understanding of truth, justice, and correctness. These sources include printed material, verbal messages, personal experiences, etc.

  There is no one person who is "the leader" of the United-Independent Compensatory Code/System/Concept. Each individual person "leads" him or her **self**, each minute, of each day and night, according to what he or she **has chosen** from one or more parts of the Code/System/Concept, that he or she judges to be of value.

There is no "organization" associated with the United-Independent Compensatory Code/System/Concept that a person can "join", and/or become a "member" of. A person who says or does anything that helps to promote justice or correctness, and/or, who says or does anything that helps to eliminate Racism (White Supremacy) is, **during that time**, an "organ" of the Code/System/Concept. During all other times, that person is not such an "organ" (Supporter).

There is no "formal" meeting place and/or "headquarters" associated with the United-Independent Compensatory Code/System/Concept **except** the brain and/or mind of each individual person while he or she is saying or doing something that helps to promote the objectives of the Code/System/Concept.

There are no mandatory "collections", "donations", "loans", and/or "transfers" of money associated with the United-Independent Compensatory Code/System/Concept.

To "contribute" to the United-Independent Compensatory Code/System/Concept, all a person has to do, is say, or do, something in a manner that helps to eliminate Racism (White Supremacy), and/or, that helps to promote the practice of justice and correctness.

A supporter of the United-Independent Compensatory Code/System/Concept seeks to speak and/or act to eliminate Racism (White Supremacy) each and every day, and each and every night, in at least **one** area of activity. Examples: economics, education, entertainment, labor, law, politics, religion, sex, war, etc.

A supporter of the United-Independent Compensatory Code/System/Concept **avoids** speaking, and/or acting, against any people, or persons, who are **not** practicing White Supremacy (Racism), as long as White Supremacy is the dominant motivating force among the people of the known universe.

There are no restrictions applicable to **any** persons who seek to help to promote the objectives of the United-Independent Compensatory Code/System/Concept in regards to the **ages** of those persons.

There is no person who speaks "for another" in association with the United-Independent Compensatory Code/System/Concept. **Each person** speaks his or her views and is not responsible for the remarks of others.

No **non-white** person is "responsible" for anything that **any** person says or does in "association with" the United-Independent Compensatory Code/System/Concept.

It is just and correct for **any** person, white, or non-white, to speak and/or act in support of the United-Independent Compensatory Code/System/Concept.

The **basic** "author" of the United-Independent Compensatory Code/System/Concept is the Law of Compensation itself.

It is the **existence** of White Supremacy (Racism), and other forms of non-justice and incorrectness that "authors" and/or "authorizes" the existence of the United-Independent Compensatory Code/System/Concept.

White Supremacy breeds opposition to White Supremacy.
Non-justice breeds opposition to non-justice.
Incorrectness breeds opposition to incorrectness.
This is the Law of Compensation.

One of the basic goals of every supporter of the United-Independent Compensatory Code/System/Concept, is, and must be, to evolve a universal "Way of Life" in which

(1) No person, will put to death, another person, for **any** reason, and,

(2) Every person will seek to help every other person for no other reason than, that help is needed in order to **maintain** justice and correctness.

SPECIAL INTRODUCTORY

INFORMATION GUIDE

Three (3) Basic Types of People in the Known Universe:

1. White people.

2. Non-White people.

3. White Supremacists (Racists).

Explanation:

1. **"White" people** are people who classify **themselves** as "White", and have been classified as "White", accepted as "White" by other people classified as "White", and who **generally function** as "White" in all of the nine major areas of activity, including economics, education, entertainment, labor, law, politics, religion, sex, and war.

2. **"Non-White" people** are people who have been classified as "Non-White", and/or who **generally function** as "Non-White" in their relationships with each other, and with people classified as "White", in all of the nine major areas of activity, including economics, education, entertainment, labor, law, politics, religion, sex, and war.

3. **White Supremacists (Racists)** are people who classify themselves as "white", and who **generally function** as "white", and, who practice racial subjugation (based on "White"-"Non-White" classifications) against people classified as "Non-White", at any time, in any place, in any one, or more of the nine major areas of activity, including economics, education, entertainment, labor, law, politics, religion, sex, and war.

Nine (9) Major Areas of People Activity in the Known Universe:

1. Economics
2. Education
3. Entertainment
4. Labor
5. Law
6. Politics
7. Religion
8. Sex
9. War

Explanation:

Area 1 = **Economics**, which means the correct distribution of, and/or balance between, all animals, persons, places, plants, things, etc. "Economics", in the **correct** sense, is the sum-total of **all** of the thought, speech, and/or action used to produce **maximum efficiency** in revealing **truth** in a manner that promotes the establishment of **justice** and **correctness** in **all** areas of activity, including education, entertainment, labor, law, politics, religion, sex, and war.

"Economics" also means using all things, thought, speech, and/or action, with **maximum efficiency** with the objective of eliminating Racism (White Supremacy).

"Economics" does not mean simply acquiring, saving, and/or spending **money.** "Economics" is not a tool of money. Money is a tool of "economics". "Economics" is the result of a person or persons speaking and acting effectively in the production of **justice** and **correctness.** It is not simply how **money** is handled that determines "Economics". It is a matter of how **everything** is handled —— and to what **ends.**

In order for a person who is a victim of Racism (victim of White Supremacy) to practice "Economics", that person must speak and act to produce justice and correctness in the **sum total** of everything that he or she says and/or does. This includes the use of **time,** the consumption of food and drink, sexual intercourse and/or thoughts of sexual intercourse, the use of music, the manner and use of labor, etc. For example, if listening to a particular "type" of sound "inspires" a person to **think** better while performing some function that helps to eliminate Racism (White Supremacy), then that type of sound becomes "music", and that person, at that time, serves an "Economical" purpose. The same is true for any other thing and/or function pertaining to a person in any of his or her day-to-day activities.

As regards action against Racism (White Supremacy), "Economic Correctness" **is not** determined by any **one** or more things that a victim of Racism [non-white person] **does,** and/or **doesn't** do, but by the **sum total** of **everything** that that victim does, and/or doesn't do, in terms of **effective results** against Racism.

Area 2 = **Education,** which means the **process** of learning **all** things about **all** things, and/or, the process of learning **all** things about **one** thing.

[Note: If **all** is known about **one** thing, then **all** is known about **all** things, because **all** things are interrelated**].**

Area 3 = Entertainment, which means **any** activity that is desired and/or "enjoyed", including that which is just and/or **un**just, and that which is correct and/or **in**correct.

Area 4 = Labor, which means any act of using energy to accomplish an objective.

Area 5 = Law, which means **anything that is done.**

Area 6 = Politics, which means **people relations,** and/or any relations between people, at **any** time, in **any** place, in **any** area of activity.

Area 7 = Religion, which means the **sum total** of **everything** that a person **thinks**, plus, **everything** that he or she **says**, plus, **everything** that he or she **does.**

A "Religion" includes **all parts** of a person's existence, each and every minute of each and every day—even if those parts are never put into "words", they are still a "part" of a person's religion, **if** that person willfully and deliberately speaks and acts according to those parts. Religion is **not separate** from existence, nor separate from any "part" of existence.

Anything that a person **says** or **does,** that is **willful** and **deliberate**, is a part of that person's "Religion".

Area 8 = Sex, which means any socio-material interrelationship between male and female.

Area 9 = War, which means any willful and deliberate **unjust** speech and/or action that is used effectively against any creature.

[Note: All of the nine major areas of (people) activity are **interrelated].**

What happens in **one** area of activity affects all other areas of activity. What a person does in the area of "Economics" affects what that person does in the area of "Religion"— or "Sex", or "War", etc.

The Racists (White Supremacists), by dominating their victims [Non-White people] in **one** area of **major** activity, also, at the same time, dominate them in **all** areas of **major** activity.

Four (4) Basic Motivating Factors in People Behavior in the Known Universe

1. Racism (White Supremacy)

2. Re-action to Racism

3. Sexual Expression

4. Re-action to Sexual Expression

Explanation:

Racism, in the form of White Supremacy, is the **greatest** motivating force, **by** people, that exist among the people of the known universe.

Every person in the known universe is either **practicing** White Supremacy (Racism), or, he or she is **compelled**, at all times, to re-act to those persons who are practicing it.

Both the practice of White Supremacy, and the re-action to it, affects **all** people, in **all** areas of activity, including economics, education, entertainment, labor, law, politics, religion, sex, and war.

Sexual intercourse, and/or "sexual play" is the **second greatest** motivating force, **by** people, that exist among the people of the known universe.

Every person in the known universe is either engaging in acts of sexual intercourse and/or "sexual play", or, he or she is, at **all** times, directly or indirectly re-acting to those who are so engaged.

Both the acts of sexual intercourse and/or "sexual play", and the re-actions to such acts, affects **all** people, in **all** areas of activity, including economics, education, entertainment, labor, law, politics, religion, sex, and war.

Summary:

No other socio-material forces, by people, affect so many people, in so many places, so much, in so many areas of activity, as the factors of **race** (Racism), and **sex.**

Two (2) Basic Problems Among the People of the Known Universe:

1. Lack of knowledge and understanding of the **reason** for existence, and/or for non-existence.

2. Racism (White Supremacy).

Explanation:

Every "problem" among the people of the known universe can, today, be traced to:

1. A lack of knowledge and understanding of the **reason** for existence and/or non-existence, compounded by and promoted by

2. The practice of Racism in the form of White Supremacy.

This is true in all areas of activity among people, including economics, education, entertainment, labor, law, politics, religion, sex, and war.

Five (5) Major "Political Isms" in the Thought, Speech, and/or Action of All People in the Known Universe:

1. **Racism** = One or more white persons using deceit, direct violence, and/or the threat of violence, to promote falsehood, non-justice, and/or incorrectness, against non-white people, on the basis of "color", in order to "satisfy" white people, in one or more areas of activity, including economics, education, entertainment, labor, law, politics, religion, sex, and/or war.

2. **Me-ism** = Any**one** person, thinking, speaking, and/or acting, to "satisfy" him or her self, with little or no concern for others, in one or more areas of activity, including economics, education, entertainment, labor, law, politics, religion, sex, and/or war.

3. **Two-ism** = Any **two** people, thinking, speaking, and/or acting to "satisfy" **each other**, with little or no concern for others, in one or more areas of activity, including economics, education, entertainment, labor, law, politics, religion, sex, and/or war.

4. **Tribal-ism** = Any **three**, and/or sometimes more than three people, thinking, speaking, and/or acting to "satisfy" **each other** with little or no concern for others, in one or more areas of activity, including economics, education, entertainment, labor, law, politics, religion, sex, and/or war.

5. **Universal-ism** = Any one or more persons, thinking, speaking, and/or acting to promote the revelation of truth, and using the truth revealed, in such manner as to promote justice and correctness, at **all** times, in **all** places, in **all** areas of activity, including economics, education, entertainment, labor, law, politics, religion, sex, and war.

Two (2) Basic "Classes" of People in the Known Universe:

1. The Power**ful** "Class" (White Supremacists)

2. The Power**less** "Class" (all **Non**-White people, and those White people who are **not** White Supremacists).

Explanation:

Since the establishment of White Supremacy (Racism) among the people of the known universe, the terms "upper class", "middle class", and/or "lower class", have become so meaningless that to use such terms to describe **any** people does not promote justice, but serves only to promote great confusion.

It is therefore best not to use such terms to describe **any** people now in existence in the known universe.

Under White Supremacy, and/or, as long as White Supremacy exists, the best and most accurate way to describe people by using the category of "class" is to describe their **power** relationship to each other.

By so doing, **all** white people who **practice** White Supremacy (Racism) must be recognized as the **only** people in the known universe who are the "powerful class".

All **Non**-White people, being **subject** to the "power**ful** class", are, therefore, the "power**less** class".

In addition, those white persons who **do not** practice White Supremacy are **also** the "powerless class". These white people who **do not** practice White Supremacy **are not subject** to the White Supremacists ("The Powerful Class"). The fact that no white person is subject to White Supremacy (Racism) greatly confuses many non-white poeple.

Some non-white people think that some **white** people are victims of White Supremacy. They believe this when they see or hear about some white people doing things to harm other white people. They then conclude that some white people practice "White" Supremacy against each other. Such a conclusion is incorrect.

White people **do** practice acts of **non**-justice against each other, but it is not possible for a white person to practice the **major** unjust act of **White** Supremacy against a **white** person. **All** people, however, both white and non-white, practice **non**-justice against each other, **all** of the time, in **all** places, in **all** areas of activity, including economics, education, entertainment, labor, law, politics, religion, sex, and war. The master injustice, however, is White Supremacy, and it is only practiced by **white** people, against **non**-white people.

No **white** person is subject to **White** Supremacy. It is possible, however, for a white person to be "powerless" to do anything that is effective **against** the practice of White Supremacy. Some examples of such persons are white people who are "infantile", and/or, who are so "senile" in mind and body that they are **completely dependent** on others for **all** of their care, and are completely "incapable" of doing **harm** to others.

Since all of the white people who practice White Supremacy are "The Powerful Class", it generally serves no useful purpose for a non-white person to worry about which **individual** white person is "more powerful" than another **within** that class. A White Supremacist is a White Supremacist [powerful person].

How one White Supremacist relates to another White Supremacist at any particular moment should be of no major concern to a non-white person, since **all** White Supremacists are committed to the practice of Racism (White Supremacy).

In any event, the White Supremacists, who, as individuals, are "smarter" than many other White Supremacists, will, in all matters involving the maintenance of White Supremacy, give effective support to those who are "not so smart".

This guarantees that all people classified as "white" are automatically "entitled" to receive benefits **special** only to people classified as "white" in a world socio-material system dominated by White Supremacists ["The Powerful Class"].

Also, the very existence of White Supremacy (Racism) automatically eliminates the possibility of any **non**-white person being so-called "upper-class" or "middle-class" in his or her relationship to **any** person, **any** place. Such persons are all "subject class", and/or "The Power**less** Class".

As long as White Supremacy exists, it is false and incorrect to say that any Black and/or non-white person is "upper-class" or "middle-class". How can they be? If they are "upper-class", or "middle-class", "Upper" or "Middle" of **what** — as compared to what? As compared to who? Certainly not white people, and **definitely** not White Supremacists.

In matters of "class" non-white people "compare" with **each other**, which, under White Supremacy, is not only meaningless, pitiful, and an admission of weakness, and subservience, to White Supremacy, but an acknowledgement of their fear to admit it openly.

Though **all** non-white people are functional "lower-class" — meaning they are **all** "lower" in comparison to the white people of the known universe — it is better not to say that they are "lower-class". To do so would be to promote questions regarding the confusing terms "upper-class" or "middle-class". Therefore, in referring to the "class" status of **all** non-white people, it is better to say that they are "The Power**less** Class".

As long as White Supremacy exists, it is incorrect for any non-white person to pretend that he or she is **any** "Class" of person other than "The Power**less** Class".

<u>Four (4) Basic Types of Power Among the People of the Known Universe</u>:

1. **All Power** - Power exercised by the "known and unknown" (God, the Creator, etc.)

2. **Superior Power - (and/or White Supremacy)** Power exercised by the collective White Supremacists (Racists) over/against the non-white people of the known universe.

3.	**Inferior Power - (and/or "Zero Power")**	Power exercised by the non-white people who exist in subjugation to the White Supremacists.
4.	**Immediate Power - (and/or Individual Power of Elimination)**	Power exercised by any person, animal, insect, etc., to **directly** cause (and/or effectively threaten to cause) the **death** of, and/or serious injury to, any person, animal, insect, etc.

<u>**Explanation(s)**</u>:

All-Power = The force that is most often referred to as "God", and/or "the Creator", etc., and is the greatest force in the known universe.

This force (the **sum total** of all that is known and unknown) is generally thought to be a power that is greater than all other "powers" in the known universe.

Whereas there has been great disagreement about the **form** of this force, there is little disagreement as regards the **existence** of this power, and/or the existence of a "closely interrelated" combination of forces that "cause" this power.

Superior Power = White Supremacy (Racism). This power is second only to **All-Power** among the people of the known universe. It is the power exercised by those "White" people who practice "White" Supremacy against **all** of the people of the known universe who are classified as "non-white".

Those white people who practice White Supremacy **are not** the **supreme** power in the universe over **all** things at **all** times.

They do, however, exercise **superior** power over all of the **non**-white **people** of the known universe in **all** things, at **all** times.

The ability to cause non-white people to think, speak, and/or act according to the will, dictates, and/or requests of White Supremacists (Racists) is what makes White Supremacists **supreme** over the non-white people who **submit to**, and/or who **cooperate with**, them.

The power of the White Supremacists to **dominate** the non-white people of the known universe is **proof** of the **superior** power of the White Supremacists.

Inferior Power = The lack of will, and/or the lack of ability of non-white people to do **anything** of **comparative** significance without the direct and/or indirect force, approval, and/or voluntary support, of White Supremacists (Racists) and/or, of white people in general.

Immediate Power = The power that a person has, as an individual, that enables him or her to act **immediately** and **effectively** without the consent of other persons.

This is the power that **most** people, as **individual persons,** have, that they can employ immediately. This power consists of:

The **will,** plus
The **means,**
of causing the **death** of persons,
animals, plants, insects, etc.

Most people, regardless of "Racial Classification", are usually able to eliminate, execute, and/or cause the death of animals, plants, insects, and/or other persons.

To eliminate the existence of self or others, **at will**, is one of the few powers that an individual person can exercise that can change, **immediately,** the current status of, and/or halt the thought, speech, and action, of others.

Immediate Power is the **most direct** form of power that can be utilized by an individual person, since it does not require the permission of, and/or the cooperation of, any other person.

Immediate power, like very few other forms of "power", can be used for purposes that are either **just** or **non**-just. [Immediate power should **never** be used for non-just and/or incorrect purposes. Nor should it be used in an incorrect **manner,** even in an attempt to accomplish a just or correct goal].

One (1) Basic Type of "Government" in the Known Universe:

Incorrect "Government"

Explanation:

Incorrect "Government" is any thought, speech, and/or action, by people that **has not produced** justice and correctness in **all** areas of activity, including economics, education, entertainment, labor, law, politics, religion, sex, and war.

No people in the known universe have produced a "government" that **has eliminated** injustice and incorrectness in **any** area of activity. There is no such thing as a just or correct government among the people of the known universe.

There is only **Incorrect Government.**

Two (2) Basic Racial Systems in the Known Universe:

1. Racist speech and action (White Supremacy).

2. Counter-racist speech and action (Resistance to White Supremacy).

Explanation:

1. Racist speech and action is **injustice** practiced by one or more persons based on factors "associated with" the "color", or "non-color", of persons.

   At present, the only form of **functional** Racism practiced in the known universe is White Supremacy.

2. Counter-racist speech and action is a combination of words and deeds that help to eliminate racist speech and action, and/or, that helps to establish justice and correctness.

In any socio-material system dominated by Racism (White Supremacy), the victims of Racism [non-white people] are neither "separate" from the racists, nor are they "integrated" with the racists. Therefore, under this condition, the victims of Racism have two, and **only** two, choices as long as they are victims:

- They can continue to speak and act in **support** of the practice of Racism, or,

- They can speak and act to **eliminate** the practice of Racism.

Four (4) Basic Stages of Racism (White Supremacy):

1. Establishment of -- (White Supremacy).

2. Maintenance of -- (White Supremacy).

3. Expansion of -- (White Supremacy).

4. Refinement of -- (White Supremacy).

Explanation:

- The **Establishment** of White Supremacy =
  The sum total of all speech and/or action, by those white persons who seek to dominate [through the practice of Racism] those persons "classified" as "non-white".

- The **Maintenance** of White Supremacy =
  The sum total of all speech and/or action, by those white persons who practice Racism (White Supremacy), and who seek to **continue** the practice of Racism, at all times, in one or more areas of activity.

- The **Expansion** of White Supremacy =
  The sum total of all speech and/or action by those white persons who practice Racism (White Supremacy), and who do so in a manner that directly, or indirectly, helps to promote an **increase** in the **number** of non-white persons made subject to Racism (White Supremacy).

- The **Refinement** of White Supremacy =
  The sum total of all speech, and/or action, by those white persons who practice Racism (White Supremacy) in a manner that **improves the methods** that help make the practice of Racism more efficient, and/or, more "acceptable" to the Victims.

Additional Information About the Four Basic Stages of Racism (White Supremacy):

What is meant by "establishing" White Supremacy?

The term "establishment of" White Supremacy means to **make** White Supremacy a **reality.**

At some point in the past, an effective number of persons classified as "white" began promoting the idea of **dominating** all of the "non-white" people of the known universe, entirely on the basis of "color" and/or factors "associated with" color.

These persons developed ways and means of establishing the domination through trial and error, based primarily, on the use of **deceit** and **violence.** The skillful use of these methods proved to be totally effective in dominating **all** of the non-white people of the known universe, in **all** of the Nine Major Areas of (People) Activity, including economics, education, entertainment, labor, law, politics, religion, sex, and war.

Each **individual** white person who supported the concept of White Supremacy, contributed that support in some form of direct or indirect speech and/or action, that **resulted** in non-white people, being subordinated to white people, on the basis of "color" and/or factors "associated with" color.

This "color code" of thought, speech, and action, by **individual** white persons, resulted in a **pattern** of ("Racist") thought, speech, and action by an effective number of white people, which, in turn, resulted in what can now be correctly called "White Supremacy".

Since White Supremacy (Racism) came into existence through a "process", evolving through the thought, speech, and action of white persons as **individual persons**, there is no known "code" of White Supremacy that can be formally recognized as such in a single "set" of words or pictures.

The basic "code" of White Supremacy is the **total pattern** of everyday thought, speech, and action of the individual white persons who practice it.

Thus, **everything** that each white person says or does, that helps to promote White Supremacy (Racism) is all a part of the "White Code" and all parts of the "White Code" is for the purpose of maintaining White Supremacy.

What is meant by "maintaining" White Supremacy?

The term "maintenance of" White Supremacy means to **keep** White Supremacy a **reality.**

The people who practice White Supremacy (Racism) do so by **constantly** thinking, speaking, and/or acting in a manner that directly, or indirectly, keeps **all** of the non-white people of the known universe subjugated on the basis of color, at **all** times, in **all** places, in **all** areas of activity, including economics, education, entertainment, labor, law, politics, religion, sex, and war.

[Note: White Supremacy (Racism), in order to be correctly called "White Supremacy", **is** and **must be** practiced against **all** of the people of the known universe classified as "non-white". This includes forms of White Supremacy that are practiced both directly and indirectly.

It is not necessary for White Supremacists to be within sight of, and/or to be in "direct contact" with, non-white persons, in order for those White Supremacists to maintain White Supremacy].

What is meant by "expanding" White Supremacy?

The term "expansion of" White Supremacy means to **increase** the **number** of people who are **subject to** White Supremacy.

Since the establishment of White Supremacy, the White Supremacists have **expanded** and/or added strength to their power by acting to make sure that all "non-white" persons born into the known universe are made subject to the will of the White Supremacists at **all** times, in **all** places, in **all** areas of activity.

In a world socio-material system dominated by White Supremacists (Racists), each and every non-white person born into the known universe, **immediately** becomes a victim of, and a subject to, the system of White Supremacy. This happens automatically — the reason being that Racist Man, and Racist Woman, are the direct, and/or indirect, **functional** masters of **all** of the non-white people in the known universe, in all areas of activity.

The expansion of White Supremacy also means that the **longer** White Supremacy is maintained, the **greater effect** it has on the **thinking** of the non-white people. Thus, if the thinking of non-white people is **dominated** by persons who practice White Supremacy, and these thoughts cause non-white people to function in **greater support** of White Supremacy, the **effects** of White Supremacy are "expanded".

Since White Supremacy is the most **masterful** expression of falsehood, non-justice, and incorrectness among the people of the known universe, any "expansion" of White Supremacy only helps to promote falsehood, non-justice, and incorrectness.

What is meant by "refining" White Supremacy?

The term "refinement of" White Supremacy means to **improve the methods** of maintaining White Supremacy.

This means that the White Supremacists (Racists) strive to **decrease** the **necessity** for using direct violence and/or the threat of direct violence against non-white people. They, instead, strive to **increase** the use of **deceit** as the basic means of causing their victims to "enjoy", and/or not resist, their subjection to White Supremacy.

The **refinement** stage of White Supremacy is the "ideal" stage of racial subjugation to those White Supremacists who strive to produce it. They prefer a condition in which their victims **willfully** support being the subjects of the White Supremacists as they become accustomed to believing that this is the best possible arrangment between white and non-white people.

The White Supremacists (Racists) promote the refinement of White Supremacy by speaking and/or acting in a manner that makes the practice of White Supremacy more acceptable and/or more "appealing" to the victims.

[Note: White Supremacy (Racism) is a **non-just** and **incorrect** socio-material practice — no matter how it is practiced, and no matter how appealing or acceptable it may be to it's victims].

The **refinement** stage of White Supremacy is generally promoted through the systematic use of falsehood and/or "flattery". Sometimes the flattery takes the form of material objects distributed among the non-white people of the known universe to be used as so-called "status" symbols.

The **refinement** stage of White Supremacy includes speech and/or action by White Supremacists that appears to be **against** White Supremacy, but, in truth, is only the promotion of White Supremacy in a different and/or more deceitful form.

Two (2) Basic Methods of Practicing Racism (White Supremacy):

1. Deceit ["Subtle" and/or Indirect Violence].

2. Violence, Direct [Including the **Threat** of Violence].

Explanation:

Deceit = Saying things that are false, and influencing **non**-white people to believe things that are **not** true. This is done in such a skillful manner that **all** non-white people, either directly, or indirectly submit to, and/or cooperate with, the **practice** of White Supremacy (Racism).

Violence = Using direct or indirect **bodily harm**, or **threatening** to use direct or indirect bodily harm, against non-white people who do not submit to, and/or cooperate with, White Supremacists (Racists) in a "satisfactory" manner.

White Supremacy is **always** practiced with **deceit**, or with direct **violence**, or with a greatly sophisticated combination of both.

Six (6) Most Important Things to Remember About the Characteristics of Racistman and Racistwoman:

1. Racistman, or Racistwoman, is generally, any "White" person, who speaks and/or acts in such manner as to produce, or promote, the practice of White Supremacy (Racism), at **all** times, in **all** places, in one, and/or all, areas of activity, including economics, education, entertainment, labor, law, politics, religion, sex, and/or war.

2. Racistman and Racistwoman, are, collectively, the **smartest, most powerful, most malicious, most deceitful, most technical, most efficient, most inventive, and most skillfully violent,** of all of the people of the known universe.

3. Racistman and Racistwoman have, as their **ultimate objective**, the eternal promotion of their pride, ego, and arrogant incentive by practicing the eternal domination and abuse of people whom they classify as "non-white".

4. Racistman and Racistwoman **always** use **deceit** [indirect violence], **direct violence**, or the **threat of direct violence** to accomplish their ultimate objective of establishing, maintaining, expanding, and/or refining the practice of Racism (White Supremacy).

5. Racistman and Racistwoman **do not**, at **anytime**, willfully and deliberately do, or say **anything**, without the **intention** of establishing, maintaining, expanding, and/or refining, the practice of White Supremacy (Racism), in **all** areas of activity, including economics, education, entertainment, labor, law, politics, religion, sex, and war.

6. Racistman and Racistwoman, by practicing Racism (White Supremacy) are the **greatest** promoters of falsehood, non-justice, and incorrectness, among the people of the known universe.

Three (3) Basic Characteristics of White Supremacists (By Comparison With, and In Relationship To, Non-White People)

1. Power**ful**

2. Smart, and/or Sophisticated

3. Malicious, and/or Hostile

Explanation:

The White Supremacists (Racists) are the **most powerful** of all of the people in the known universe. They are **willing** and **able** to dominate all non-white people, in **all** places in the known universe, and in **all** areas of activity, including economics, education, entertainment, labor, law, politics, religion, sex, and war.

The White Supremacists are **smart**. They are also very **"sophisticated"**. They are not naive, or "simple-minded". They have very great knowledge and understanding of many things. Their thought, speech, and actions are **usually** complex or greatly developed in form and technique.

They are very misleading of others, and very clever in doing so. The White Supremacists are **malicious**. They are **hostile**.

They willfully and deliberately practice great deceit, and great violence, against people classified as "non-white". They do this for purposes of maintaining permanent domination, and to "glorify" "White Supremacy" as being the best of all "possible" forms of existence, in **any** place, at **all** times, throughout the universe, both known and unknown.

Three (3) Basic Characteristics of Non-White People (By Comparison With, and In Relation To, White People)

1. Powerless, and Pitiful

2. Primitive, and/or Ignorant

3. Stupid, and/or Silly

Explanation:

1. Non-white people, by comparison with, and in relationship to, White Supremacists (Racists), are power**less**, and pitiful.

   Non-white people are pitiful because of their lack of power, and/or because of their lack of **will**, and **ability**, to think, speak, and act effectively against injustice.

   In a world socio-material system dominated by White Supremacists, the words **"powerless"** and **pitiful"** are terms that best describe **all** non-white people and persons, both individually and collectively, at **all** times, in **all** places in the known universe, in **all** areas of activity. Some may, or may not, be **primitive.** Some may, or may not, be **stupid or silly.** But **all** are power**less** and pitiful.

   Of all the white people in the known universe, it is those who practice White Supremacy (Racism) who have the greatest **will**, and the greatest **ability**, to do whatever they choose to do in all areas of activity, including economics, education, labor, law, politics, religion, sex, and war. They have also shown, through the practice of White Supremacy, that they have **great** will, and **great** ability to subjugate non-white people, basically through the skilled use of deceit and violence. They maintain this subjugation through a day-to-day "code" of thought, speech, and action, utilizing a variety of words and deeds in a manner that promotes falsehood, non-justice, and incorrectness.

   Non-white people, however, because of a lack of will and ability, in one or more areas of activity [economics, education, etc.], are both power**less** and pitiful in comparison to the White Supremacists who are subjugating them.

   The term "Pitiful People" best describes **all** non-white people.

2. Non-white people, by comparison with, and in relationship to, White Supremacist (Racists) are, most of the time, in most areas of activity, "primitive". This means that they are relatively simple and elementary in thought, speech, and action. It means that they are, comparatively, not greatly developed in knowledge and understanding of most things, in most areas of activity, including economics, education, entertainment, labor, law, politics, religion, sex, and war. They are not smart or sophisticated in their attempts to prevent being subjugated by White Supremacists. They are usually easily fascinated, deceived, and victimized by any white person who believes in and knows how, to practice Racism.

   "Primitive" people are not necessarily "savage" or brutal. Many of them are very non-offending. Many of them are very, very meek. But those non-white people who best fit the description of "primitive", are people who do not know or understand very much as compared to a "smarter" and "more sophisticated" people such as the White Supremacists. They lack both the will **and** the ability to do most of the things that need to be done to **produce justice and correctness.**

   The White Supremacists, by comparison, only lack the **will**. They have the **ability**, but refuse to use it. In this respect, the White Supremacists are not as "primitive" as their subjects, but they are more "savage".

3. Non-white people, by comparison with, and in relation to, White Supremacists (Racists), are, most of the time, in most areas of activity, **stupid** and/or **silly**. Most of them, most of the time, do not think, speak, and/or act seriously and effectively in a manner that helps to promote the elimination of Racism and the establishment of justice and correctness.

   Since it is they who are the **victims** of the injustice and incorrectness that is greatly promoted through Racism (White Supremacy), the non-white people of the known universe can be correctly judged as "stupid" and/or "silly" when compared to the Racists.

   The Racists are powerful, smart, and malicious. They are unjust. But they are not stupid, and they are not silly. They know what needs to be done, and they are smart enough, and powerful enough, to do it. They know that justice should be produced, but they **refuse** to produce it. Their victims — the non-white people — when willing, simply do **not know how** to produce it. It is, however, correct for them to always try. It is their **duty** to always try.

Considering the circumstances, the establishment of justice may be the "assigned" mission of the non-white people of the known universe.

The Most Destructive Act Committed by White Supremacists Against Non-White People

- Sexual Intercourse,
  "Sexual Play", and/or
  Sexual Confusion

Explanation:

Next to White Supremacy (Racism) itself, "sexual activity" is the **second strongest** motivating force among the people of the known universe.

The persons who have dominant functional control or influence over the sexual expressions and/or desires of other persons [animals, etc.], also have dominant control over the basic motivations of those same persons in other areas of expression, including economics, education, entertainment, labor, law, politics, religion, and war.

Any white person, who engages in **sexual intercourse** with a non-white person, **under conditions dominated by White Supremacy**, has done more to promote the maintenance, expansion, and/or refinement of White Supremacy, than he or she could have done by any other means, in any other area of activity. This is also true when a white person, under conditions dominated by White Supremacy, commits a **counter-sexual act** [so-called "homosexual" act] with/against a non-white person. Anything that a white person says or does that helps to promote such behavior, and/or anything that a white person says or does that helps to promote sexual confusion of any kind, among non-white people, is, by so doing, practicing Racism in it's most destructive form.

Two (2) Basic Re-Actions to Racism (White Supremacy):

1. Cooperation With -- (White Supremacy).

2. Resistance To -- (White Supremacy).

__**Explanation**__:

- "Cooperation With" White Supremacy (Racism) means any thought, speech, and/or action, by persons, that directly, or indirectly, helps to promote White Supremacy.

- "Resistance To" (White Supremacy (Racism) means any thought, speech, and/or action that is effective **against** White Supremacy, and is intended to be.

- In a world socio-material system dominated by White Supremacy, each and every person who is physically and/or mentally **able** to do so, is either **cooperating** with White Supremacy, or **resisting** it.

- Each and every **white** person who is physically or mentally **able** to willfully and deliberately **cooperate** with White Supremacists, and, who does so **is**, him or her self, a White Supremacist (Racist).

- Each and every **white** person who willfully **resists** White Supremacy is **not** a White Supremacist — but this is **only** during the period when he or she is actually speaking, and/or acting, **effectively** against White Supremacy.

- No **non**-white person is, or can be, a "White" Supremacist. As long as White Supremacy exists, no **non**-white person is, or can be, a Racist.

  As long as White Supremacy exists, **all** non-white persons are **victims** of White Supremacy. Those who willfully and deliberately **cooperate** with White Supremacy are Victims, as well as those who **resist** it.

  No **white** person, however, is, or can be, a **victim** of "White" Supremacy. This is true of those who practice White Supremacy, **and** those who **do not** practice it.

[Note: Under socio-material conditions dominated by White Supremacy, any white person who practices Racism is a Racist (White Supremacist).

Also, any white person who is **able** to speak and/or act **against** White Supremacy, even under threat of death, and who **does not do so**, is, during any period when he or she is **not** doing so, a White Supremacist].

Four (4) Basic "Show-Offisms" By/Among the Victims of Racism

1. "Showing-Off" (to each other) the **things** that white people have allowed them to obtain.

2. "Showing-Off" (to each other) the **information** that white people have allowed them to obtain.

3. "Showing-Off" (to each other) their ability to **belittle** (each other).

4. "Showing-Off" (to each other) their ability to make **sexual impressions** on each other.

Explanation:

Many non-white people spend much time/energy/money "showing-off" to each other.

They do this as a means of trying to make the overall effects of Racism (White Supremacy) on their "personal affairs" seem unimportant and/or non-existent.

This "show-offism" serves no constructive purpose. It only helps non-white people to become more pitiful, primitive, stupid, and/or silly in comparison to the activities of White Supremacists, and/or, in comparison to white people in general.

Two (2) Basic Methods of Resisting Racism (White Supremacy):

1. "Four-Wallism"

2. "Open-Airism"

Explanation:

The "Four-Wall" method of fighting White Supremacy (Racism) is the general title given to the concept of having a special "meeting place" for those persons who seek to resist White Supremacy. For the most part, this also includes the following:

- "Regular meetings" by two or more persons.

- The renting and/or buying of "meeting halls" and/or buildings.

- Repeated fund-raising.

- Centralized and/or "closed-in" activities.

- **Formal** acquisition and storage of supplies to be distributed and/or sold for support of "organizational" activities.

- **Mandatory** and regular payment of "dues".

- Payment of salaries, and/or giving of "awards" to "organizational" personnel.

- Regular accumulation of funds for "legal" fees, etc.

- Designated "leadership": persons who regularly give "orders" or directives.

- Designatged "followship": persons who regularly "follow" the orders and/or directives of the persons who are designated as "leaders".

- Promoting the practice of thinking, speaking, and/or acting as if a "particular" number of people, situated in a certain place, at a certain time, and calling themselves a particular name or title, constitutes an "organization".

- Promoting the practice of calling an area of **land** by a specific name or title, and/or referring to **it** as a "country", "nation", "state", etc.

- Promoting the practice of calling **persons** by a specific name and/or title, and then "associating" that name and/or title with the name and/or title "associated" with a particular area of land.

- Promoting the practice of "associating" a **person** with a **thing** by speaking and/or acting as if the person and the **thing** are **one and the same,** and/or that the **person** and the **thing** "represent" each other.

  Examples: Buildings, Pictures,
  Flags, Statues,
  Maps, Words, etc.

The "Four-Wall" method is the standard and/or traditional procedure used by the Victims of White Supremacy in their resistance to White Supremacy.

It is called the "Four-Wall" method because the non-white people who use the method, plan, talk, and generally try to inspire each other by "meeting" each other regularly in a building that usually has four or more "Walls". The "Walls" may be of stone, wood, wire, or some other structure that is erected by people. The "effectiveness" of the meetings in the accomplishment of their purposes are ofttimes judged on the basis of the **numbers** of people that appear within a "walled" area at the same time. If the same people assemble often enough, they are usually asked or expected to assemble regularly. They may be "awarded" a "name" and/or "title", and told that they are "members" of an "organization" of people. The structure, building, etc. in which the "members" meet is usually considered to be a "headquarters" and/or central "meeting place". **The "power" of the people attending a meeting at this "headquarters" is ofttimes measured by the total number of people who appear regularly at that particular place.** Those persons who appear regularly are usually expected to contribute money, "socialize", and use names and/or titles that are associated with that particular assembly of people at that particular place of assembly.

In a world socio-material system dominated by White Supremacists (Racists), the "Four-Wall" method of resisting White Supremacy (Racism) has the following weaknesses:

- Ofttimes, many of the **most effective** people who attend "counter-racist meetings" do not intend to help eliminate Racism but are sent by, and/or are financially assisted by White Supremacists to work to defeat the purposes of the meetings.

- When money is collected, much of it is stolen and/or used for purposes other than the elimination of Racism.

- Most of the time, too much time/energy/money, etc. is spent trying to obtain and/or maintain the "Four-Walls" and/or the "regular" structure, or place, where the people assemble to talk about what they should or should not be doing to accomplish their goal.

- "Power" is too often judged on the basis of the **number** of people who attend a particular meeting, and/or on the basis of "how crowded" with people a particular "walled" structure was at a particular time.

- **Squabbling** is usually **increased** as the number of people attending meetings increases, usually because of the development of "personality clashes".

- Those who are lax in attending meetings, and/or those who are not considered to be "members" of the organization, are generally treated as "unimportant", uncooperative, and/or as "outsiders".

- Promoting the **appearance** of being substantially effective against White Supremacy (Racism) **without** being substantially effective against White Supremacy.

The "Open-Air" method of resisting White Supremacy (Racism) is practically the **functional opposite** of the "Four-Wall" method. The "Open-Air" method is generally characterized by:

- Informal communication and/or association.
- No regular "meetings".
- No renting or buying of "meeting halls" and/or buildings.
- No repeated fund-raising activities.
- No formal acquisition and storage of supplies to be distributed and/or sold for support of "organizational" activities.
- No payment of "organizational" dues.
- No payment of salaries, and/or giving of "awards" to "organizational" personnel.
- No regular accumulation of funds for "legal" fees, etc.
- No designated "leadership": every person speaks and/or acts as his or her own "leader" according to individual selections from a "code" of thought, speech, and action.
- No designated "followship": every person speaks and/or acts as his or her own "follower" according to individual selections from a "code" of thought, speech, and action.
- No thought, speech, and action that is "dictated" by one person and/or by a "special-designated" **group** of persons.

In a world socio-material system dominated by White Supremacists (Racists), the "Open-Air" method of resisting White Supremacy (Racism) has the following basic weakness:

- It is initially difficult to **communicate** the idea of a "Counter-Racist Code" to **all** of the Victims of Racism [non-white people], in a manner that effectively **motivates** all, or most of them to think, speak, and act according to the suggestions of that "Code".

Summation:

The **basic difference** between the "Four-Wall" method of resisting Racism, and the "Open-Air" method is as follows:

> The "Four-Wall" method, generally, is characterized by **two** or more persons attending regular "meetings" at the same time, in the same place(s) according to a mutual "agreement" they have made with **each other**.
>
> The "Open-Air" method, generally, is characterized by **one** or more persons, thinking, saying, or doing **specific** things, at **all** times, in different places, according to an individual "agreement" with a specific "code" of thought, speech, and/or action.

[Note: The United-Independent Compensatory Code/System/Concept is an "Open-Air" method of resisting Racism].

Two (2) Basic Objectives of Correct Law Enforcement:

1. To **Promote Justice**

2. To **Eliminate Injustice**

Explanation:

A "Law" is a tool.

A "Law" is a tool that can be used to produce and/or maintain justice.

A "Law" can also be used as a tool to produce, and/or maintain injustice.

Any "Law" that is enforced, by people, in a manner that **does not** promote **justice**, and/or, is enforced in such manner that **injustice** is not eliminated, is a "non-law". Any person who enforces a "non-law" is acting as an "out-law".

A person who acts as an "out-law" should **not** be allowed to **enforce** "Law".

Three (3) Basic Steps Toward Racial Subugation Compensation:

1. **Ask** for what **should be given.**

2. **Accept** what is **granted.**

3. **Compensate** for the **difference**
   (between what was **asked for,** and what was **granted**).

__Explanation__:

1. **Ask** for what **should be given.**

   This means that non-white people should **ask** the White Supremacists (Racists) to reveal **truth** (not just "facts"), and to produce **justice**, and **correctness**, in **all** things, at **all** times, in **all** areas of activity, including economics, education, entertainment, labor, law, politics, religion, sex, and war.

   Those white people who practice White Supremacy (Racism) have established and maintained the practice through **falsehood**, **non-justice** and **incorrectness.** Therefore, the revelation of truth, **plus** the production of **justice** and **correctness** can best be established by **first** eliminating "White" Supremacy, and **replacing** it with thought, speech, and action that uses **truth** in such manner that **justice** and **correctness** is produced.

   This is what should be **asked** for.

2. **Accept** what is **granted.**

   This means that since it is the White Supremacists (Racists) who are **supreme** over **all** of the non-white people of the known universe, in **all** areas of activity, it is, therefore, **correct** for the Victims of White Supremacy to **accept** whatever the White Supremacists choose to grant them, that is of **constructive value.**

   The non-white people of the known universe have **nothing** that is not subject to the power of the White Supremacists. Therefore, the non-white people should accept from the White Supremacists whatever they grant that is of **constructive value**, even if that which is granted is **less** than that which was **asked for.** As long as that which is granted is **less** than that which was **asked for,** then non-white people should **continue** to ask for that which **should be granted** — namely, the revelation of truth, **and** the establishment of justice and correctness in **all** areas of activity.

3. **Compensate** for the **difference.**

   This means that "after" the Victims of White Supremacy (non-white people), **ask** [repeatedly] for what **should be given**, and, after they **accept** what is granted, they should study what was granted to see if it is the **same** as that which was asked for. If what was **granted** is **not the same** as that which was **asked for**, non-white people should then speak and act to **compensate** for the **difference** between what was asked for, and what was granted.

They can do this by thinking, speaking, and acting according to a "code" of behavior that promotes the revelation of truth, and the use of truth in such manner that justice and correctness is produced in all areas of activity, including, economics, education, entertainment, labor, law, politics, religion, sex, and war.

Four (4) Basic Entitlements Toward the Promotion of Justice:

1. Adequate **teaching/learning** facilities for constructive communications, so that **every** person knows the **truth** about everything that he or she needs to know in order to do, or have done, anything that **should be** done.

2. Adequate **housing**, and constructive **control** over adequate **space, land,** etc.

3. Adequate and progressive **health** facilities and nutritional products.

4. Adequate, safe, comfortable, convenient, and efficient **transportation.**

Three (3) Basic Requirements in the Establishment of "Peace"

1. Truth [The Revelation Of]

2. Justice

3. Correctness

Explanation:

"Peace" is the result of the revelation of truth, **and** the use of truth, in a manner that produces justice and correctness.

Truth is **that which is.**

Justice is **balance between people.**

Correctness is **balance between people,** and all things, animals, plants, minerals, etc., **other** than people.

When **all** people speak and/or act to use truth, in a manner that produces justice and correctness at **all** times, in **all** places in **all** areas of activity (economics, education, entertainment, labor, law, politics, religion, sex, and war) "Peace" is the result.

Two (2) Basic Qualifications for Producing and/or Promoting Justice:

1. Speaking and acting to find and reveal **truth** in regards to the relationship(s) between **all** people, in **all** aspects, of **all** areas of activity, including economics, education, entertainment, labor, law, politics, religion, sex, and war.

2. Upon finding truth, speaking and acting to **promote justice** on the basis of the truth found.

Three (3) Basic Goals Sought by Most of the People in the Known Universe:

1. To **survive** by any means necessary.

2. To **dominate others** through deceit and/or violence [including the **threat** of violence].

3. To **establish** "Peace".

Explanation:

- **Most** people in the known universe have no "major" goal greater than to survive, by any means necessary.

- **Most** of the **smartest** and **most powerful** people in the known universe have no "major" goal greater than dominating and abusing others through deceit, direct violence, and/or the threat of violence.

- A **few** people have no "major" goal greater than the establishment of "Peace".

Ten (10) "Basic Stops" That Victims of Racism Should Practice in Speech and/or Action:

1. **Stop "Snitching".**

   Reason(s)/Explanation(s):

   To "snitch" is to **willfully** and **deliberately** "volunteer" information about a person, or persons with the specific intention of gaining direct or indirect "personal" favors, and/or praise, from **Racists.** When Victims of Racism [non-white people] carry messages about, and/or witness against, any person or persons, in a manner that gives aid and comfort to Racists, such actions only help to promote **injustice.**

   It is just and correct for all persons, to the best of their will and ability, to avoid situations wherein they believe they may be tempted to, and/or expected to, "snitch".

   "Snitching" does not mean speaking to **protect** yourself from false accusations, or from other unjust acts.

   "Snitching" does mean to **say** something to try to "get ahead" of someone else by taking **unjust advantage** of his or her lack of correct judgment.

2. **Stop "Name-Calling".**

   Reason(s)/Explanation(s):

   To "name-call" is to call a person by any name **other than** the name [title, etc.] that that person chooses to be called, and/or chooses to call him or her **self.**

   "Name-calling"is a simple but **major** act that promotes serious conflict between one person and another. Among Black people, it ofttimes leads very quickly to fighting and killing.

   The **result** of "name-calling" is never worth the grief that such practices promote.

   To avoid "name-calling" a person, it is better to practice **describing** what it is that a person **does** or **says.**

Example(s):

Instead of calling a person a "liar", repeat what it was that the person said, and say that what was said was "not true". Then explain **why. Always** explain **why.**

Instead of calling a person a "Racist", **describe** what it is that that person says or does that is **characteristic** of a Racist. Say that it is the **type** of thing that a Racist says or does. Do not, however, call the **person** a "Racist".

It is also important to know and understand what to **not** do when a person calls **you** a "name":

- Do not **say anything.**
- Do not **fight.**
- Do not **kill.**

3. **Stop "Cursing".**

Reason(s)/Explanation(s):

To "curse" people is to use "profanity" toward them in a manner that is likely to be thought of as insulting or demeaning. This often results in the promotion of hostility.

The hostility promoted ofttimes serves no constructive purpose. The use of "curse" words ofttimes promote "name-calling", discourtesy, and unnecessary fighting and/or killing.

4. **Stop Gossiping.**

Reason(s)/Explanation(s):

To "gossip" about a person is to say something about that person, to someone **other than** that person, that you would **not** be willing to say **directly** to that person, at the same time and place, with those other persons listening.

"Gossip" promotes injustice. Ofttimes it leads to hostility, which, in turn, often leads to snitching, name-calling, cursing, fighting, and/or killing.

"Gossip" promotes confusion and unnecessary suspicion. It serves no constructive purpose.

5. **Stop Being Discourteous.**

Reason(s)/Explanation(s):

To be "discourteous" is to say or do something that shows a lack of consideration for what a person is doing or saying, or trying to do, or say, to promote knowledge or understanding of his or her thought, speech, or action(s).

To be "discourteous" means to not allow a person to reveal, and/or to explain, his or her intentions. It means for a person to speak and/or act as he or she chooses, with little or no regard as to how others will be affected.

Discourtesy often breeds hostility and/or confusion.

Discourteous speech and/or action often promotes name-calling, cursing, fighting and/or killing.

[Note: If someone is discourteous to you, **do not help to promote it by speaking and/or acting with discourtesy toward him or her.**

Try to avoid contact with such persons. Say only to them that which is absolutely necessary].

6. **Stop Stealing.**

Reason(s)/Explanation(s):

To steal, from any person, for any reason, is to promote injustice. To steal — even to survive — is to promote injustice.

To steal — even from one who has stolen from you — is to promote injustice.

To steal — even from an enemy — is to promote injustice.

To steal — even from a Racist — is to promote injustice.

Stealing causes a person to put a greater value on the **things** stolen, than on the value of justice. Also, once a person starts stealing, he or she develops a tendency to continue to do so.

In a world socio-material system dominated by White Supremacists (Racists), **all** people are encouraged to steal, or to condone stealing, by some people, under some conditions. Those white people who practice White Supremacy (Racism) have stolen more things from people, and have stolen more people "from themselves", than any other category of people in the known universe.

Under White Supremacy, stealing is particularly condoned if it is done through the **very skillful** use of deceit. If a person can steal from another, by gaining his or her confidence, and/or by skillful trickery, it is ofttimes considered to be not "stealing", but the so-called "game" of so-called "living".

When stealing helps to maintain, expand, and/or refine the practice of White Supremacy, it is **not** generally considered to be "stealing". It is ofttimes called "progress".

The system of White Supremacy functions in such manner that non-white people are not only **expected** to steal, but are also **encouraged** to steal. They are trained, bribed, and/or enticed from the time that they are small infants. They are taught to want many things that will **deliberately** be made difficult for them to obtain. After being "encouraged" to want certain things, they are then **denied** the **means** of acquiring them without robbing, stealing, and/or killing, in order to get them. They are, in many instances, very deceptively encouraged to want many things that are of no constructive value — things that they do not "need", and that no person can use **constructively** in the manner that is generally considered "acceptable".

Racists ofttimes ridicule their subjects because they do not have, or do not want to have many things that the Racists say that a subject should strive to get. The Racists say that their subjects [non-white people] are "backward" if they do **not** want, and strive to get, all of the things that Racists say that a subject should have. The Racists then proceed to encourage their subjects to develop a desire for those things. Once the subjects develop the desire, the Racists act, **deliberately**, to directly, or indirectly, **discourage** the subjects from getting the things desired by any means other than stealing, robbing, and/or killing.

The Racists then act to **punish** their subjects because of the "manner" that they, the subjects, used to acquire the things that they were trained to desire.

Under White Supremacy (Racism), non-white people are directly or indirectly encouraged to steal those things that are of use for a relatively short period.

All things considered, it is better that no person steal from, or rob, anyone, at any time, for any reason. It is "better" for a non-white person, [as long as he or she is subject to White Supremacy] to **beg** for his or her needs, than to **steal** anything, at any time, for any reason. This is one of the best ways to start to produce **justice**, and to show how **nothing** is important without it.

7. **Stop Robbing.**

Reason(s)/Explanation(s):

To **rob** a person is to use **direct** bodily harm, and/or, to use the threat of **direct** bodily harm, to take from a person, any one or more **things**, that he or she possesses, and then to use the thing(s) taken to "please" the mind, and/or to "make comfortable" the body of the person doing the taking.

To **steal** from a person is to **take something** from that person, without that person knowing one or more of the following, at the exact time of the taking:

- **What** was taken
- **When** it was taken
- **Where** it was taken
- **How** it was taken
- **Why** it was taken
- **Who** took it.

A person who **robs** has the same basic intentions as a person who **steals.** Neither robbing nor stealing helps to promote justice.

A person should not rob, for the same reasons that he or she should not steal.

8. **Stop Fighting.**

Reason(s)/Explanation(s):

People should not fight as long as they can talk to each other, and they should talk to each other in such manner as to **minimize conflict**, and/or to better **promote justice.**

When people cannot talk to each other without trying to maim or do other bodily harm to each other, they should then do everything that they can to **minimize or eliminate contact with each other.**

When people have no **contact** with each other, directly or indirectly, they cannot have **conflict** with each other.

There is no **justifiable violence,** by persons, against each other. There is only justifiable **counter**-violence.

It is correct for all persons to do all that they can to **avoid** being involved in any form of "violence".

It is also correct for all persons to try to keep circumstances from becoming so imbalanced that **counter**-violence is required in order to promote justice. People who exist in subjugation to White Supremacy (Racism) should only use **counter**-violence, and they should use it only for the following purposes:

- To **protect** themselves, or others, from acts of **deliberate, immediate, direct**, and functionally **unavoidable** violence, by **any** person, or persons. In protecting themselves, or others, only a **minimum** of necessary **counter**-violence should be used.

- To enact Maximum-Emergency Compensatory Justice.

[Note: See detailed description of "Maximum-Emergency Compensatory Justice" in portion of this work entitled "Area 9: War".]

9. **Stop Killing.**

[Exceptions: When "forced" to do so in **direct** defense of self, others, and/or major property, or, except when "forced" to do so through the enactment of Maximum-Emergency Compensatory Justice**]**.

Reason(s)/Explanation(s):

Even in direct and immediate defense of self, of others, and/or in the direct protection of major property, it is best to **avoid** killing or maiming. Killing **any** aggressor should only be done when there is apparently no other known way to put an immediate stop to his or her aggression, and/or, when every reasonable effort has been made to escape the immediate fury of the aggression.

It is correct for a Victim of Racism [non-white person] to **willfully** and **deliberately** kill and/or execute **no** person(s) except Racists (White Supremacists), and, when done, that Victim of Racism should then kill him, or her **self.**

Such killings and/or executions should **never** be done unless the Victim of Racism is made subject to Racism (White Supremacy) in a manner that is **totally unbearable,** and **apparently inescapable**, except through **non-existence.**

[Note: See a detailed description of "Maximum-Emergency Compensatory Justice" in portion of this work entitled "Area 9: War"].

10. **Stop Squabbling Among Yourselves and Asking Racists (White Supremacists) to Settle It.**

Reason(s)/Explanatons(s):

One of the major non-just acts that Racists (White Supremacists) commit is to establish situations that cause, and/or encourage non-white people to squabble among themselves.

Racists **do not approve** of **any** fights or arguments between non-white people that non-white people settle among themselves without the so-called "help" of the Racists.

Racists do not, knowingly, allow any non-white person, or persons, to do **anything** that does not directly, or indirectly, help to promote Racism (White Supremacy).

Racists approve of, and encourage non-white people to fight each other, kill each other, squabble with each other, "name-call" each other, and/or do anything that best helps non-white people to remain confused, and non-constructive.

Racists, however, are **not** in favor of the **extermination** of **all** non-white people. They are in favor of **many** non-white people being killed, but not **all** of them. They have no desire for non-white people to become **extinct.** If "non-white" people became extinct, there could be no way for "white" people to practice "Racism" — at least they could not practice it in the form of "White" Supremacy. Racists want non-white people to continue to exist. It is not possible to **practice** "White Supremacy" if "non-white" people do not exist.

The Racists want non-white people to continue to be their subjects and victims. While using non-white people as victims, the Racists particularly want the non-white people to squabble among themselves, and they want the non-white people to beg them, the Racists, to "settle" the squabbles. This is one of the major ways that the Racists have of maintaining their power. They also do this to "prove" their power, feed their ego's, and amuse themselves.

A Summary of the "Ten (10) Basic Stops"

In order to help to eliminate Racism and to produce justice, all Victims of Racism should, in all of their relationships with **each other**, think, speak, and act in support of the following three-word suggestion:

"Minimize the Conflict"

SPECIFIC SUGGESTIONS

FOR

THOUGHT, SPEECH, AND/OR ACTION

AREA 1: ECONOMICS

▮ PREFACE ▮

The following pages present suggestions that pertain to what a Victim of Racism [non-white person] **should**, or **should not**, choose to do in the First Major Area of [People] Activity: Economics.

Each person should choose to speak, and/or act, according to one or more of the suggestions presented — but only if he or she decides to do so. No person should speak and/or act according to **any** suggestion presented herein unless he or she has judged that the suggestion chosen is of **current** and **correct** value in helping to eliminate Racism (White Supremacy), and/or, in helping to better promote justice.

It is important to know and understand that one or more suggestions selected from one Major Area of [People] Activity, should be used in constructive combination with one or more suggestions selected from other Major Areas of [People] Activity.

If an individual person chooses to utilize any suggestion presented herein, he or she should do so in a manner, and at a specific time, and specific place, that will produce the **most constructive results** in the revelation of truth, and/or, the production of justice or correctness.

▮ ▮ ▮ ▮ ▮ ▮

As long as Racism (White Supremacy) exists, use **all** of your time/energy doing no more than the following, and, do not **willfully** make or maintain contact with other persons **except** for these purposes:

1. Producing, building, repairing, improving, and/or cleaning those things that have [constructive] value, and using those things for **constructive purposes only**.

2. Studying, writing, asking questions, and/or exchanging views with others, about **all** aspects of how to **eliminate Racism**, and/or how to **produce justice**, in **all** areas of activity, including economics, education, entertainment, labor, law, politics, religion, sex, and war/counter-war.

3. Eating and sleeping, correctly, and **only as necessary**.

ECONOMICS

4. Engaging in sexual intercourse no more than twice every seven (7) days,, and using a **minimum** amount of **time** and **resources** in association with such engagements.

Reason(s)/Explanation(s):

If each Victim of Racism [non-white person] would limit **all** of his or her activities to no more than the aforementioned, most of his or her problems will be greatly **minimized**, in a very short period of time.

Victims of Racism who are **serious** about eliminating Racism (White Supremacy), and/or, who are **serious** about producing justice, cannot "afford" to engage in **any** activities, **other** than the aforementioned.

The **voluntary** and **constructive** use of time and/or energy, by substantial numbers of the Victims of Racism would have a very damaging effect on the continued practice of Racism. Racism could continue to exist for a while, but only with great difficulty. A great improvement in the promotion of justice would be immediately evident. At the same time, each Victim of Racism would quickly develop into a stronger and greatly improved person. Victims of Racism, would, no longer, with relative ease, be side-tracked into, and/or burdened with, activities which at best are useless rituals, and/or destructive "fads". By using [their] time and energy in accords with the aforementioned four suggestions, Victims of Racism [non-white people] would eliminate doing those non-constructive and mostly "non-satisfying" things that are usually the product of indoctrination and/or long-standing habit.

Their overall functions, as constructively-progressive persons, would be greatly simplified. Thought, speech, and action would be much healthier and characterized by less confusion, frustration, and clutter. The maintenance and refinement of Racism (White Supremacy) depends greatly on the ability of the Racists (White Supremacists) to keep their vicitms constantly engaged in a great variety of activities that are wasteful of time and energy, and/or, that are, otherwise **directly supportive** of the continuation of White Supremacy. Therefore, each Victim of Racism should use all of his or her time and energy in a manner that **results** in the

least amount of waste and frustration, while, at the same time, greatly improving his or her ability to counteract Racism in all areas of activity.

Victims should, **at all times** be engaged in one, or more, of the aforementioned four interrelated uses of time and/or energy. As long as Racism (White Supremacy) exists, no Victim of Racism [non-white person] should, at **any** time, be engaged in any other use(s) of time and/or energy.

Important: At no time should any person seek the "company" of, make deliberate contact with, and/or voluntarily remain in the presence of, other persons, except for the purpose of speaking, and/or acting, in support of the suggested four-point [Economic] format.

Avoid Excess.
Avoid acquiring things that you must serve more than they serve you. Avoid "being possessed" by the things in your possession.
Don't "worship" the "toys" that you or others possess.

Reason(s)/Explanation(s):

When a person spends too much time/energy arranging, cleaning, counting, repairing, and/or protecting his or her "material possessions", he or she will have too little time/energy for anything else. Too little time/energy would be used to think, speak, and/or act to produce justice. Too little time/energy would be used in thinking, speaking, and/or acting to eliminate Racism.

All "material possessions" should be used to eliminate Racism, and/or, to produce justice.

All time/energy should also be used for those purposes. In a known universe dominated by Racism (White Supremacy), and by other injustices, no time/energy and/or "material possessions" should be wasted on other purposes.

Do not buy anything with the intention of using it for "show-offish" purposes.

Reason/Explanation:

"Showing-off" serves no constructive purpose for people (non-white) who are subject to Racism (White Supremacy).

ECONOMICS

The people who would be "impressed" **do not "count"**, and the people who "count" would not be "impressed". With all that you "have", you, as a Victim of Racism, do not have as much as you **should have had** long before you had it. With all that you "have" you still do not have **justice**, which is the basic thing that must be had in order to give **value** to all that you "have".

Avoid the production of off-spring:

- Until you **know**, and **understand**, what White Supremacy (Racism) is, and how it works in **all** areas of activity including economics, education, entertainment, labor, law, politics, religion, sex, and war.
- Until you have the **will** and the **ability** to adequately feed them, clothe them, and house them.
- Until you have the **will**, and the **ability** to explain to them, in a manner that they will understand, what White Supremacy (Racism) is, and how it works in all areas of activity, including economics, education, entertainment, labor, law, politics, religion, sex, and war.

Do not, under any circumstance, engage in sexual intercourse and/or "sexual play" for purposes of gaining financial, monetary, and/or material support, either for self, or others, including off-spring.

Reason/Explanation:

As long as White Supremacy (Racism) exists, there are two (2), and **only** two [correct] reasons for sexual intercourse and/or "sexual play" between persons. They are as follows:

- To help to provide **comfort for, incentive to,** and promote **constructive communication between,** those Victims of Racism [non-white people] who repeatedly strive to speak, and/or act, to resist or eliminate Racism (White Supremacy).
- Production of off-spring.

Avoid borrowing anything, from anybody, at any time.
If you must borrow, try to borrow from white people, rather than non-white people.
Avoid lending a non-white person more money than you can afford to give him or her.

ECONOMICS

Reason(s)/Explanation(s):

In a socio-material system dominated by White Supremacists (Racists), white people are the greatest producers of money. White people are the **masters** of money. They are the only people who have "enough" money to **lend.** White people can better afford to "take chances" by making loans. Many, many white people can afford to take "losses" on loans made to non-white people, whereas, non-white people can least afford to take losses on loans made to each other.

In a socio-material system dominated by White Supremacists, **all** non-white people are in a weak "economic" condition. None of them can "afford" to borrow from, or lend to, the other. Also, because of White Supremacy (Racism), Black people are more likely to return what they borrow from white people, than what they borrow from each other.

Under White Supremacy, many, many people classified as "Black" [and/or "Negro"] are **extremely** insecure. They tend not to return what they borrow unless they are forced to. Therefore, to minimize conflict, it is better to "give" to a non-white person that which you can **afford** to give. **Avoid lending.** By so doing, you not only will help to minimize conflict and animosity among non-white people but you will also help to minimize dishonesty and the tendency to steal.

As long as White Supremacy (Racism) exists, ask white people, including the White Supremacists, to help you to provide material care for your off-spring, as well as for yourself.

Reason(s)/Explanation(s):

As long as White Supremacy exists, **all** persons who are subject to the White Supremacists (Racists) are **greatly limited** in the quality and quantity of all that is of **constructive value.**

Since it is the White Supremacists who are **functionally responsible** for directly, or indirectly, providing constructive care for their victims [non-white people], it is just and correct for all victims of White Supremacy to seek this care **first** from the White Supremacists. They should next seek it **from** the Creator **and** through themselves, in spite of, and/or in opposition to, the dictates of the White Supremacists.

At no time, however, should anything be obtained by robbing or stealing.

ECONOMICS

Do not expect any white person who is a Racist (White Supremacist), or expect any non-white person who is A Victim of Racism, to do what needs to be done for any off-spring that you produce.

Reason(s)/Explanation(s):

A white person, who is a Racist, **will not** do what **needs** to be done for your off-spring.

A non-white person, who is a Victim of Racism, **can-not** do what **needs** to be done for your off-spring.

As long as White Supremacy (Racism) exists, no person, or persons, in the known universe, **will do**, or **can do**, what **needs** to be done, for your off-spring.

Don't take a "vacation". Don't wait for a "vacation". Make a "vacation" — and make one everyday — wherever you happen to be.

Do something that will **constructively** stimulate and/or "freshen" your mind and body.

Examples: Sit quietly and think constructive thoughts.

Write a plan for future constructive activity.

Engage in some constructive physical work of your choice.

Read, in a relaxed manner, some writings that will give you constructive information.

Engage in constructive conversation.

Engage in sexual intercourse (but no more than twice every seven days).

Quietly look at, and **see**, and quietly listen to, and **hear**, the sights and sounds of all things around you — people, plants, animals, etc.

Ask yourself, and/or others, **why** everything is, what it is, and for what **ultimate** purpose.

ECONOMICS

Wear the "latest styles" by wearing the clothes that you have.

Reason/Explanation:

If your clothes are **clean, simple** in design, and **neat** in appearance, they are always "appropriate", and always "in style".

Buy land, if you can, and sell land only to buy other land.

Make a habit of saving some part of all monies that regularly comes into your possession.

Reason/Explanation:

To save, regularly, helps to prevent waste, and helps a person to be better prepared for emergencies and for opportunities.

Do not accuse any non-white person, or persons, of being responsible for any of your "Economic" problems.

Reason/Explanation:

In a socio-material system **dominated** by White Supremacists (Racists), the White Supremacists are responsible for **all** problems involving the people who are subject to them.

AREA 2: EDUCATION

■ PREFACE ■

The following pages present suggestions that pertain to what a Victim of Racism [non-white person] **should**, or **should not** choose to do in the second Major Area of [People] Activity: Education.

Each person should choose to speak, and/or act, according to one or more of the suggestions presented — but only if he or she decides to do so. No person should speak and/or act according to **any** suggestion presented herein unless he or she has judged that the suggestion chosen is of **current** and **correct** value in helping to eliminate Racism (White Supremacy), and/or, in helping to better promote justice.

It is important to know and understand that one or more suggestions selected from one Major Area of [People] Activity, should be used in constructive combination with one or more suggestions selected from other Major Areas of [People] Activity.

If an individual person chooses to utilize any suggestion presented herein, he or she should do so in a manner, and at a specific time, and specific place, that will produce the **most constructive results** in the revelation of truth, and/or, the production of justice or correctness.

■ ■ ■ ■ ■ ■

Try to learn something about everything. Take an interest in everything that happens, and in everything that exists in the universe.

Reason(s)/Explanation(s):

All people, both white and non-white, have persons among them who have great knowledge and understanding of many, many things. But non-white people do not **consolidate** and constructively utilize, and efficiently exchange, the variety of things that they learn from time to time. They do not record and "store" what they learn. They allow what they learn to "filter away". They do not pass on constructive information willingly, deliberately, constantly, and efficiently, to those who need it most. This is one of the reasons much of what non-white people once "knew" was "lost", and/or forgotten.

EDUCATION

Non-white people do not keep long-lasting records that can readily be used in an efficient manner, for great and constructive purposes. Racists do.

Racists (White Supremacists) do not have to greatly tax themselves to remember past mistakes. They do not have to repeat experiments involving people, things, animals, plants, insects, etc. They have records of these experiments, records of the results, and records of suggestions of how the results can be used in the future in any one or more areas of activity.

Racists do not discard records simply because they have no **current** use for the information contained in them. They do not destroy, or allow to decay, any records of information, simply because they have not been used in a "long" time. They keep them, re-examine them, and develop newer uses for them.

Non-white people, however, generally are not interested in learning about **everything**, and/or in keeping detailed records about **all** things.

Non-white people, generally, have no great desire to know **everything** there is to know about the universe. They have no great desire to dominate the universe and **all** that is in it, or a part of it. They are mostly, content to "survive" in it.

The lack of interest, by most non-white people, in doing anything other than "surviving" in the universe, explains why non-white people lack the **will** to keep themselves from being dominated by White Supremacists (Racists). The White Supremacists encourage their subjects to limit their interest and desires to nothing more constructive than "survival". While permitting and encouraging non-white people to concern themselves mostly with "survival" from day to day and year to year, the Racists continue to improve their own ability to think, and to explore, and to develop greater and more efficient means of dominating non-white people. They seek more non-white people to dominate as they travel through the unknown.

Though most non-white people do not understand the thoughts and desires of those white persons who practice White Supremacy, they are, generally, not opposed to being subjugated by them, as long as they can survive, and be allowed to acquire a degree of food, clothing, and housing that prevents them from becoming extinct. They also enjoy "socializing" and/or "showing-off" among themselves. Among Black people, "showing-off" is ofttimes equated with power and intelligence.

Because of this, many of them do not try to learn anything or acquire anything that cannot be soon used for "show-off" purposes. This is why too many Black people know or remember little that is of constructive value.

Study White Supremacy (Racism), and learn how it works in all areas of activity:

Economics	Labor	Religion
Education	Law	Sex
Entertainment	Politics	War

Study what you learn about White Supremacy, and use what you learn in a manner that helps to promote justice and correctness.

Reason(s)/Explanation(s):

Nearly all of the knowledge that Black people have received while existing among, or in contact with, white people, has been presented to them **by** White Supremacists (Racists), **for** the purpose of **serving** White Supremacy (Racism).

It is correct for all victims of White Supremacy to know and understand **all** that the White Supremacists teach, as well as **why** they teach what they teach.

It is correct for all victims of White Supremacy to know and understand **all** that the White Supremacists know and understand.

Knowledge is neutral. It is **how** knowledge is used, and for what **purpose** it is used, that determines it's value.

Do not use the term "racial de-segregation" to describe any situation.
Do not use the term "racial integration" to describe any situation.
Use the term "elimination of Racism".

Reason(s)/Explanation(s):

There is no such process as "racial desegregation" or "racial integration". There is, and only can be, the **existence** of Racism, **or,** the **non-existence** of Racism.

EDUCATION

Racism either **exists**, or, it **does not** exist. There is no way to "de-segregate" racism. There is no way to "integrate" Racism. Racism can only be **practiced**, or **not practiced.**

Readily admit, to yourself and others, that there are no people in the known universe who are "smarter" than those white people who practice White Supremacy (Racism).

Reason(s)/Explanation(s):

There are no people in the known universe who are "smarter" (have greater knowledge and understanding), collectively, then those white persons who practice White Supremacy (Racism). Therefore, there are no people in the known universe who are as **powerful** as those persons.

In order to establish, maintain, expand, and/or refine the practice of White Supremacy, it was **necessary** for those white persons (who chose to participate in the practice) to learn more, know more, and understand more, than **all** of the non-white people combined. It was necessary for those white persons, collectively, to dominate all non-white people, at **all** times, in **all** areas of activity, including economics, education, entertainment, labor, law, politics, religion, sex, and war.

No matter how "smart" a non-white person may be as an individual person, so far, none of these persons have proven to be "smart enough" to **not** be subject to the power of the collective White Supremacists. Unlike the White Supremacists, non-white people have never developed a desire to become "all-knowing". Non-white people, generally, have not shown a desire to learn many things for the basic purpose of dominating others on the basis of "color" and/or factors "associated" with "color", or "non-color". They have, collectively, shown no interest in becoming Racists. They have, collectively, shown no interest in subjugating white people because white people are "white". In not wanting to be Racists they have been **correct.** In **failing** to dedicate **all** of their efforts toward the elimination of Racism, they have been **incorrect.**

As a result, **all** of the non-white people of the known universe are now the every-day victims of, and the direct or indirect subjects to, the only form of **functional** Racism: White Supremacy.

Teach (smaller/younger) people the truth about everything that you know about economics, education, entertainment, labor, law, politics, religion, sex, and war.

Teach them in such manner that they fully understand what you are saying.

Tell them that the correct **purpose** for learning about anything, at anytime, is to use what is learned to help produce **justice** and **correctness**. Tell them **specific ways** that they can best use what they learn.

Also, avoid guess-work. Tell them the truth about anything that you **do not** know. Say to them "I do not know. I will help you to try to find out".

Reason(s)/Explanation(s):

Learning **truth** (that which is), and, promoting **justice** (balance between people), and promoting **correctness** (balance between people and things other than people) is the best basic investment for **any** people, any place in the known universe.

A person — any person, of any age — should have the **truth** about any and all things revealed to him or her about **anything,** as soon as it is perceived that he or she is likely to **understand** that **truth**, and is likely to use that understanding to promote justice and correctness.

The aforementioned activity, for the aforementioned purposes, is the greatest, and most constructive, that any person can do to help another.

Study the past (history) for one basic purpose:

> To learn about the **mistakes** that were made in the past, so as to be better prepared not to make the same type mistakes in the future.

As long as you exist, refer to yourself as a "permanent student". Act as if you are a permanent student. Be **willing** to learn everything about anything that is constructive. If you can see a thing, try to learn how that thing is put together. Try to learn what is does, and **how** it does what it does. Start by **looking** at the thing — and keep looking at it until you "see" it.

Make a habit of asking questions about anything and everything that you do not know, but may be worth knowing.

Ask many people the same question, and/or ask many questions of the same people. When studying history, study the history of **all** people — not just **some** people.

Reason(s)/Explanations(s):

All people should learn about all of the **mistakes** that were made by all the people who existed before them. They should learn about all of the things that **should not** have been done, by people, in all areas of activity. This includes the areas of economics, education, entertainment, labor, law, politics, religion, sex, and war.

The mistake that many **white** people made upon contact with non-white people was to take advantage of their ignorance, in order to practice injustice against them, and promote injustice among them.

The mistake that most **non-white** people made upon contact with white people was to submit to, and cooperate with, people who were very smart, but who had no intentions of doing justice. The non-white people, for the most part, showed that they were willing to submit to injustice, if by so doing, they would be allowed to "survive". They did so because of their ignorance of the importance of justice.

Any people who value **survival** more than justice, do not understand that survival, without justice, is **valueless**.

Any people who **do not know** the value of justice are an **extremely** ignorant people. This mostly pertains to Black and/or non-white people.

Also, any people who **know** the value of justice, but who **deliberately prefer** to practice injustice, are an **extremely** non-just people. This mostly pertains to those white people who practice White Supremacy (Racism).

EDUCATION

Victims of Racism (non-white people) do not know and understand **enough** about **anything** of constructive value. If they did know and understand enough, they would not be Victims of Racism.

Therefore, Victims of Racism have an obligation to the promotion of justice, and to the "meaning" of existence, to try to learn **everything** that is, or may be, of constructive value.

While trying to learn, **non**-white people should not hesitate to ask white people — including White Supremacists — to help them. They should ask for this help even if they know that White Supremacists do not **intend** to help their victims do anything of constructive value. They should ask for the simple reason that the White Supremacists owe them this help as an effort to compensate for the injustice that they practice against non-white people, and to help compensate for the "benefits" that Racists receive as a result of the practice.

Do not say that any person in the known universe is "wise".

Reason(s)/Explanation(s):

A person who is "wise" does not practice injustice.

A person who is "wise" does not submit to the will of anyone who practices injustice.

A person who is "wise" does not tolerate the existence of injustice, and, at **all** times, does that which is necessary to eliminate it.

When any person in the known universe becomes "wise", **injustice** in the known universe, will immediately, cease to exist.

Pay attention to white people. Pay attention to what they do. Listen to what they say. Look at all that they do. When talking with white people, let them talk to you about anything that is constructive. Don't act as if you are a "know it all".

Reason(s)/Explanation(s):

White people, most of the time, know many useful things. They, most of the time, say some things that **can** be used for a **constructive** purpose. If you are talking about anything of **constructive** value, white people usually know and understand more about what you are talking about than you do.

Among the people of the known universe, white people, generally, are the greatest "source" of immediate information, on the greatest variety of subjects.

Practice making and keeping written notes of all possibly useful ideas as swiftly as they come to mind.

Record them under nine (9) distinct areas of activity — Economics, Education, Entertainment, Labor, Law, Politics, Religion, Sex, and War. Keep a reference file, and/or a listing of titles and authors of all publications which are, or may be, of basic value in helping to produce knowledge and understanding that can be used constructively.

Read the writings of many writers — and record the essentials.

Listen to the words of many speakers — and record the essentials.

Observe all that you can observe — and record the essentials.

Then, by utilizing the best of your knowledge and understanding, translate these essentials into "codes" for thought, speech, and/or action, for everyday use.

Always seek the truth — about all things, events, etc.

Seek the source(s) of all information received. "Accept" no "praise" for yourself for anything that you have learned.

Accept all challenges to, and/or tests of your knowledge and understanding.

Know and understand **why** you do whatever you do, and know and understand **why** you want to do, whatever it is that you want to do.

Study words and/or terms in order to learn their:

> Current definitions, past definitions, "double" meanings, "philosophical" meanings, etc.

EDUCATION

Give these words and/or terms the most accurate compensatory definitions that you can think of, that, when used, will best reveal and/or promote truth, justice, and/or correctness. Try to use words that promote knowledge and understanding in a simpler and more efficient manner.

Do not call yourself an "expert" in the knowledge or understanding of any subject.

Do refer to yourself as being a "student", and/or, an "advanced student" of the **truth** (that which is).

Speak and act as if the entire "universe" is the true "school" ("university").

Do not fear to look at anything in the universe that does not do harm to your ability to "see", and/or to think, constructively.

Support by word and/or deed, the invention, modification, re-modification, and/or utilization of any words, terms, definitions, and/or forms of speech, or writings, which are more effective in helping to eliminate Racism and helping to promote truth, justice, and correctness.

Practice Asking People These Three (3) Important Questions:

1. What is your **ultimate** objective?

2. What do you think **my** ultimate objective should be?

3. In what ways should the accomplishment of **your** ultimate objective involve **me**, and in what ways should the accomplishment of **my** ultimate objective involve **you**, in which of the following areas of activity: Economics, Education, Entertainment, Labor, Law, Politics, Religion, Sex, and/or War?

Speak and write precisely, clearly, simply, and constructively.
Avoid the use of unnecessary words.
Avoid the use of "slang" expressions.

Reason/Explanation:

The most constructive forms of speaking and writing are those forms that reveal a maximum amount of information with a minimum of confusion and "wasted" words.

EDUCATION

Never say, or imply, that any question is "stupid", "silly", "crazy", etc.

Reason(s)/Explanation(s):

There is no such thing as a **question** that is "stupid", "crazy", "silly", etc.

Every question has an **answer.**
Every question has a **correct answer.**
If there was no answer, there could be no question.

Therefore, **no** question can be correctly regarded as "stupid", "silly", "crazy", etc.

Seek the truth in answers to the following questions, and use the truth found, in such manner as to help to produce justice.

1. **What** is a "race of people?"
2. **How** did a "race" of people become a "race" of people?
3. **Why** did a "race" of people become a "race" of people?
4. **How** many "races"of people exist in the known universe?
5. **What** is the **purpose** of a "race" of people?
6. **What** is **"Racism"?** What isn't "Racism"?
7. **What** are the purposes of "Racism"?
8. **When** did the practice of "Racism" begin?
9. **Where** did the practice of "Racism" begin?
10. **Who** started the practice of "Racism"?
11. **Why** did the practice of "Racism" start?
12. **What people** practice "Racism"?
13. Is "Race" and "Racism" the same?
14. **Why** is "Racism" practiced by those who practice "Racism"?
15. **Where** is "Racism" practiced?

EDUCATION

16. **When** is "Racism" practiced?

17. **How** is "Racism" practiced in each area of activity: Economics, Education, Entertainment, Labor, Law, Politics, Religion, Sex, and War?

18. **What people** practice "Racism" the "most"?
Why is "Racism" practiced by that particular people more than by any **other** people?
How is "Racism" practiced by **that** particular people more than by any **other** people?

19. **Where** is "race" a problem?

20. **What causes** "race" to be a problem?

21. **Who** causes "race" to be a problem?

22. **What** is the total number of **known** "systems" of "racism"?

23. **What** is the **name** and/or title of each known "system" of "Racism"?

24. **What** is the **just** and **correct** thing to do in regards to "race", and/or "Racism", in each area of activity, including Economics, Education, Entertainment, Labor, Law, Politics, Religion, Sex, and War?

Before speaking and/or writing about any matter of basic importance, plan everything that you are going to say, and how you are going to say it.
Always arrange for enough time to do it correctly.
Always speak and/or write in a manner that is both simple and effective.

Reason(s)/Explanation(s):

It is better to say nothing, than to say something in a manner that produces misunderstanding of what is said.

Every word that a person uses should be chosen carefully. It is correct to use every word in such manner that it has the **correct effect** toward the accomplishment of a **correct objective.**

Many people are motivated by **words** more often than by **deeds.**

Every word is, within itself, a "neutral" word.

EDUCATION

The "value" of a word or an act can only be measured by the **effect** of the word or act. Every word, like every act should be especially designed to accomplish a **correct** objective or effect. The use of a word, like the commission of an act can only be justified if such usage results in the planned effect toward the accomplishment of a correct objective.

A word is a **tool**, and like any other tool should always be used to accomplish a **just** and **correct** objective.

In the spoken or written word, it is the revelation of truth that counts more than the grammar or the mechanics of language.

All written words, **all** pictures, and **all** images are neutral.

A written word is not the "same" as a spoken word, and a picture or image of a person, place, or thing is **not** the same as the person, place, or thing itself.

The actions and/or re-actions of a person, plant, animal, or thing, upon being exposed to any written word or any picture or image of any person, plant, animal, or thing, are **not** caused by, nor in any way "connected with" the word, picture, or image itself. The actions and/or reactions resulting from such "exposure", if any, are the **results** of the current "conditioning" of the person, plant, animal, or thing, that is acting and/or reacting according to the "training" previously received through the sum total of the environment.

A **conception** of a person, animal, place, or thing **is not** the same as the person, animal, place, or thing conceived.

A "symbol" of a person, animal, place or thing **is not** the same as the person, animal, place, or thing "symbolized".

A "symbol" can only "symbolize" that which is the **same** as **itself.**

Do not worship "symbols", "images", "insignias", "emblems", etc.

Reason/Explanation:

People sometimes become so fascinated with images, reflections, symbols, insignias, emblems, etc., that they begin to think, speak, and/or act in support of falsehood, non-justice, and incorrectness in the belief that they are doing the opposite.

EDUCATION

Increase your will power by increasing your knowledge and understanding.

Reason(s)/Explanation(s);

Where does **will power** come from?

Will power comes through knowledge and understanding of **truth** (that which is), **justice** (balance between people), and **correctness** (balance between people, and things other than people).

Will power also comes through knowledge and understanding of the opposite — **falsehood, non-justice,** and **incorrectness.**

The more a person knows and understands about any of the aforementioned, the more will power he or she will exercise as a result of that knowledge and understanding.

[It is correct, also, to seek knowledge and understanding of anything in the known universe when there exists a powerful enemy who possesses that knowledge and understanding].

Use your "education" only for the correct purpose. Use all that you learn in such manner as to best promote justice and correctness.

Reason(s)/Explanation(s):

The **correct** purpose for learning anything is to help a person to find truth, and to use truth in a manner that best promotes justice and correctness, at all times, in all places, in all areas of activity.

"Education" should **not** be used to treat people unjustly. If one person is "smarter" than another, that does not mean that the "smarter" person is a "better" person than the "not-so-smart" person.

If one person has a greater knowledge, and greater understanding, of a particular subject, that does not mean that he or she has the "right" to use that knowledge and understanding to **mistreat** a person who has less knowledge and understanding of that particular subject.

The **greater** a person's knowledge and understanding, the **greater** is that person's **responsibility** to speak and act in support of the use of truth to help produce justice and correctness.

EDUCATION

Persons who have learned much should not "poke fun" at persons who have not learned as much. Persons who have great knowledge and understanding should help others to know and understand **all** that **they** know and understand.

A person who has learned more than others should not adopt an attitude of "prideful arrogance" and "contemptous superiority" toward those others. He or she should, instead, seek to use all that has been learned to render constructive service to those who are in need of it.

Every person should know and understand what "education" is. It is a process. No person is "educated" until he or she knows and understands **everything** about **everything**, and/or, knows and understands **everything** about **one** thing.

Study and practice ways of improving your memory.
Put what you learn into effective practice.

Reason(s)/Explanation(s):

An efficient memory is essential to an effective education. To learn and not remember is **not** to learn. Education without **application** is useless.

Practice recognizing, knowing, and understanding all words which have no simple and/or clearly-defined meaning(s) — especially when such words are used by any people directly or indirectly associated with any socio-material system dominated by White Supremacists (Racists).
Examples of such words are as follows:

American	Cultured	Law	Public
Aryan	Democracy	Left-Wing	Qualified
Asian	Devil	Legal	Race
Bad	Educated	Legitimate	Racist
Beautiful	Enemy	Liberal	Red
Black	European	Liberty	Religion
Brotherhood	Evil	Love	Right
Brown	Extremist	Moral	Right-Wing
Capitalist	Freedom	Nation	Savage
Caucasian	Friend	Natural	Sinner
Christian	God	Negro	Slavery
Civilized	Good	Nigger	Sport
Civil Rights	Hate	Non-White	Theft
Colored	Human	Owner	Ugly
Communist	Humanitarian	Peace	Uncivilized
Conservative	Indecent	Possession	War
Country	Independent	Poverty	White
Crime	Indian	Private	Wrong
Criminal	Justice	Property	Yellow

EDUCATION

Avoid confusion. Seek truth. Practice presenting words or terms that have "opposite meanings" in a manner that will raise questions as to whether the words or terms truly mean what they are generally thought to mean. Some examples of what to say to people when you are seeking such information:

That I may gain knowledge and understanding, **tell** me the difference between an "educated person", and an "uneducated person", and **show** me one of each.

That I may gain knowledge and understanding, **tell** me the difference between a "laborer" and/or "worker", and one who **is not** a "laborer" and/or "worker", and **show** me one of each.

That I may gain knowledge and understanding, **tell** me the difference between a "poor" person and a "rich" person, and **show** me one of each.

That I may gain knowledge and understanding, **tell** me the difference between a person who is a "fool", and a person who **is not** a "fool", and show me one of each.

That I may gain knowledge and understanding, **tell** me the difference between a "capitalist" and a "communist", and **show** me one of each, as he or she functions in each area of activity, including Economics, Education, Entertainment, Labor, Law, Politics, Religion, Sex, and War.

That I may gain knowledge and understanding, **tell** me the difference between a "civilization", and a "non-civilization", and **show** me one of each.

That I may gain knowledge and understanding, **tell** me the difference between a "Christian", and a White Supremacist (Racist), and **show** me one of each.

That I may gain knowledge and understanding, **tell** me the difference between a "Jew", and a White Supremacist (Racist), and **show** me one of each.

That I may gain knowledge and understanding **tell** me the difference between a "Muslim", and a White Supremacist (Racist), and **show** me one of each.

That I may gain knowledge and understanding, **tell** me the difference between a white person who **is** a White Supremacist (Racist), and a white person who **is not** a White Supremacist (Racist), and **show** me one of each.

EDUCATION

That I may gain knowledge and understanding, **tell** me the difference between a "good" white person, and a white person who is a "White Supremacist (Racist)", and **show** me one of each.

That I may gain knowledge and understanding, **tell** me the difference between a "high-class" Black person, a "middle-class" Black person, and a "low-class" Black person, and **show** me one of each.

That I may gain knowledge and understanding, **tell** me the difference between a person who is an "Uncle Tom", and a person who **is not** an "Uncle Tom", and **show** me one of each.

That I may gain knowledge and understanding, **tell** me the difference between a "racially-segregated" Black person, and a "racially-integrated" Black person, and **show** me one of each.

That I may gain knowledge and understanding, **tell** me the difference between a "Christian" and a "sinner", and **show** me one of each.

That I may gain knowledge and understanding, **tell** me the difference between a "married" person, and a "non-married" person, and **show** me one of each.

That I may gain knowledge and understanding, **tell** me the difference between a "war criminal", and a "non-war criminal", and **show** me one of each.

That I may gain knowledge and understanding, **tell** me the difference between "war-time", and "peace-time", and **show** me one of each.

AREA 3: ENTERTAINMENT

▪ PREFACE ▪

The following pages present suggestions that pertain to what a Victim of Racism [non-white person] **should**, or **should not**, choose to do in the Third Major Area of [People] Activity: Entertainment.

Each person should choose to speak, and/or act, according to one or more of the suggestions presented — but only if he or she decides to do so. No person should speak and/or act according to **any** suggestion presented herein unless he or she has judged that the suggestion chosen is of **current** and **correct** value in helping to eliminate Racism (White Supremacy), and/or, in helping to better promote justice.

It is important to know and understand that one or more suggestions selected from one Major Area of [People] Activity, should be used in constructive combination with one or more suggestions selected from other Major Areas of [People] Activity.

If an individual person chooses to utilize any suggestion presented herein, he or she should do so in a manner, and at a specific time, and specific place, that will produce the **most constructive results** in the revelation of truth, and/or, the production of justice or correctness.

▪ ▪ ▪ ▪ ▪ ▪

When possible, avoid all forms of "entertainment" that requires that you be directly involved with others. When possible, seek to "entertain" yourself alone. Minimize and/or eliminate all unnecessary time spent in the company of others for purposes of "entertainment".

Reason/Explanation:

Under White Supremacy (Racism) non-white people usually spend too much time, energy, and money "entertaining" each other. They spend too much time in each other's company, doing too many things that produce little of constructive value.

Such contacts usually serve to do little more than promote animosity, conflict, "show-offism", dishonesty, gossip, and other forms of unnecessary and destructive activity.

ENTERTAINMENT

Do not engage in sexual intercourse and/or "sexual play" as a means of "showing off".

Reason(s)/Explanation(s):

As long as White Supremacy (Racism) exists, no non-white person should ever do **anything** for purposes of "showing off".

An act of sexual intercourse should not be used for such purposes.

Under conditions dominated by Racism, it is correct for non-white persons to engage in sexual intercourse **only with each other**, and **only** for one or more of the following three purposes:

- Production of off-spring.
- Improvement of communications.
- Minimizing the amount of time/energy spent thinking about, and/or planning for, sexual intercourse.

Do not gloat, cheer, and/or express gladness about the death and/or injury of any person, animal, etc.

Reason(s)/Explanation(s):

Death and/or injury is never a reason to rejoice.

To "celebrate" the death and/or injury of any person, animal, etc. is unjust and incorrect.

It is incorrect to regard killing and/or maiming as "entertainment".

Do not kill or maim for purposes of entertainment or sport.

Reason/Explanation:

Any person who kills or injures any creature for the primary purpose of providing entertainment or "sport" is guility of promoting injustice and incorrectness.

Except for counter-racist educational purposes, do not support, participate in, and/or be a paying spector to, any form of "entertainment" or "sport" which has as it's basic objective the glorification of the White Nation (White Supremacy).

ENTERTAINMENT

Stop acting as if you should be the "entertainment committee" when in the presence of white people.

Reason: If they are Racists, they will be laughing **at** you — not **with** you.

Do not use racial subjugation as a subject for "funny" remarks in such manner that Racists (White Supremacists) are helped to feel "more comfortable" in their practice of Racism (White Supremacy).

Stop "swapping jokes" with members of the White Nation (White Supremacists).

Reason: Such so-called "joking" serves no constructive purpose. It usually ends with the telling of a "joke" that isn't a "joke", and the "joke" that isn't a "joke" is usually a joke on you.

Listen to "music".
Avoid Listening to "noise".

Reason(s)/Explanation(s):

"Music" is those sound that help a person to **think constructively.**

"Noise" is those sounds that **hinders** a person in thinking constructively.

Too many non-white people spend too much time and/or effort making, listening to, and/or responding to noise.

Very seldom do they choose to listen to music. Because of the choice of sound to which they listen, many non-white people are seldom inspired to **think constructively**.

A person who chooses to listen to "non-constructive" sound, will have non-constructive thoughts.

A person whose mind is dominated by non-constructive thought will speak and/or act in a non-constructive manner.

People who **listen** to "music", and **hear** "music" will become smarter than people who listen to, and hear, "noise".

ENTERTAINMENT

While listening to "noise", a person does not gain the correct use and control of his/her "brain" power.

"Noise" sometimes contributes to a person's inability and/or lack of desire to think constructively, and/or to speak or act in a manner that best reflects the will and ability to do constructive things.

"Noise" ofttimes contributes to people speaking and/or acting to harm themselves, or unjustly harming others.

Avoid helping to promote "beauty contests".

Reason(s)/Explanation(s):

It is incorrect to attempt to "contest" **beauty**. **Beauty** is the revelation of **truth**, and the promotion of **justice** and **correctness.** Also, it is incorrect to directly or indirectly make a sport of, and/or to make jest of talent, ability, disability, physical appearance, etc. It is incorrect to directly, or indirectly, promote arrogant "pride", belittling division, envy, greed, jealously, (falsehood, injustice, incorrectness) etc.

Since no person in the known universe is the quality of person that he or she **should** be, there is no person in the known universe that is "beautiful".

There is not now, nor will there ever be, a justifiable reason for a so-called "beauty contest".

Seek to be "comfortable" only for the purposes of producing justice, and/or correctness.

Reason(s)/Explanation(s):

In a world that is not perfect, no person should have any more "comfort" than is necessary to help him or her to think, speak, and/or act to find truth, and use truth in such manner as to promote justice and correctness.

Do not promote, or participate in, any part of a "social gathering", for purposes of "fun" or "entertainment", in which more than two (2) persons are present. Always make sure that one of those persons is yourself, and the other person is a non-white person of opposite (complimentary) sex.

ENTERTAINMENT

Reason(s)/Explanation(s)

Non-white people waste too much time, energy, and money by promoting, and/or participating in, frivolous or **non-constructive** "parties" and "social gatherings".

As long as Racism (White Supremacy) exists, any deliberate "gathering" of **more** than **two** people should always be for the purpose of **doing constructive labor**, and/or, for the purpose of **exchanging constructive information.**

Most so-called "social gatherings" of non-white people are none other than excuses to "show-off" or gossip, and/or to engage in nit-picking, or malicious plotting.

An "entertainment party" that is limited to one male [non-white] person, and one female [non-white] person, should produce the following constructive results:

- Less money, time, and/or energy spent preparing and comparing clothing, trinkets, and other material possessions.
- Less time and/or energy spent comparing so-called "educational backgrounds", and/or social or financial "status".
- Less time and/or energy spent preparing to become familiar.
- Less time, energy, and/or money wasted in the effort to make "sexual impressions" while **pretending** not to intend to do so.
- Less hypocrisy, deception, and/or "show-offism" in any act associated with sexual intimacy, sexual intercourse, and/or "sexual play".
- Less dishonesty, and the promotion of an easier and more relaxed exchange of views that best helps to reveal the true objectives of the persons present.
- Fewer persons involved in the direct spead of gossip, idle talk, "nit-picking" or malicious plotting.

AREA 4: LABOR

▮ PREFACE ▮

The following pages present suggestions that pertain to what a Victim of Racism [non-white person] **should**, or **should not**, choose to do in the Fourth Major Area of **[People]** Activity: Labor.

Each person should choose to speak, and/or act, according to one or more of the suggestions presented — but only if he or she decides to do so. No person should speak and/or act according to any suggestion presented herein unless he or she has judged that the suggestion chosen is of **current** and **correct** value in helping to eliminate Racism (White Supremacy), and/or, in helping to better promote justice.

It is important to know and understand that one or more suggestions selected from one Major Area of [People] Activity, should be used in constructive combination with one or more suggestions selected from other Major Areas of [People] Activity.

If an individual person chooses to utilize any suggestion presented herein, he or she should do so in a manner, and at a specific time, and specific place, that will produce the **most constructive results** in the revelation of truth, and/or, the production of justice or correctness.

▮ ▮ ▮ ▮ ▮ ▮

Do not depend on other persons to help you to speak and/or act against injustice in matters of labor or employment.

Minimize conflict between yourself and others with whom you must contact in a work environment.

Offer to help others, but do not insist on doing so against their will.

In job situations, be polite to everyone, but always avoid being either overly familiar, or unnaturally rigid in your manner.

Avoid all talk about anything that does not directly or indirectly help to produce justice and correctness.

LABOR

Do not accuse any non-white person of being "the cause" of another non-white person "getting in trouble", and/or getting "fired", in regards to any employment situation that is directly or indirectly dominated by White Supremacists (Racists).

Reason(s)/Explanation(s):

As long as White Supremacy (Racism) exists, it is the White Supremacists (Racists) who are the cause of, and/or who are responsible for, all "problems" that involve any and all non-white people, in any and all areas of activity. This includes economics, education, entertainment, labor, law, politics, religion, sex, and war.

In a socio-material system dominated by White Supremacists, all "jobs" that are established and/or maintained by white people, are dominated, either directly or indirectly by those white people who practice White Supremacy (Racism).

Therefore, no person can be hired, fired, promoted, and/or get "in trouble" on a job unless it is the will of the White Supremacists (Racists).

In addition, there is no such thing as a **non**-white person being a "supervisor" (super/superior-advisor) on a job, in any socio-material system that is dominated by White Supremacists. Only **white** persons are "supervisors" (superior-advisors and/or **masters** of all advice-giving). Non-white persons, however, may have "supervisory" titles but, in truth, only serve as **messengers** (carriers of messages). Their assignment, functionally, is to act out the will of Racists (White Supremacists) by carrying messages, and/or instructions from Racist sources, to other persons whose "job" is to support those messages, and/or to follow those instructions.

In a socio-material system dominated by White Supremacists, **all** non-white persons either directly, or indirectly submit to, and/or cooperate with White Supremacy, each and every day of their existence.

Therefore, no non-white person is justly "qualified" to "name-call" and/or denounce any other non-white person because of his or her submission to, and/or cooperation with Racism (White Supremacy).

All non-white persons help to support White Supremacy.

Each non-white person does his or her part. They are all equal **servants** to the Racists. They are all equal **victims** of the Racists. They are all fearful. They are all weak. No one of them can justly blame the other.

Do not use the term "working class".

Reason(s)/Explanation(s):

Everyone "works".
Therefore, there is no such thing as a "class" of people that can correctly be called "**working class".**

Some people work with a greater purpose than others.
But **all** people, everywhere, do some form of "work".

Even those who only sit and wait for others to lead them are "working" for the leaders by **waiting** to be led by the leaders. But everybody **does** "work". Since everybody "works", there is no such thing as a working "class". There are only "working people" — some of whom "work" with **greater efficiency** and for a **greater purpose** than others.

Both the racists (White Supremacists), and their victims (non-white people) "work", in order to **survive**, so that they can "have fun".

The Racists work, in order to survive, so that they can "have fun" by practicing Racism (White Supremacy).

Many of the victims of the Racists, particularly those classified as "Black" and/or "Negro", work in order to survive, so that they can "have fun" by doing anything that they **think** may be "fun", from one moment to the next.

Most victims of White Supremacy work in order to "get in position" to "have fun". The White Supremacists build their fun into their work [White Supremacy] so that their "work" and their "fun" are one and the same.

The "work" of the White Supremacists is designed to make and/or keep them the masters of all non-white people, in all areas of activity, in all parts of the known universe.

By having a **greater purpose** for their "work" [Racism], the White Supremacists (Racists) have made their "work" [White Supremacy] the dominant motivating force among the people of the known universe.

LABOR

There is no "working class"
There are only **superior workers** (White Supremacists), and **inferior workers** (Victims of the White Supremacists).

Never say that any person is "unemployed".

Reason(s)/Explanation(s):

Every person in the known universe is "employed". All persons are either employed in the production of **justice**, or, they are employed in the maintenance, expansion, and/or refinement of **non-justice.**

Try to get things done by:

- Concentrating on what you know best.
- Choosing a situation that needs improvement.
- Getting all the facts.
- Interpreting the facts.
- Thinking of possible improvements.
- Choosing the better way.
- Convincing others that it is an improvement.

Before starting a project, ask yourself these questions:

- What should be done?
- Why should it be done?
- Where should it be done?
- Why should it be done there?
  Would another place be better?
- When should it be done?
  Would another time be better?
- How should it be done?
- How **much** time should be spent doing it?
- What should be the volume?
- Why do what should be done "this" way? Could it be done faster, cheaper, and more efficient some other way?
- **Who** should do it?

When putting an idea to work:

- Get a thorough understanding of the idea.
- Set a time limit in which to try the idea.
- Set a definite number of times to try the idea.
- Analyze the results.
- Improve the technique.

LABOR

Do not speak and/or act as if you are "better" than other persons because of the type of work [job/employment] that they are required to do, in order to try to function in a constructive manner. Do not try to "belittle" people because of the work that they are required to do. Do not "poke fun" at the low or inadequate pay that others receive for the work that they do.

Do not speak and/or act as if other persons are "better" than you because of the type of work that they do, or because of the amount of pay that they receive for that work.

Reason(s)/Explanation(s):

All constructive work is worthy of great regard. Those who try to belittle those who do constructive work, belittle themselves. Those who "poke fun" at the low or inadequate pay that others receive for the work that they do, are by so doing, showing a contempt for justice.

AREA 5: LAW

▮ PREFACE ▮

The following pages present suggestions that pertain to what a Victim of Racism [non-white person] **should**, or **should not** choose to do in the Fifth Major Area of [People] Activity: Law.

Each person should choose to speak, and/or act, according to one or more of the suggestions presented — but only if he or she decides to do so. No person should speak and/or act according to **any** suggestion presented herein unless he or she has judged that the suggestion chosen is of **current** and **correct** value in helping to eliminate Racism (White Supremacy), and/or, in helping to better promote justice. It is important to know and understand that one or more suggestions selected from one Major Area of [People] Activity, should be used in constructive combination with one or more suggestions selected from other Major Areas of [People] Activity.

If an individual person chooses to utilize any suggestion presented herein, he or she should do so in a manner, and at a specific time, and specific place, that will produce the **most constructive results** in the revelation of truth, and/or the production of justice or correctness.

▮ ▮ ▮ ▮ ▮ ▮

In the event you willfully and deliberately put to death any Racist(s), and/or any suspected Racist(s), you should then eliminate yourself before being forced to commit any act of violence and/or bodily harm against any people who are not Racist(s) or suspected Racist(s), but who are directly or indirectly sent by Racists to maim, kill, or put you in greater confinement [jail].

Reason(s)/Explanation(s):

As long as Racism (White Supremacy) is the dominant motivating force among the people of the known universe, every effort should be made to avoid violent conflict between all people who **are not** Racists (White Supremacists). It is also correct to avoid conflict with Racists, if it is at all possible to do so while trying to reveal truth, and/or while trying to promote justice or correctness.

LAW

To kill is a serious and terrible act. No animal, person, insect, or any thing generally recognized as "animate" or "alive" should be killed for any reason other than to establish and/or maintain justice, and/or correctness.

To kill for any other "reasons", and/or to consider killing for any other "reasons" is to help to keep the animals, people, insects, etc., of the known universe in the state of non-justice and incorrectness that now exists.

No person should seek, find, and **willfully** and **deliberately** put to death any other person without, also, putting him or her **self** to death. No person should, willfully, seek, find, and deliberately end the existence of another person without ending his or her own existence. Eliminating one's own existence after willfully and deliberately eliminating the existence of another person is just and correct.

Such an act makes a person sincere in his or her belief in justice, and in his or her regard for the value of existence and non-existence. The willful and deliberate ending of the existence of another has, in too many instances, been a "game". Some methods of making war are ofttimes referred to as "war games". Fighting and killing has, in many ways, been treated as sport and entertainment.

The destruction of a person's existence has been made to appear "natural", "heroic", and "glamourous". Killing people has ofttimes been considered as nothing more than a mature form of frivolity. All such acts are unjust and incorrect.

To seek, find, and willfully and deliberately put Racists and/or suspected Racists to death, and then, to surrender to captivity by Racists, suspected Racists, and/or the Victims of Racism recruited for such purposes, is not only unjust and incorrect but defeats the purpose of taking counter-violent action against the Racists.

If a Victim of Racism [non-white person] does this, it indicates that he or she has chosen to take counter-violent action against Racists that was **not absolutely necessary.** It indicates that the person engaging in such action was making a temporary protest rather than engaging in an emergency act of **maximum necessity**. Such action is unjust.

When non-white persons do anything that is unjust or incorrect, do not comment without explaining that under White Supremacy (Racism) it is the White Supremacists, and only the White Supremacists, who are "responsible" for what was done.

Reason(s)/Explanation(s):

White Supremacists (Racists) are the **smartest** and **most powerful** people in the known universe.

White Supremacy (Racism) is **unjust** and **incorrect.**

Therefore, nothing **unjust** happens among the people of the known universe unless the White Supremacists **cause** it to happen and/or **allow** it to happen.

Ask all people to help to produce justice. Particularly, ask white people to help to produce justice. But avoid attempting to produce justice by spending large amounts of money in your possession to play "games" with "laws".

Reason/Explanation:

In a socio-material system dominated by people who practice Racism (White Supremacy), it is **unjust** and **incorrect** for any Victim of Racism (non-white person) to "pay" to **ask** for justice.

Avoid helping any person, whom you suspect may be a Racist (White Supremacist), to do anything against another person, unless the other person is doing, and/or is attempting to do, something that is obviously unjust and/or incorrect.

If you are not absolutely certain that a particular white person does not practice White Supremacy (Racism) in Economics, Education, Entertainment, Labor, Law, Politics, Religion, Sex, or War, try to avoid helping that person to say or do anything against any person who is a Victim of White Supremacy [non-white person].

Reason/Explanation:

As long as White Supremacy exists, it is non-just and incorrect to help a person who you think may be a White Supremacist to do anything that is likely to give greater support to White Supremacy (Racism/non-justice).

LAW

Before doing, or saying, anything, ask yourself this question:

Will it help to promote justice?

If so, do it. If not, don't do it.
If in doubt, wait until there is no doubt.

Reason/Explanation:

As long as non-justice exists, the only **correct** reason for doing or saying **anything** is to promote justice.

Never hire, force, or order, any person, to kill, or maim a person.

Never allow any person to hire, force, or order, you to kill, or maim, a person.

Kill only those **persons that you know should be killed, and who should be killed by you, in order to promote justice.**

Reason(s)/Explanation(s):

It is non-just and incorrect for any person to hire, force, and/or order any person to kill, or maim, a person.

Do not say or do anything in such manner that someone else is suspected of, and/or accused of, saying or doing what you alone, said or did.

Do not confuse "comfort" with justice.

Reason(s)/Explanation(s):

Persons who are **subject** to injustice sometimes may feel "comfortable". At other times they may feel "uncomfortable".

Persons who **practice** injustice sometimes may feel "comfortable". At other times they may feel "uncomfortable".

Because a person is "physically" or "mentally", "comfortable", or "uncomfortable", does not necessarily mean that that person, is or is not, a **victim** of injustice.

Because a person is "physically" or "mentally" "comfortable", or "uncomfortable", does not necessary mean that that person is, or is not, **practicing** injustice.

LAW

Example:

On a cold, rainey, day, a Black slave may feel "comfortable" in the warm kitchen of a White Master.

On that same day, the White Master may feel very "uncomfortable" riding to a slave auction in an open coach.

The Black slave, however, though "feeling" more "comfortable" than the White Master, is, none-the-less, a victim of injustice. In spite of the relative "comfort" of the moment, he, or she, is **still** a slave to the White Master.

Do not enforce, support, and/or promote any "law" unless you can do so in a manner that promotes justice.

Reason(s)/Explanation(s):

The correct purpose for **any** law is to promote **justice.**

Any law that is enforced in such manner as to promote **injustice** is an **unjust** law.

Any **person** who enforces an unjust law is an **out-law.**

Do not "blame" any place or any thing for practicing Racism, and/or for committing any unjust act.

"Blame" only persons.

Reason(s)/Explanation(s):

It is not possible for **places** or **things** to commit **unjust** acts.

Only **people** can commit unjust acts.

People sometimes say that a particular **place** is "Racist", and/or that a person was "mistreated" by a particular **town** or **city** or **country.** People will sometimes say, or imply, that they were "treated badly" by the "United States". They will sometimes say that "Russia practices Racism", or that "Mississippi is Racist". People will sometimes say that a particular automobile plant "does not do justice".

Remarks of this type are **never** correct.

"Places" and/or "things" should never be identified as being "Racist" or "unjust". Only a **person** can practice **Racism.** Only a **person** can practice **injustice.**

LAW

When Victims of Racism (non-white people) mention Racism and/or injustice, it is correct and just for them to make use of one or more of the following type statements:

- "To the extent that Racists are operating in this (that) area of the world, they are responsible for the unjust activity".
- "To the extent that Racists have influence in this (that) area of the world, they are responsible for the unjust activity".
- "To the extent that the Masters of Injustice (Racists) have influence in this area of the world, they are responsible for the unjust activity".
- "If Racists (White Supremacists) have direct or indirect domination over this (that) area of the world, they are responsible for any and all unjust activity".
- "If a Racist (White Supremacist) was involved, he or she most certainly was responsible for most of the unjust activity".

Never refer to a policeman or policewoman as being Racist. Also, avoid using the term "police" to describe any person now in existence.

Practice using the term "enforcement officials" to describe any person who uses "force" to enact the will of those who have dominant power.

Reason(s)/Explanation(s):

It is **not possible** for any person to be a "policeman", or a "policewoman", and, at the same time, be a Racist.

"Policemen", and "policewomen" are people who seek and find truth, and who use the truth in such manner as to produce justice and correctness, at **all** times, in **all** areas of activity.

Racists, however, are people who practice White Supremacy (Racism).

White Supremacy is the promotion of falsehood, non-justice, and/or incorrectness based on factors "associated with" the "color" and/or the "non-color" of people.

LAW

Do not steal —— even from the Racists (White Supremacists).

Do not steal —— even from those who have stolen from you.

Reason(s)/Explanation(s):

To "steal", generally, means to take possession of material(s) by deceitful and/or "sneaky" methods.

"Stealing" —— even from the Racists —— is **incorrect.**

The self-confidence of racial subjects is greatly weakened when they rely on stealing as a means of gaining material things from the Racists (White Supremacists). Though **everything** that a Racist has in his or her possession is a direct or indirect **result** of the practice of Racism (White Supremacy), no Victim of Racism (non-white person) should take any material possessions (other than his or her personal existence) from the Racists, **without the consent** of the Racists.

If a Victim of Racism (non-white person) wants something from the Racists, he or she should **ask** for it. But no Victim of Racism should ever ask the Racists or anybody else, for **anything** that does not promote the revelation of **truth**, and the practice of **justice** and **correctness.**

Try to eliminate the harm that people deliberately do to each other by exchanging views with people in such manner that understanding is best promoted, and that conflict is minimized.

If **minimizing conflict** by exchanging views fails, then try to **minimize non-constructive contact** with persons who deliberately seek to do harm to yourself and/or to others who seek to promote justice.

If you cannot avoid non-constructive involvement with persons who **willfully** and **deliberately** seek to do harm to you, and/or to others who seek to promote justice, you should then try to stop them by using the just/most-effective, means.

"Blame" the White Supremacists (Racists) for all unjust acts that Victims of White Supremacy (non-white people) commit against each other.

LAW

Reason(s)/Explanation(s):

Whereas the victims of White Supremacy who commit unjust acts, **are guilty** of having **committed** the acts, they **are not responsible** for the acts.

In any socio-material system dominated by White Supremacists (Racists), the White Supremacists are responsible for all unjust acts committed by persons who are subject to the power of the White Supremacists.

White Supremacy (Racism) **itself** is an unjust socio-material **dictatorship.** Therefore, the persons who are **responsible** for all unjust acts committed by persons who are subject to White Supremacy **are not** the persons who committed the acts [non-white people]. The persons responsible for the acts are the White Supremacists who are **in charge** of the persons who committed the acts.

Since the White Nation (White Supremacists, collectively) is in charge of all of the non-white people in the known universe in **all** areas of activity, it is also in charge of **all** parts of the socio-material system (White Supremacy) that permits and/or encourages non-white people to commit unjust acts against one another. This system also inspires non-white people to value injustice rather than justice.

Therefore, whereas **each** and **every** Victim of White Supremacy (non-white person) should be **stopped immediately** from committing major unjust acts, it is **each** and **every** White Supremacist (Racist) who should be made to **compensate** for **all** unjust acts committed by **any** person, **any** place, at **any** time, since the establishment of White Supremacy.

When any non-white person commits any act of injustice against anyone while existing subject to White Supremacy, all White Supremacists are guilty of causing that act of injustice to be committed. It is the same as if they, themselves, committed the act, in person, rather than through the person of their subjects. The White Supremacists **themselves** are **essentially** the persons who actually committed the act of injustice.

Under White Supremacy (Racism), non-white people serve as tools and/or instruments through which major acts of injustice are committed.

LAW

Anytime that any non-white person does anything that is unjust and incorrect, it is those white people who practice White Supremacy who are responsible, and/or to "blame". They are the only people responsible. They are the only people to "blame". They are the people who have the dominant power to do the most to produce justice, and/or to allow others to produce it.

Speak and/or act to use "law" only in such manner that justice is promoted. Do not under any circumstance speak and/or act in such manner that "law" is promoted but justice is opposed or ignored.

Reason(s)/Explanation(s):

Laws change, but justice remains the same.

Laws are made and unmade. Laws are sometimes promoted, sometimes opposed, and sometimes ignored. **Justice**, however, is **"constant"**.

A **correct** law is made for one purpose:

> To help **people**, to produce **justice**, in order to produce **correctness**, in order to provide "peace".

Any law that is used in such manner as to promote injustice is a **non**-law.

Any **person** who willfully and deliberately utilizes a law in such manner as to promote **in**justice is an **out**law.

It is the **basic duty** of every person in the known universe to promote the production of justice. In order to do so, each person must use all laws **correctly**. This includes all laws that are "recorded" and all laws that are **not** "recorded".

Make a major effort to avoid being put into "Greater Confinement" [jail, prison, small and inadequate areas, etc.]. Avoid doing anything that you have reason to believe may result in your being put into "Greater Confinement".

Reason(s)/Explanation(s):

In a socio-material system dominated by Racism (White Supremacy), **all** non-white people are confined, retarded, and restricted, in thought, speech, and/or action, in all places, at all times, in all areas of activity, including Economics, Education, Entertainment, Labor, Law, Politics, Religion, Sex, and War.

Too many Victims of Racism (non-white people) spend too much time/energy in "Greater Confinement".

Too many jails, prisons, concentration camps, etc., are established for the basic purpose of "warehousing" non-white persons — including many of the unborn.

The White Supremacists know that a world system based on Racism (White Supremacy) requires that substantial numbers of non-white people be greatly restricted in their movements from place to place. The White Supremacists restrict the movements and activities of non-white people so as to keep them idle, and/or to keep them from becoming constructively self-sufficient.

The Racists (White Supremacists) make certain that substantial numbers of non-white people exist under conditions that will most likely cause them to do things that will give the Racists an "excuse" to put them in Greater Confinement.

The Racists cause this by using a variety of tactics — many of them based on deception, through pretention.

Examples:

- **Pretending** to provide "economic" progress, while working to hinder it.

- **Pretending** to provide "educational" progress while working to hinder it.

- **Pretending** to promote justice, while working to continue, and refine, the practice of injustice.

As long as White Supremacy (Racism) exists, avoid using the term "husband", the term "wife", or the term "parent", to describe any non-white person. Instead, practice using the terms:

- **"Acting husband", and/or "attempt husband".**
- **"Acting wife", and/or "attempt wife".**
- **"Acting parent", and/or "attempt parent".**

LAW

Reason(s)/Explanation(s):

No person [non-white] can be subject to White Supremacy (Racism) in anything that he or she says, or does, in **any** area of activity, and, at the same time, be a "husband", a "wife", or a "parent", to any other person — white or non-white. **All** persons [non-white] who are subject to, and/or, who are victims of White Supremacy (Racism) are, also, functionally, **Racist**-retarded "children". A functional, and/or **Racist**-retarded "child" is not "qualified" to be a "husband".

A functional, and/or **Racist**-retarded "child" is not "qualified" to be a "wife". A functional, and/or **Racist**-retarded "child" **can** produce off-spring. He or she is **not** "qualified" to be a "parent".

It is important to know and understand that one of the basic functions of a Racist is to retard and confuse non-white people. Under White Supremacy, **all** non-white people function as **retarded children.**

As long as White Supremacy (Racism) exists, avoid speaking and/or acting as if any person classified as "white" is a "husband", a "wife", or a "parent", to any person who is classified as "non-white".

Reason(s)/Explanation(s):

In a socio-material system dominated by White Supremacy (Racism), **no person** can function as a "husband", a "wife", or a "parent" to any **non**-white person.

In a socio-material system dominated by white Supremacy, **all** non-white persons are direct, or indirect, **subjects** of White Supremacists (Racists).

A system of White Supremacy does not permit any **non**-white person to function as a "husband" a "wife" or a "parent". Also, a system of White Supremacy functions in such manner that any **white** person who attempts to be a "husband", a "wife", or a "parent" to a **non**-white person, cannot do so. Those who attempt to do so become White Supremacists in the process of the attempt. They become White Supremacists because any attempt by a white person to act as a "husband", "wife", or "parent", to a non-white person, under a condition dominated by White Supremacy, only helps to maintain and refine White Supremacy. White Supremacists (Racists) can only function as the Master-Custodians and/or so-called "Race Parents" of non-white people. Therefore, simple but important titles such as "husband", "wife","father", "mother", or "parent" are meaningless. Such titles do not correctly apply to any person [non-white] who is subject to White Supremacy.

AREA 6: POLITICS [PEOPLE RELATIONS]

▮ PREFACE ▮

The following pages present suggestions that pertain to what a Victim of Racism [non-white person] **should,** or **should not,** choose to do in the Sixth Major Area of [People] Activity: Politics [People Relations].

Each person should choose to speak, and/or act according to one or more of the suggestions presented — but only if he or she decides to do so. No person should speak and/or act according to any suggestion presented herein unless he or she has judged that the suggestion chosen is of **current** and **correct** value in helping to eliminate Racism (White Supremacy), and/or, in helping to better produce justice.

It is important to know and understand that one or more suggestions selected from one Major Area of [People] Activity, should be used in constructive combination with one or more suggestions selected from other Major Areas of [People] Activity.

If an individual person chooses to utilize any suggestion presented herein, he or she should do so in a manner, and at a specific time, and specific place, that will produce the **most constructive results** in the revelation of truth, and/or, the production of justice or correctness.

▮ ▮ ▮ ▮ ▮ ▮ ▮

Study, know, and understand **all** of the characteristics of Racism Man and Racism Woman [White Supremacists, collectively]. Do not forget what is learned from studying **all** of the ways and means by which, and through which, Racist Man and Racist Woman practice the science of Racism (White Supremacy).

Constantly watch for the methods used by the Racists that enable them to practice Racism with greater ease through the use of more **deceptive techniques.**

Study, try to understand, and try to remember everything that is said or done by Racist Man or Racist Woman, in **every** area of activity, that **directly**, or **indirectly**, helps to support or promote Racism (White Supremacy) any place in the known universe.

Study, try to understand, and try to remember, **all** of the basic characteristics of Racist Man and Racist Woman, in all

POLITICS

of the Nine Major Areas of (People) Activity — Economics, Education, Entertainment, Labor, Law, Politics, Religion, Sex, and War. Utilize the following initial outline as a beginning format for your own recordings of the basic characteristics of Racist Man and Racist Woman. Add details of further information to your recordings, as pertains to each area of activity, as soon as such details are revealed to you, through your experiences, or the experiences of others:

Economics

Racist Man and Racist Woman speak and act to **make certain** that non-white people, will, at **all** times, depend on white people for most, or all, of their needs.

Education

Racist Man and Racist Woman **discourage**, and/or speak and act to **prevent** non-white people from seeking knowledge, and/or maintaining records of knowledge to the **same** extent that White Supremacists do. They take unjust advantage of the fact that non-white people, generally, do not strive to "know everything", nor strive to know what they need to know to produce justice and correctness throughout the known universe.

Racist Man and Racist Woman construct, define, re-define, and use, all words and/or the meanings of all words, in such manner that they promote and/or "justify" the condition of White Supremacy (Racism) and/or the deeds of White Supremacists (Racists).

Entertainment

Racist Man and Racist Woman make a special effort to promote the abuse of non-white people by utilizing them as "things of entertainment". They do this by promoting, depicting, and/or utilizing non-white people as personal "pets", as "toys", as the "butt" of derogatory jokes, as sexual "trash", as sexual "toilets", and/or as ego-building "status symbols" based on the so-called "ownership" of non-white people by white people.

Labor

Racist Man and Racist Woman are the **superior** "workers" among the people of the known universe. They do **more** "work" than any people in the known universe.

POLITICS

The "work" of Racist Man and Racist Woman is to establish, maintain, expand, and/or refine the practice of Racism (White Supremacy). In addition, Racist Man and Racist Woman use deceit, direct violence, and/or the threat of violence as a means of getting **non-white** people to labor in direct or indirect support of the establishment, maintenance, expansion, and/or refinement of Racism (White Supremacy). The major result of such "work" as based on the color/non-color of people, is the promotion of falsehood, non-justice, and incorrectness among the people of the known universe.

Law

Racist Man and Racist Woman make, define, interpret, and/or practice all "law" **only** in a manner that directly or indirectly helps to establish, maintain, expand, and/or refine the practice of Racism (White Supremacy).

Politics

Racist Man and Racist Woman, at no time, say anything, or do anything, that is not intended to establish, maintain, expand, and/or refine the practice of White Supremacy (Racism). Racist Man and Racist Woman speak and act in such manner as to promote **confusion** [imbalance] in the thought, speech, and action of their victims (non-white people) at **all** times, in **all** places, in **all** areas of activity, including, Economics, Education, Entertainment, Labor, Law, Politics, Religion, Sex, and/or War. The Racists speak and act as **supreme** leader, teacher, father, mother, priest, queen, guide, god, critic, dispute-maker, dispute-settler, judge, prosecutor, provider, so-called "protector", etc., of all non-white people, in all places in the known universe, in all areas of activity.

Religion

Racist Man and Racist Woman practice, promote, and advocate the practice of **one** "religion" **only**. The name of that "religion" is White Supremacy (Racism).

Racist Man and Racist Woman, also, at all times, both directly and indirectly, use the names and/or rituals of any, or all, other religions, to promote, through **deceit**, and ofttimes through direct violence, the "religion" of White Supremacy.

Sex

Racist Man and Racist Woman claim absolute "ownership" of, and practice direct, or indirect, **master** power over, the sexual activities of **all** non-white people. Their claim includes a so-called absolute "right of access" to the sexual activities of any and all non-white male or female persons.

The Racists do **whatever is necessary to make sure** that any or all non-white persons are available, and vulnerable, **at all times**, to, and for, sexual experiment, and sexual abuse by white people.

War

Racist Man and Racist Woman do not fight, kill, and/or speak against, or for, any person, place, or thing, without the intention of directly or indirectly establishing, maintaining, expanding, and/or refining White Supremacy (Racism).

Summary of Some of the Major Characteristics of Racist Man and Racist Woman

Racist Man and Racist Woman (White Supremacists) are the Master Subversive Elements of the known universe, and the Master Subversive Elments of the known universe are Racist Man and Racist Woman. Because of their tremendous energy and great ability combined with their devotion to unjust and incorrect objectives, they have become the master promoters of falsehood, non-justice, and incorrectness. They are, collectively, the greatest enemies of, and the most skilled opposers to, the production of peace among the people of the known universe.

Racist Man and Racist Woman are the direct and/or indirect functional "cause" of all widespread and long-lasting malice and confusion, and all hunger and envy among all of the people of the known universe.

As long as White Supremacy (Racism) exists, it is extremely important for all Victims of Racism (non-white people) to remember, at all times, that Racist Man and Racist Woman do not, at **any** time, willfully and deliberately do, or say, **any** thing, in **any** area of activity, that does not directly or indirectly help to establish, maintain, expand, and/or refine the practice of Racism (White Supremacy).

It is extremely important for Victims of Racism to remember that **everything** — repeat — **everything** — that a Racist (White Supremacist) says or does, that is willful and deliberate, is **intended** to **unjustly** subjugate, dislocate, deceive, deny, deprive, destory, and/or retard, one or more persons classified as "non-white".

It is correct to know, understand, and remember, that, as long as White Supremacy exists, **every person** classified as "white" should be "suspected" of being a Racist (White Supremacist).

The only exceptions should be those "white" persons who are "infantile", "senile", and/or "acutely helpless" because of mental or physical disabilities.

It is correct to know, understand, and remember, that the basic tools and/or weapons of a Racist Man or a Racist Woman are **deceit** (indirect violence) and/or **direct violence**. A Racist Man, or a Racist Woman, will **at all times** seek to **deceive** his or her victims [non-white persons], and/or he or she will seek to do violence to them **directly**. The deceit and direct violence usually takes many different forms, and affects and dominates every area of activity of the violated.

Racist Man and Racist Woman are the Masters of Deceit and the Masters of Direct Violence.

Speak and act as if the current "reason" for the existence of Black people in the known universe is to produce justice, and that everything that Black people say and do be for that purpose.

Reason(s)/Explanation(s):

It seems that the current "reason" for the existence of white people in the known universe is to do great and useful things through science and technology.

It seems that the current "reason" for the existence of **non**-white people in the known universe is to **use** the things that are developed through science and technology in a manner that helps best in producing **justice** and **correctness.**

This seems to indicate that the current "reason" for the existence of non-white people is, apparently, to **make sure** that **justice** and **correctness** is established and maintained in **all** areas of activity. These "areas", as a matter of course, would automatically include Economics, Education, Entertainment, Labor, Law, Politics, Religion, Sex, and War [conflict].

The evidence seems to show that, so far, too many white people who know, and understand, how to do many things, with great efficiency, have **refused** to use that knowledge and understanding to produce **justice** and **correctness.**

Likewise, the evidence seems to show that, so far, too many Black people have shown **too little interest** in, and/or, not enough knowledge and understanding of **how** to produce justice and correctness.

"White" people, on the whole, seem to have a greater "talent" for, and/or a greater interest in, great accomplishments in science and technology. The smartest and most powerful of white people do a variety of great and complex things on a broad scale, and with relative ease.

"Black" people, when showing an interest in activities that are constructive, seem to, on the whole, show a great interest in those activities that are considered more "social" and/or "religious".

Great numbers of Black people seem to enjoy those activities that are directly related to the production of justice.

Many of the great accomplishments by white people, through science and technology, have helped many white people, and Black people, to increase their mental and physical abilities. Much of what has been done however, has helped many white people, and many Black people to develop habits and intentions that are **opposed** to the production of justice and correctness. The promotion of incorrect habits and intentions of many Black people, on a grand scale, has been the result of the activities and intentions of many of the smartest and most powerful of white people. Many of the smartest of white people have established the most powerful socio-political science in the known universe. This socio-political science has become their "reason" for existence. It is called "White Supremacy" and/or "Racism". These extremely smart people have developed a desire to use their great knowledge and understanding of people, beings, and things, to practice a system of supremacy over, and injustice against, all people who are classified as "Black" or "non-white". They have used their "whiteness" as a basic so-called "justification" for subjugating and mistreating Black people. As White Supremacists (Racists), many white people have made a maximum effort to use their technical and scientific capabilities to treat non-white people as "things" rather than as people. They value Black people only as objects, tools, and/or "toys", rather than as people. They have made Racism their religion, and made the use and abuse of non-white people the "most worthy" of all possible activities among the people of the known universe. They have deliberately used their great skills to get many things done, in order to do many things that should **not** be done. Through their great knowledge and understanding, the White Supremacists, have, so far, been able to nullify the feeble and confused efforts of those Black people who seek to promote justice and correctness.

Too many white people have shown that they prefer White Supremacy (Racism) to justice and correctness. Too many Black people have shown that they do not care enough about justice and correctness to make a **maximum effort** to produce it.

Justice and correctness cannot exist, at the **same** time, in the **same** "universe", with Racism. As long as Racism exists, it is **impossible** to have justice and correctness.

Do not speak and/or act as if you are doing what you are supposed to be doing [your "duty"] during any period in which you are not promoting justice.

Reason(s)/Explanation(s):

Each person in the known universe, is, each minute, of each day and night, engaging in **one** of the following **Two (2) Major Types of People Activity:**

1. Promotion of Justice [Promoting Balance Between People]

2. Maintenance of the Status Quo [Maintaining Injustice and/or Wasting Time]

Since justice **does not exist** among the people of the known universe, it should be understood that **each person** in the known universe is, at each moment, either "trying" to produce justice, or, he or she is "trying" to maintain the **Status Quo.**

POLITICS

The people of the known universe are **not in balance** with one another.

To try to produce justice is to try to produce balance between each and every person in the known universe.

To produce balance between the people of the known universe is to **eliminate** the **Status Quo.**

To try to maintain the Status Quo, and/or, to allow the Status Quo to be maintained, is to **maintain injustice.**

To "spend time" doing anything **other than** trying to produce justice by eliminating the Status Quo is to **waste time.**

"Wasting time" is none other than maintaining the Status Quo.

Never say that any white person is not a Racist.
Never say that any person is a Racist. However, as long as White Supremacy (Racism) exists, always be alert. Always be suspicious. Assume, at all times, that any white person that you meet, or hear about, is most likely to be a person who directly, or indirectly, practices Racism (White Supremacy).

Do not assume that any (white) person is not a Racist because you have "known" him or her a long time. Do not assume that a (White) person is not a Racist because you have been intimate with him or her. Do not assume that a (white) person is not a Racist because you have sexual intercourse with him or her. Do not assume that a (white) person is not a Racist because of "personal favors" that he or she has done for you.

Reason(s)/Explanations(s):

White people, collectively, are the smartest people in the known universe.

Among the white people are people who practice White Supremacy (Racism). Those white people who practice White Supremacy are smarter than **all** the other people of the known universe combined — both white and non-white. The white people who practice White Supremacy are, also, the most violent, the most powerful, and the most deceitful people in the known universe. They are the collective Masters of Deceit, and they usually deceive non-white people with great skill and great ease. Their deceit is ofttimes accompanied by smiles, or handshakes, or "gifts", or promises, or by many "kind" words. They know how to deceive people in every area of activity, and have repeatedly done so. They have done so, and still do so, in **Economics, Education, Entertainment, Labor, Law, Politics, Religion, Sex, and War**. They do not, however, do the same things, the **same way**, all of the time. This too, is a part of their strategy of deceit.

For these reasons, it is important that each and every non-white person be **constantly suspicious** of **everything** that a suspected Racist says or does. This suspicion of suspected Racists should be dominant when looking at, or hearing about, anything that they say, or do, in any area of activity, including Economics, Education, Entertainment, Labor, Law, Politics, Religion, Sex, and War. This is the first, and most important step, toward counter-acting and eliminating Racism and making possible the establishment of justice.

As long as White Supremacy (Racism) exists, do not speak, and/or act, as if any non-white person is responsible for any unjust and/or incorrect thing that happens, as a result of the acts of people, white or non-white. Speak, and/or act, as if the White Supremacists(Racists) are responsible.

Reason(s)/Explanation(s):

Those white people who practice White Supremacy (Racism) are the smartest, and most powerful people in the known universe. Their power and influence is greater than that of all other people **combined**.

Non-white people do nothing that is not endorsed, allowed, supported, and/or promoted by the White Supremacists (Racists). Racist Man and Racist Woman (White Supremacists, collectively) have more direct and/or indirect control over the bodies, brains, and general environment of **all** non-white people than the non-white people have over themselves or each other. It is, primarily, the Racists who can, and, so far, **do**, determine what **all** non-white people do, or don't do.

Since **everything** that a White Supremacist does is designed to dominate non-white people through deceit and/or direct violence, and/or through the general promotion of falsehood, non-justice, and incorrectness, it is, then, just and correct for any person who is a victim of White Supremacy to speak and/or act as if the White Supremacists are "responsible" for all non-just and/or incorrect speech or action by non-white people.

Under White Supremacy (Racism), any non-white person who says or does anything that **effectively** helps to promote justice, and/or correctness, becomes a target for **greater** deceit, and/or direct violence, by Racists Men and/or Racist Women.

Practice Asking People the Following Questions:

- **What** is your **ultimate** objective?
- **Why** is this [that] your ultimate objective?
- **How** do you intend to accomplish your ultimate objective?
- Will the accomplishment of your ultimate objective help to produce **justice**? If so, how?
- In what ways will the accomplishment of **your** ultimate objective **involve me?**
- In what ways will the accomplishment of **your** ultimate objective **affect me?** Will I be affected in the area of Economics? In Education? Entertainment? Labor? Law? Politics? Religion? Sex? War?

Reason(s)/Explanation(s):

It is correct to not only look at what people do, but, also, to ask yourself and others, **why.**

People do things for "reasons".

People have **objectives** for what they do, and say.

It is correct to seek, to know, and to understand the "reasons" people do what they do, or say what they say.

It is correct to seek, to know, and to understand the **ultimate objective** of every person whom you encounter, whose words or deeds may directly, or indirectly, affect your activities or existence.

Females: **Practice referring to yourselves as females. Avoid calling yourselves women.**

Males: **Practice referring to yourselves as males. Avoid calling yourselves men.**

Reason(s)/Explanation(s):

Racism is the greatest form of **injustice** in the known universe.

POLITICS

White Supremacy is the only **functional** expression of **Racism** in the known universe. White Supremacy is designed to subjugate people classified as "non-white" through the masterful promotion of falsehood, non-justice, and incorrectness.

Through the skillful use of deceit, and/or direct violence, the people who practice White Supemacy force **all** people classified as "non-white", to function as "children", in all of their relationships with people classified as "white".

They also force all people classified as "non-white" to function as "children" in all of their relationships with each other.

Any person [non-white], who is directly or indirectly subject to White Supremacy (Racism) is a "child".

It is not possible for a person [non-white] to be subject to White Supremacy, and, be a "man" or a "woman".

All persons who exist in subjugation to White Supremacy are either **male**, or **female**, "children".

All persons who exist in subjugation to White Supremacy are required, encouraged, and forced to function in a silly, primitive, and/or "child-like" manner, in all areas of activity, including Economics, Education, Entertainment, Labor, Law, Politics, Sex, and War.

When commenting on any event (past, present, or future) that likely involves Racists or Racism, always precede your comments with these exact words:

> "To the extent that a Racist has [or had] anything to do with it"--- [followed by comment].

Examples:

"To the extent that a Racist has anything to do with it, justice will not be done".

"To the extent that a Racist had anything to do with it, the peace talks could not lead to peace".

"To the extent that a Racist had anything to do with it, non-white people should not have been surprised at the outcome".

POLITICS

"To the extent that a Racist has anything to do with it, the new teaching procedures will only be used to give more strength to the status quo".

Explanation:

The dominant motivating force among the people of the known universe is White Supremacy (Racism). Therefore, nothing of significance happens among the people of the known universe that does not, directly or indirectly, involve the power of the White Supremacists (Racists). It is correct for Victims of White Supremacy [non-white people] to mention this fact during any discussion of importance in the area of people relations.

Do not say, or imply, in any manner, that any people, white or non-white, are now, or ever were, the quality of people that should exist in the known universe.

Reason/Explanation:

The "quality" of people [perfect people] that **should** exist, do not exist, in the known universe.

Such people are yet to be developed.

Help destory deceit, by helping to promote, the revelation of truth.

Examples:

Do not say **anything** that is **not true.**

Do not hesitate to say what is true, at a **time** that it **must** be said, in order to promote **justice.**

Do not say anything that is the **opposite** of what you are **thinking.**

Do not talk to a person, with the primary intention of engaging in sexual intercourse, while **pretending** to talk without having that intention.

Never criticize without making a constructive suggestion, and always strive to present the suggestion in detail, and in a manner that is easily understood.

Always give the reason for each suggestion made.

POLITICS

Reason/Explanation:

To criticize, without making a constructive suggestion, promotes hostility and/or confusion, and does little or nothing to solve a problem in a constructive manner.

If you agree to talk about something that a person said or did, always agree, or disagree, with the specific thing that the person said or did.

Avoid criticizing the person.

Try to minimize conflict. Avoid being "personal" in your comments on matters being questioned or discussed. Focus your talk in a manner that promotes ideas, concepts, and/or systems of doing things, and getting things done.

Example:

If you are asked to comment on something that a person did or said, make your remarks in a manner similar to those shown in the following exchange (with yourself as the 2nd person):

1st Person: What do you think of Mr. Smith?

2nd Person: What about Mr. Smith?

1st Person: You do know Mr. Smith don't you?

2nd Person: I've heard of him.

1st Person: Well, what do you think of his policies?

2nd Person: His policies as pertaining to what?

1st Person: Race.

2nd Person: What specific racial policy?

1st Person: His policy pertaining to the resettlement of Black people.

2nd Person: I disagree with that policy.

1st Person: Why?

2nd Person: Because it is the type of policy that helps promote Racism.

POLITICS

1st Person: Do you mean to say that Mr. Smith is a Racist?

2nd Person: I mean that the policy that Mr. Smith proposes is a policy that helps to promote Racism.

1st Person: But isn't that the same as calling Mr. Smith a Racist?

2nd Person: I do not name specific persons as being Racists. I point out specific things that are said or done that help to promote Racism.

1st Person: But isn't Mr. Smith's speech and action characteristic of the speech and action of a Racist?

2nd Person: I do not name specific persons as being Racists. I point out specific things that are said or done that help to promote Racism.

1st Person: But that's what you just did.

2nd Person: I just did what?

1st Person: Call Mr. Smith a Racist.

2nd Person: I did not do that. I would not do that.

1st Person: But you may as well have.

2nd Person: But I did not do that. I would not do that.

1st Person: Well, as far as **I'm** concerned that's exactly what you did.

2nd Person: You are entitled to your opinion.

[etc. ---]

Never call anyone a "liar".
Never say that someone is "a liar".
Don't say that a person is "lying".
When a person makes a remark that you know is not true, say:

"That [remark] is not true".

Reason(s)/Explanation(s):

POLITICS

To call someone a "liar" is "name-calling". It is incorrect to call anyone by any name and/or title except the name and/or title that he or she asks to be called.

When a person makes a remark, it is best to try to concentrate on the truth or non-truth of the **content** of the **remark**, rather than to place a "label" on the person making the remark.

Practice using the terms "correct government" and/or "incorrect government".

Avoid, and/or discontinue the use of any other terms pertaining to "types", and/or "kinds" of government.

Reason(s)/Explanation(s):

People make government.

All government by any people is either **correct** government or **incorrect** government.

Correct government is **any** person, and/or persons, who **effectively** speak and/or act to promote **justice.**

Incorrect government is **any** person, and/or persons, who **effectively** speak and/or act to promote **injustice.**

The **correct** name and/or title for **correct** government is "correct government".

The **correct** name and/or title for **incorrect** government is "incorrect government".

It is not necessary to use titles and/or names of so-called "countries", "systems", "states", "cities", "towns", etc., to describe and/or mention correct government or incorrect government. It is better and much less **confusing** to simply describe any action and/or inaction by any person or persons, any place, at any time, if effective, as either "correct government" or "incorrect government".

Any person, who, at any time, says, or does, **anything,** that has a substantial effect on what **other** people say or do, is either promoting **correct government, or, incorrect** government.

A person is acting as, and/or promoting, correct government, **only** when he or she is speaking and/or acting to effectively promote **justice.** At all other times, that person is speaking and/or acting to promote **injustice.**

POLITICS

If injustice exists, justice does not exist. It is not possible for justice and injustice to exist at the same time.

Since justice is not effectively promoted by any people, any place, then it is correct to conclude that injustice is either, directly or indirectly, **supported** by all people, in all places.

It is correct to say that there is, at present, **no** correct "government" in the known universe. There are only **some** people, who, **sometimes, try** to produce correct government.

Do not assume that you can keep a "secret" from White Supremacists (Racists).

Reason(s)/Explanation(s):

White Supremacists (Racists) are the direct-functional masters of **all** of the non-white people in the known universe. Of all the people in the known universe, those white people who have chosen to practice White Supremacy are the most powerful.

White Supremacists are also the **smartest** people in the known universe.

It is not likely that a **victim** of White Supremacy [non-white person] can prevent the White Supremacists from knowing anything that they want to know.

It is correct to always assume that if any person (other than yourself) has knowledge of what you know, then, what you know **is no secret.**

Do not refer to people as being "rich" or "poor". Refer to them as being "powerful" or "poor".

Reason(s)/Explanation(s):

All persons in the known universe, are, in their relationships to each other, either "powerful" or "poor". None are "rich".

"Rich" people are people who use truth, to practice justice, and correctness, at all times, in all places, in all areas of activity.

"Powerful" people are people who have massive power over many others. [**Example**: Racists (White Supremacists)].

"Poor" people are people who have little or no power when such power that they have is compared to the power of the Racists (White Supremacists).

Do not make remarks to any people — white or non-white — with the intention of being insulting. Do not belittle or try to embarrass people. Greet all people with a "good morning", a "good evening", etc.

Greet them, even when they repeatedly do not "return" the greeting. Continue to greet them until they **ask** you **not** to do so.

Reason(s)/Explanation(s):

Under most circumstances, it is always correct to try to be as friendly as possible, even to persons whom you suspect may be enemies.

Hostile speech or action should always be initiated by the enemies of justice — never by the major victims of injustice.

Do not refer to yourself as a "grown" person. Do not make remarks like, "don't talk to me like I'm a child. I'm grown".

Reason(s)/Explanation(s):

No person [non-white], who is subject to White Supremacy (Racism) is "grown". All persons [non-white] who exist in subjugation to White Supremacy are in a **relatively** primitive, retarded, and/or "undeveloped" condition, in all areas of activity, including Economics, Education, Entertainment, Labor, Law, Politics, Relgion, Sex, and War.

It is not correct for them to pretend that they do not.

As long as you are a Victim of Racism, avoid using the expressions "my child", "my children", etc.

Practice using the expressions "the children", and/or, "my off-spring" [those who sprang from, and/or away from me, into the domination of others].

Reason(s)/Explanation(s):

In a socio-material system dominated by White Supremacy (Racism), all non-white people are subject to the will of the White Supremacists (Racists).

Therefore, no **non**-white person can **truthfully** claim that he or she has **functional** "ownership" of, and/or "general power" over, any person, place, animal, thing, etc.

When a person makes a remark about you that you think may be important, do the following:

- Write and/or record **each word** of the remark.

- Study **each word** of the remark and seek, and find, the **true** definition [functional meaning] of **all words** that the person making the remark intended to be **applicable to you**.

- Find if the remark is **true**. Compare what you have said, and/or done, with the **true** definition of the words used by others to **describe** what you have said and/or done.

- Compare what you do, and/or say, with what others do, and/or say.

  Find if the **words** used to describe what others do, and/or say, are the **same** as the words and/or, **mean** the same, as the words, used to describe what **you** do and/or say.

  If the words are the **same**, and/or **mean** the same, find why.

  If the words **are not** the same, and/or, do not **mean** the same, find **why not**.

Don't be "stand-offish" in your relations with white people. Try to communicate. Try to be friendly.

Greet them, and don't be ill-at-ease when talking to them. Be casual without being disrespectful. Do not react with anger and/or discomfort when they make "insulting" and/or "Racist-sounding" remarks. Continue talking in a courteous and constructive manner.

Don't "nit-pick" or "be-little".
Exchange views with them on a variety of subjects. Be serious without being too formal. Be relaxed without being too frivolous.

Ask questions, and seek answers about all matters that may be of constructive value.

Reason(s)/Explanation(s):

White people are people who are worthy of great interest.

They are, generally, people who are attractive, fascinating, industrious, inventive, and "deep thinking".

They are generally not an aimless people. They are generally a people who constantly strive to do great things.

They are mentally alert and more questioning "in depth" than any other people.

They are generally more capable of answering questions that have long been unanswered, but asked many times by many people.

They have shown great ability to solve many problems much faster and with greater efficiency than non-white people.

They are proven masters of organization. They are proven masters of "arrangement" in the affairs of things, people, animals, insects, vegetation, etc.

They are people who cannot be avoided, and should not be ignored.

They are people who, to non-white people, are still the **most** "familiar mystery" in the known universe.

Avoid "croneyism", "cliqueism", "tribalism", "nationalism", "clanism", "clubism", etc., to the extent that such functions interfere with the revelation of truth, and/or the promotion of justice or correctness.

Reason(s)/Explanation(s):

The **basic duty** of every **person** in the known universe is to find, and use truth in such manner as to promote justice and correctness at all times, in all places, in all areas of activity.

Therefore the basic duty of every "group" of persons — "cronies", "cliques", "clans", "clubs", "nations", "tribes", etc. — is to do likewise.

There is no reason to "join" any group of people who do not have, and **show**, the basic intention of finding truth, and using the truth found in such manner as to promote justice and correctness.

Do not brag about anything that any person, or persons, have done, are doing, or are attempting to do, no matter how constructive it was, is, or may be.

Help people to do what should be done.

Encourage people to do what should be done. But do not brag, and do not help or encourage others to brag.

Reason(s)/Explanation(s):

Bragging is not a constructive activity. Revealing and/or using truth in such manner as to promote justice and correctness **is** constructive activity.

It is incorrect and unnecessary to **brag** about the truth.

It is incorrect to **brag** about anything that is learned, or about anything that is acquired, or about anything that is accomplished, by any person, animal, insect, etc.

It is incorrect to use **bragging** as a "reward", either to yourself, or to others. Constructive activity — the use of truth to produce justice and correctness — does not need to be bragged about. The practice of justice and correctness does not need to be bragged about.

Bragging tends to make many people think that constructive activity is something other than a "natural" occupation.

Bragging, most times, causes envy and/or animosity among people.

The people of the known universe do not need to do anything that **unnecessarily** increases the envy and/or animosity that they already have toward one another.

Do not speak or act in such manner as to promote hatred of white people.

Reason(s)/Explanation(s):

"White" people are **people.**
Generally speaking, they are smart people.
They are industrious people.
They are a people who question, and explore, and examine, and experiment.
They are great arrangers.
They study everything in great detail.
They are great builders.

POLITICS

Their knowledge and understanding is extensive in all areas of activity, including Economics, Education, Entertainment, Labor, Law, Politics, Religion, Sex, and War.
They are, generally speaking, the smartest people in the known universe.
As such, they are, generally speaking, very attractive and exceedingly fascinating — both in appearance and performance.

As a people who can usually be recognized by their extreme lightness of skin, "white" people have shown a distinct capability for engaging in an awesome number of grand and difficult activities. They apparently achieve whatever they achieve with an ease that is ofttimes startling, but most times taken for granted by "non-white" people.

"White" people, as people, are capable of great compassion — or great fury.
As **people**, they clearly display the possible capacity for unmatched humanitarian accomplishment.
But as people who have chosen to be Racists (White Supremacists), large numbers of them have utilized their intellect to practice deceit and violence on a scale that has made falsehood, injustice, and incorrectness, a "normal" condition, and a **basic requirement** for existence, among the people of the known universe. Still, it is just as **incorrect** to "hate" white people who practice White Supremacy as it is to "hate **any** people, anywhere.

"Hatred" of any person serves no constructive purpose. Nor is it necessary to devote the power of the mind to a "hatred" of not only any person, but of any place, thing, or idea. It **is** correct, however, to **oppose falsehood, injustice,** and **incorrectness** — particularly when it is expressed in such a massive and destructive form as Racism (White Supremacy).

Since White Supremacy has proven to be the most powerful means of promoting falsehood, injustice, and incorrectness, then it is the duty of all people to use truth, to promote justice and correctness, and thereby, oppose White Supremacy (Racism).

The opposition to White Supremacy should be massive and effective.
All people should speak and/or act against it in all areas of activity, including Economics, Education, Entertainment, Labor, Law, Politics, Religion, Sex, and War.
But it can, should, and **must**, be done without hatred.

POLITICS

Do not taunt, curse, provoke, "name-call", fight, or otherwise confront, Racists, and/or suspected Racists, and then expect them to show mercy toward you, and/or to relate to you in a humane manner.

Reason(s)/Explantion(s):

To get, and keep, their power, Racists (White Supremacists) **must** practice falsehood, non-justice, and incorrectness.

To be a Racist, a person **cannot** be humane. It is not possible for a person to be a Racist, and be humane, at the same time.

Racists (White Supremacists) are masters of **deceit** and **violence**.

When Racists are not violating their victims [non-white people] through the use of deceit, they violate them through **direct** physical abuse. It is incorrect to expect a Racist to be **humane**. It is correct to expect them to be **deceitful** and/or violent — either directly or indirectly.

It is correct to expect them to be this way **all** of the time.

When asked to discuss the "causes of Racism", present, and/or repeat, the essentials of the following points of view:

- "White" people, generally, produce more questions, **and** more answers, about more things, than all of the "Black" and/or "non-white" people of the known universe combined.

- In the process of producing many questions and many answers, great numbers of "white" people discovered that they had learned more, and knew more, about more different things, than all of the "Black" and/or "non-white" people of the known universe **combined**.

- In the process of learning, many "white" people discovered that when they had sexual intercourse with "Black" people, any off-spring produced were usually not a nearer "like-ness" of themselves. The off-spring were "non-white" in appearance, and/or "classification", **most** of the time.

- Being, collectively, "smarter" than Black people, being incapable of producing "white" off-spring through sexual intercourse with them, and "fearing" the ability of Black people to produce people of all "colors" as well as the "non-color" ["white"], many "white" people decided to **subjugate** "Black" people — using "color" as a basis, or "reason".

POLITICS

- The subjugation of people based on color, and/or, by using factors "associated with" color, has resulted in the establishment, maintenance, expansion, and ofttimes refinement of the greatest and **most effective** form of **injustice** in the known universe.

  This injustice is ofttimes referred to as "Racism", and, more specifically referred to as "White Supremacy".

- In the process of making "non-white" people subject to them, those "white" persons who participate in the practice of White Supremacy do so through the greatest and most sophisticated use of deceit, direct violence, and/or the threat of violence, ever devised by people, among the people of the known universe.

- White Supremacy (Racism) is now the dominant socio-material force among the people of the known universe. **No** major problem(s) in the areas of Economics, Education, Entertainment, Labor, Law, Politics, Religion, Sex, or War can be solved as long as White Supremacy exists.

Do not speak and/or act in support of any "formal" system of birth control, for the non-white people of the known universe, until such time, as the births of all white people come to a complete halt.

Reason/Explanation:

Many white people practice Racism (White Supremacy).

Those white people who practice Racism do not intend for any **non**-white people to be born without their permission. Such a restriction by such people is non-just and incorrect.

Therefore, as long as White Supremacy (Racism) exists, non-white people should be wary of all birth-control programs that are suggested by, and/or controlled by others.

Do no participate in Riots.
Do not willfully and deliberately assist others in committing any act that, because of confusion, is likely to result in injury to those to whom injury is not intended.

Do not seek help from others in your commission of any willful and deliberate act that promotes "non-constructive" injury.

POLITICS

Reason/Explanation:

As long as White Supremacy exists, it is unjust and incorrect for any Victim of White Supremacy (non-white person) to **willfully** and **deliberately** do serious bodily harm to **any** person except through the enactment of Maximum-Emergency Compensatory Justice.

[Note: See explanation of Maximum-Emergency Compensatory Justice, Area #9: War].

Unless you personally know each and every white person in the universe, do not say that all white people are Racists. Likewise, do not say that any white person is not a Racist, unless you personally know that that particular white person never practices Racism (White Supremacy) against anyone — either directly or indirectly — at any time, in any area of activity, including Economics, Education, Entertainment, Labor, Law, Politics, Religion, Sex, and/or War.

Reason(s)/Explanation(s):

Racists (White Supremacists) are **Masters of Deceit.**

Therefore, it is not always easy for a Victim of Racism (non-white person) to "single out" those white people who practice Racism, from those who don't.

As long as White Supremacy exists, it is **just** and **correct** for any Victim of Racism to **suspect** any white person to be a Racist, if that white person has not, by both **word**, and **deed,** proven to **that** Victim of Racism, that he, or she, is **not** a Racist.

Admit your faults. Admit your fears.

Reason/Explanation:

If a person is easily willing to admit his or her faults, fears, and/or weaknesses, he or she will, by so doing, develop the will to seek truth, and to use the truth in such manner as to best promote justice and correctness.

When talking about Racists (White Supremacists), do not use these terms:

"**White People**"
"**The White Man**"
"**The White Woman**"
etc.

POLITICS

Practice using these terms instead:

Racists
Racist Man
Racist Woman
White Supremacists
Collective White Supremacists

Reason(s)/Explanation(s):

When talking about the white people who practice Racism (White Supremacy), it is correct to emphasize the Racism that they practice based on their "whiteness", rather than to seem to denounce "whiteness" itself.

Don't confuse people.
Be reliable. Avoid hypocrisy.
Do what you say you're going to do, at the time and place that you said that you would do it.
Don't make promises that you cannot, or will not, keep.

Reason(s)/Explanation(s):

It is best to promise **nothing**, and deliver **something,** than to promise **anything**, and deliver less than you promised.

Do not use the words "good" and "bad" as long as you do not possess a total knowledge and understanding of all that is "good", and all that is "bad". Instead, use the words "correct" and "incorrect".

Reason(s)/Explanation(s):

The words "good" and "bad" have been used to describe too many people, too many things, and too many situations.

Until you are absolutely certain that you **know** and **understand** what is "good", and what is "bad", and, until you speak and act according to this knowledge and understanding, at **all** times, it is best that you use the terms "correct" and "incorrect".

By using the words "correct", and "incorrect", instead of the words "good" and "bad", a person will, by so doing, help him or her self to remember that he or she does not yet know and understand **exactly** what is "good", and what is "bad". He or she may then be inspired to seek and gain that knowledge and understanding.

POLITICS

Do not participate in the doing of bodily harm to any person because you are "ordered" and/or asked to do so by any other person. Do bodily harm to a person only if you have, by your own judgement, decided that it is the correct thing to do in order to promote justice and/or correctness, and only at the time, place, and under the circumstances that you have chosen to be correct.

Reason(s)/Explanation(s):

As long as Racism exists, it is unjust and incorrect for any Victim of Racism [non-white person] to **seek** to do bodily harm to any person, except when **required** by the enactment of Maximum-Emergency Compensatory Justice. [See: Area 9: War].

Avoid answering questions about "Communism" and/or "Capitalism" unless the questioner specifices the exact "type" of so-called "Communism" and/or "Capitalism that he or she is talking about.

Ask the questioner to explain, both as a whole, and in parts, exactly what he or she means by the terms "Communism", or "Capitalism", and to do so in a manner that you and most people in the known universe can easily understand.

Ask him or her to explain "Communism" and "Capitalism", and how one is different from the other in each of the following areas of Activity:

Economics,	Politics (People Relations),
Education,	Religion,
Entertainment,	Sex, and/or
Labor,	War.
Law	

Also, ask the following:

- What does "Communism" do to **eliminate** Racism (White Supremacy)?
- What does "Capitalism" do to **eliminate** Racism (White Supremacy)?
- If "Communism" or "Capitalism" eliminates Racism, **why** is Racism still the dominant motivating force among the people of the known universe?

POLITICS

Do not permit any feelings of friendship, cordiality, respect, and/or affection toward any person, white or non-white, Racist or non-Racist, to interfere with, or take precedence over, any just and correct speech and/or action in support of the elimination of Racism (White Supremacy).

Reason/Explanation:

Racism (White Supremacy) is the greatest motivating force in the known universe in the promotion of combined falsehood, non-justice, and incorrectness.

Therefore, it is best to eliminate Racism so that "feelings" of "friendship", "cordiality", "respect", and/or "affection" can best promote **truth**, in a manner that produces **justice** and **correctness.**

Talk to people who are younger than yourself, or older than yourself, the same way that you talk to people of any age — particularly, people who are Victims of Racism. Speak the truth, but be certain to speak it in a manner that the person listening will understand what is being said.

Always say everything in a manner that will best promote justice and correctness.

Reason(s)/Explanation(s):

All Victims of Racism [non-white people], of all ages, are "children" as long as they are subject to domination by White Supremacists (Racists). Therefore, all Victims of Racism, like all other people, regardless of age, are entitled to have the truth revealed to them, and, are entitled to have the opportunity to use the truth in such manner as to promote justice and correctness.

Do not speak and/or act as a "leader" of any people, or person, in the known universe, at the same time that you are still directly or indirectly subject to White Supremacy (Racism).

Do not ask people to depend on you for "leadership" unless you are ready, willing, and able, to protect them from all who try to harm them.

Reason(s)/Explanation(s):

As long as you, yourself, are subject to the will of the White Supremacists (Racists), it is best to only offer suggestions and opinions to others.

It is just and correct to avoid speaking and/or acting as a "leader" of others.

It is just and correct under such circumstances to tell people the **truth** about yourself, and others, and encourage them to seek the truth for themselves.

It is just and correct to seek ways to encourage self and others to use truth in a manner that best promotes justice and correctness.

Avoid being "personal" in your comments on events — especially in matters that are racial.
Do not call a person a Racist.
Instead, describe a remark, or an act as "Racist" or "incorrect".

Examples:

> "The remarks made at the meeting were the types of remarks that help to maintain White Supremacy".

> "The things that were done last week were the type of things that are characteristic of Racist Acts".

Do the following when talking with a person who indicates that he or she does not intend for the talk to be constructive, either in manner, or objective:

> When the person **asks a question, answer the question.**

> When the person **makes a statement, say nothing.**

Do not call any person a "liar".
Do not "name-call".
When commenting on a person's speech or action, describe what the person is doing or saying, rather than calling the person a "name".
Take particular care not to say to, or about, any white person anything that may sound as if you are calling him or her a "liar".

The following is an example of the manner in which such dialogue should be conducted:

POLITICS

White Person: "White people don't owe **anything** to Black people! I'm white, and I don't owe Black people anything. Everything I have, I worked for, and got on my own. Is that not true?

Black Person: "No sir (Maam)".

White Person: "Are you calling me a liar?"

Black Person: "No sir (Maam). I am simply saying that the statements that you made are not true".

White Person: "That sounds like you're calling me a liar!"

Black Person: [Silence].

White Person: "What I want to know is **are you calling me a liar?"**

Black Person: "No sir (Maam), I am not calling you a liar".

White Person: "But you **are** calling me a liar!"

Black Person: [Silence].

Reason(s)/Explanation(s):

Racism (White Supremacy) is maintained through **deceit** and **violence** — both direct and indirect.

A **lie**, as a means of **deceit** is one of the basic tools of people who practice White Supremacy (Racism).

The use of lies in a skillful, scientific, and masterful manner, is the **basic** method that Racists (White Supremacists) use to **confuse** and **subjugate** the non-white people of the known universe.

To speak the **truth** about Racism, by giving a **detailed** explanation of how a Racist practices Racism in each area of activity, is one of the effective means of counter-acting Racism. A Racist dreads having his or her lies and/or deceitful activities exposed to large numbers of white and non-white people — particularly if the person revealing the truth, and exposing the lies, is a Victim of Racism (non-white person). Racists, usually become greatly, if temporarily, disturbed when their lies are exposed during a period when the lies **must** be believed, in order that a particular plan, to better promote Racism, functions effectively.

It is, never-the-less, functionally incorrect to call **any** person a "liar" —— even when the person is obviously telling a lie. To call a person a "liar" —— usually succeeds in making people angry and/or nervous, without contributing anything to the revelation of truth in the correct manner.

Without, necessarily, mentioning any persons by name, it is best to comment on false and/or incorrect remarks by simply saying that such remarks are "not true". It is correct to follow this by saying what **is** true.

Before speaking about what others are saying or doing to eliminate Racism (White Supremacy), ask yourself these questions:

- Are others doing what they **should** be doing?
- What should others be doing?
- Are others telling the truth?
- What are others saying that is not true?
- What am I doing to eliminate Racism?
- Why aren't the people who are interested in eliminating Racism following **my** example instead of following the example of those with whom I disagree?
- Instead of complaining about what **others** are doing to eliminate Racism, why haven't I put **my** ideas into **practice** the way that **others** have put **their** ideas into practice?
- If my ideas **have been** put into practice, and they are the "correct" ideas, then why haven't my ideas **succeeded** in eliminating Racism?
- What suggestions do I now have that will do the most, in a short period of time, toward eliminating Racism?

When in the presence of white people, avoid speaking and/or acting as if you are supposed to automatically serve as the "entertainment committee".

Avoid speaking or acting in such manner as to cause white people to expect you to be the "entertainment committee"

while in their presence.

Remember that many white people prefer to laugh at non-white people — not with them.

Be cordial, courteous, and generally relaxed, but avoid swapping "jokes" with Racists and/or suspected Racists.

Reason(s)/Explantion(s):

Being a "non-white" person should not necessarily mean that you are supposed to "clown" for the "benefit" of people who are white — because they are white. Neither should being a "non-white" person mean that you should present yourself as a whore to the white people that you encounter.

Swapping "jokes" is correct, but only in such manner that the results are constructive. "Jokes" should not be insults in disguise. "Joke" swapping can be constructive under some conditions. But when white and non-white people swap jokes, it ofttimes ends with the telling of a "joke" that isn't a "joke", and the "joke" that isn't a "joke" is ofttimes a "joke" on the **non**-white person. Such conduct does not and will not produce a relationship between white and non-white persons that is just and correct.

In your general conversations with white people (particularly white women) practice making the following statement, and asking the following questions:

[Statement]

"You are one of the greatest and most fascinating people in the world".

[Questions]

"What is your **ultimate** objective?"
"What do you think **my** ultimate objective should be?"
"How do you **intend** for **your** ultimate objective to relate to mine?"

When talking to white persons about racial matters, or about any matter pertaining to the promotion of justice, make the following remarks:

"Your duty is to produce justice.
My duty is to make sure that justice is produced.
Our duty is to eliminate all enjoyment, and all 'profit',

from any activity that does not help produce justice".

Reason(s)/Explanation(s):

Every person in the known universe, white and non-white, has the basic duty to produce, or help to produce, justice.

The smartest, and most powerful people (particularly White Supremacists) have the greatest **capability** for producing justice, and, therefore, have the **greatest** responsibility.

The powerless, most pitiful, and most primitive people (non-white people, collectively), have the greatest **disability** for producing justice, and therefore, have the **least** responsibility.

It is non-just and non-correct for any person in the known universe, white or non-white, to enjoy, and/or "profit" from, any activity that does not help to produce justice.

In the process of eliminating Racism (White Supremacy), do not speak and/or act to promote the extinction of "white" and/or "Caucasian" people. Do not promote the concept that "white" and/or "Caucasian" people should be forced into non-existence through war, sexual intercourse with non-white people, and/or through other means, either direct or indirect.

Reason(s)/Explanation(s):

There is no reason to believe that people who are "very light", and/or "white" in appearance should not exist.

It is incorrect for any person, or person, in the known universe, to attempt to force and/or cause any color, non-color, and/or "shade of color", of people, to become extinct. People who are generally called "white" and/or "Caucasian" are, generally, a very peculiar and very special people. They are, generally, very intelligent, curious, and energetic in ways that all other people [collectively] are not.

The **ultimate correct** purpose of white people as "white" people, and non-white people as "non-white" people, may likely be revealed when Racism (White Supremacy) is ended. Therefore, it is not correct for the Victims of Racism to try to do things that could likely result in the disappearance of "white" and/or "Caucasian" people from the known universe.

POLITICS

Speak and/or act in support of the concept that in the process of eliminating Racism (White Supremacy), there must be no "geographic", "national", "Religious", "ethnic", or "political", boundaries. Promote the concept that Racism must be eliminated wherever it exists, and that it exists wherever, and whenever, a person practices it.

Do not use the term "Black community". As long as White Supremacy exists, do not refer to any people as a "community" except those people who function as the "Racist Community" (White Supremacists, collectively).

Refer to all other people as "black", "brown", red", "yellow", and/or "white" people.

Reason(s)/Explanation(s):

In a known universe where all non-white people are dominated by White Supremacists (Racists), there is only **one** "community" —— the Racist Community.

The white people who **do not** practice Racism **are not** a "community". They are simply people who are "white" in appearance. Since, however, they are not "organized" to do anything **major** "in common", they cannot correctly be called a "community".

In a socio-material system dominated by White Supremacy, no **white** person is **subject to**, and/or a **victim of**, the Racist Community.

All white people either function **as** the Racist Community, **or** they function in opposition to the white people who function as the Racist Community.

All Black, and/or non-white people are **subject** to those white persons who function as the Racist Community ("collective", and or "communal" Racists).

As long a White Supremacy exists, no Black and/or non-white people **can** function as a "community". Should White Supremacy cease to exist, only the "Universe of Justice and Correctness" should replace it.

Avoid visiting people at their place(s) of residence [houses, huts, apartments, etc.] except for one or more of the following purposes:

POLITICS

- Exchanges of views on ways and means of eliminating Racism (White Supremacy).
- Exchanges of views on ways and means of revealing truth, and/or ways and means of using truth in such manner as to promote justice and correctness.
- Assistance in doing constructive labor.
- Sexual intercourse [between non-white persons].

Always seek to be alone, except when doing the following:

1. Doing **work** that requires the help of others.
2. Talking and/or listening to others about ways and means of eliminating Racism (White Supremacy) and producing justice.
3. Engaging in sexual intercourse (as a means of helping to improve communications in promoting activities described in items 1 and 2.

Avoid attending any "meetings", "assemblies", etc., of any kind, at which white people are not welcome at all times.

Reason(s)/Explanation(s):

The correct purpose of any "meeting", "assembly", etc. is to reveal truth, promote justice, and promote correctness. White people should be welcome at any "meeting", "assembly", etc., in which the purpose is to reveal truth, promote justice, and promote correctness.

Do not speak, and/or act, to try to establish "Black Supremacy".

Reason/Explanation:

Subjugation of any person based on the presence of "color", or the absence of "color" in the appearance, and/or the general "make-up", of that person is non-just and incorrect.

As long as White Supremacy (Racism) exists, do not speak and/or act as if any non-white person has "parental authority".

If you have off-spring, do not speak, and/or act, as if they are subject to your so-called "parental authority".

POLITICS

Tell them everything that you know that is of constructive value. Do not tell them anything, or give them anything, that does not serve a constructive purpose. Tell them the things that you **know** that they should do — and **should not** do — but also tell them that you are not their "boss". Tell them that you have no "parental authority" over them, but that you **do** want them to try to **cooperate** with you in accomplishing those things that are of constructive value. When they develop the ability to understand what you mean, tell them that it is the Racists (White Supremacists) who are their "bosses". Tell them that it is the Racists who have "parental authority" over **them**, and, over **you**. Tell them that the Racists are their functional "mothers" and "fathers" — powerful, smart, **unjust**. Tell them that the Racists also have "parental authority" over **all** people of **all** ages who are classified as "non-white". Tell them that the Racists are also **your** illegitimate, but functional "mothers", and your illegitimate, but functional "fathers". Tell them that you, **currently**, have little power over anyone, or anything, other than the **power to appear to have power**, and that that power is "granted" and/or promoted by the Racists.

Tell them that in order for **you** to **be** a "parent", and to exercise "parental authority", you **must** be **able** to **protect** all of your off-spring from the dictates of Racists, and from the injustice that is the essence of that dictatorship.

Tell them that since you have, so far, failed to provide this protection, then, you have not, so far, earned the title of "parent", or the function of being regarded as a "parental authority". Tell them that you can try to work in "partnership" with them, to try to overcome the awesome and very real power that the Racists have over your existence and theirs.

Tell them that the best way of doing this is by doing all that you can, to develop the will, to seek, and find, **truth**, and to use truth in such manner as to produce **justice** and **correctness**, at all times, in all places, among all people and things. Tell them that the production of justice and correctness should be the **only** reason for the existence, at this time, of any and all people, white and non-white, male and female, "parents" and "children".

Tell them the truth, and tell it in such manner that they can understand it.

Reason(s)/Explanation(s):

It is just and correct to tell any person, of **any** age, the **truth**, and to tell it in such manner that that person can understand it.

It is just and correct to **ask** any person, of any age, to use their knowledge and understanding of truth in a manner that best promotes justice and correctness.

Avoid using the terms "husband" or "wife" to describe any non-white persons.

Use such terms to describe only white persons, and only when such [white] persons are involved in a socio-material-sexual relationship with each other — not with non-white people.

Reason(s)/Explanation(s):

1. As long as White Supremacy (Racism) exists, only **white** male persons can function as "husbands" — but only to **white** females.

2. As long as White Supremacy (Racism) exists, only **white** female persons can function as "wives" — but only to **white** males.

3. As long as White Supremacy (Racism) exists, only **white** persons can function as "husbands", or as "wives" — **but only to each other.**

4. As long as White Supremacy exists, **no white person** can function as a "husband", or as a "wife", to any **non**-white person. As long as White Supremacy exists, white persons can, and will, function as "husbands", and as "wives", but only to **white** persons.

   Because of the existence of White Supremacy [dominant power], those white persons who **attempt** to function as "husbands", or as "wives", to non-white persons, can, and will, function only as **direct** or **indirect** masters.

   Any **white** person who is involved in such a relationship is always a **master** — never a "partner" or a "mate".

In a socio-material system dominated by White Supremacy (Racism), this is **always** true — even when it appears not to be.

5. As long as White Supremacy exists, no **non**-white person can function as a "husband", or as a "wife", to any person(s) — **white**, or **non**-white. Non-white persons who attempt to function as "husbands" or as "wives" fail to do so. They fail to do so because they are, in every major area of activity, **subject** to the direct or indirect power of the White Supremacists (Racists). Being subject to the power of White Supremacy (Racism) means that **all** major decisions that affect the functions of all **non**-white so-called "husbands", or all **non**-white so-called "wives", are directly, or indirectly, made by the Collective White Supremacists.

   Under White Supremacy, non-white people only **pretend** to be "husbands". They only **pretend** to be "wives". They only **pretend** to be "parents" to "children".

Under White Supremacy, all non-white people, regardless of age, are "children". They are the servants to, the victims of, and the "children" under the power and direction of the White Supremacists (Racists). The White Supremacists are their bosses, their masters, and their major decision-makers.

In a socio-material system dominated by White Supremacy, it is the White Supremacists (collectively) who make the major decisions that control **all** non-white people, in **all** of the Major Areas of [People] Activity. This includes Economics, Education, Entertainment, Labor, Law, Politics, Religion, Sex, and War.

In addition, as long as White Supremacy exists, no **non**-white person is the "head" of any "household", the "head" of any "family", a "member" of any "family", the "head" of any "organization", or a "member" of any "organization".

Non-white persons are **victims of** and **subjects to** White Supremacy. They are "heads" of, and "members" of **nothing.** They have a "zero" status.

It is correct for all non-white persons to know and understand these things to be true, and to **stop pretending** that they are not. Non-white people should stop pretending that they have power that they do not have.

POLITICS

If you are now involved in a "legal" so-called "marriage", or a similar arrangement, try to spend less time and energy "entertaining" one another, and more time and energy speaking and/or acting to eliminate Racism.

Reason(s)/Explanation(s):

Non-white people who are currently participating in a "legal" so-called "marriage" should study, know, and understand how to best use time and energy.

One of the **basic** purposes for a "true" marriage is to help to produce justice [balance between people]. Since the establishment of White Supremacy (Racism), all so-called "marriages" that directly or indirectly involved non-white people, have failed to promote justice.

As long as White Supremacy has existed, all "marriages", and all attempts at ["legal"] marriage, have only helped to **support** White Supremacy.

Non-white people who have attempted "marriage" while subject to White Supremacy have become devoted to a belief in a power and security for themselves that **does not exist**. By believing this, they then proceed to become more involved in, and more devoted to maintaining the status quo. To maintain the status quo however, is to [functionally] maintain White Supremacy. These so-called "marriages" become little more than a time and energy consuming exercise in avoiding the duty of promoting the elimination of Racism (White Supremacy).

The problem of White Supremacy is, and always has been serious enough to warrant a suspension of all "marriages", and of all attempts at "marriage", until such time as White Supremacy is eliminated. "Marriages", and/or attempted "marriages", require too much time, attention, and energy that can best be used to help eliminate White Supremacy. Also, any and all sexual activity of any kind should be conducted in a manner that gives the **most support** to the elimination of White Supremacy, and the least support to the continuation of it.

Until White Supremacy is eliminated, however, there should be no sexual intercourse, "sexual play", etc., between white persons and non-white persons.

POLITICS

Avoid using the expressions:

- **"My Child",**
- **"My Children",**
- **"My Son(s)",**
- **"My daughter(s), etc.**

Instead, practice using the expressions:

- **"My Off-Spring",**
- **"My Female Off-Spring",**
- **"My male Off-Spring",**

Reason(s)/Explanation(s):

As long as White Supremacy (Racism) exists, no non-white person can "possess" a child, son, daughter, etc.

They can only **produce** off-spring.

Under White Supremacy (Racism), **all** non-white people are directly or indirectly subject to the White Supremacists (Racists).

Under White Supremacy, **all** non-white people of **all** ages are the "children" ("sons" and "daughters") of the White Supremacists.

Non-white people can produce "off-spring", but the off-spring that they produce, become, at birth, subject to the will of the White Supremacists, just as the producers of those off-spring are subject to that will.

The White Supremacists, then, in effect, **function** as the boss "fathers", and the boss "mothers" of all non-white males and females, including their off-spring. This is true, and will continue to be true, as long as White Supremacy is the dominant socio-material force among the people of the known universe.

The babies that are produced by non-white people are "sprung-off" into a socio-material condition functionally dominated by White Supremacists.

Do not describe any existing condition among the people of the known universe as "good". Avoid using the word "good" except to bid a person "good morning", "good evening", "good day", etc.

POLITICS

Reason(s)/Explantion(s):

As long as White Supremacy (Racism) is the dominant socio-economic force among the people of the known universe, no situation involving the people affected by White Supremacy can be correctly called "good".

A "good" situation is one in which there is a **complete absence** of falsehood, non-justice, and incorrectness.

It is correct however, to use the word "good" to greet a person with "good morning", "good day", etc.

To wish a person a "good" morning ["good" evening, "good" day, etc], without being, in a **condition** of "goodness" is still a correct thing to do.

It is correct because such an expression shows an **intent** to wish a person a "morning" that consits of **everything** that is **just** and **correct** [a condition of perfection].

It is correct to **desire** this for each and every person, even when there is little or no indication that such a condition is immediately likely.

Do not say that any people, and/or any person, in the known universe, is an example of what any people, and/or any person, should be.

Reason(s)/Explantion(s):

Racism (White Supremacy) is the **dominant** motivating force among the people of the known universe. Every person in the known universe either practices Racism (White Supremacy), **or** he or she **re-acts** to those who practice it.

This means that Racism is the **dominant**, and therefore, **only** functioning "government" among the people of the known universe. As long as Racism (White Supremacy) is the only **functioning** "government" among the people of the known universe, no people, and/or no person, can practice justice and correctness.

Any people who do not and/or any person, who does not, practice justice, and correctness, **is not** an **example** of what **any** person should be.

POLITICS

Never say that one person is "better" than another.

Reason(s)/Explanation(s):

Many people believe that if a person is "tall", or "short", or "old", or "young", or "fast", or "slow", or "black", or "white", or "fat", or "slim", or "dull", or "smart", etc., that that person is "better", or "**not** better", than another person.

Many a person thinks that if he or she is "smarter" than another person, or "smarter" than many another person, in any one or more areas of activity, at a particular time and place, then he or she has the "right" or "duty" to take unjust advantage of the person or persons who are not as "smart". Such persons also think that people who are not "smart" should "pay" for not being "smart" by "idolizing" those persons who **are** "smart", and/or by speaking, acting, or keeping silent in support of the things that they do or say that are unjust and incorrect.

This manner of thinking is one of the major forces in support of the commission of non-just acts among the people of the known universe.

A person who is "smarter" than another person is not a "better" person.

A "better" person is a person who knows and understands truth, and who uses truth in such manner that justice and correctness is produced at **all** times, in **all** places, in **all** areas of activity, including Economics, Education, Entertainment, Labor, Law, Politics, Religion, Sex, and War.

A person who is thirty years of age is no "better" than any newly-born "infant", though a thirty-year old person may be able to **do** "more".

A person who "exists" is no "better" than a person who has ceased to "exist", though the person who "exists" may be able to **do** "more".

A person who can "see" is no "better" than a person who cannot "see", though the person who can "see" may be able to **do** "more".

POLITICS

A person who **can** do more than other persons, **should** do "more" of everything that he or she is able to do, to find truth, and to use the truth in such manner as to promote justice and correctness, at all times, in all areas of activity.

Having the **ability** to **do** "more" should always mean one thing: The persons who have the ability, should **do** "more", to produce justice and correctness. This is all that it should mean.

As long as White Supremacy (Racism) exists, do not say that any people "live".
Say that people exist.

Reason(s)/Explanation(s):

Racism (White Supremacy) is the dominant motivating force among the people of the known universe.

Racism is also non-just.

People cannot "live in a situation dominated by non-justice.

They can only exist.

Therefore, no people in the known universe "live".

The people who **practice** Racism do not "live".

The people who are **subject to** Racism do not "live".

The people who have no "knowledge" [infantile and/or senile people] of Racism do not "live".

No people "live".

They only **exist.**

If you are a non-white person with "light" complexion of skin, and/or who can easily be mistaken for a white person, do not seek advantage of others because of it. Resist the temptation to do so. Seek to promote justice.

Reason(s)/Explanation(s):

To seek advantage of persons, based on considerations of color, or non-color, of the skin of those persons, is a major promotion of non-justice.

Do not refer to any person simply as "a black". Do not refer to any person simply as "a white". Refer to both black people, and white people, as black, or white, people, or persons.

Reason(s)/Explanation(s):

Words, and how they are used, are a very important part of the production of justice. **People** should be called "people". Black people should be called "black **people**". White people should be called "white **people**". To refer to black people simply as "the blacks", or to refer to white people simply as "the whites", is to [subtlely] promote the thinking that either black people or white people, **may not be** "People". To use the terms "a black", or "a white", **without** adding the word, "people" may promote the concept that Racism (White Supremacy), is **not** a problem between **people**. Racism is **caused** by **people**. Racism is **practiced** by **people.** The Victims of Racism are **people**. The **words** that are used to help maintain Racism are produced by **people**. To simply refer to a black person as "a black",. or as "the black", is to promote the concept that a black person is not a **person**, but a **thing**. A person — **any** person — should not be seen as some type of "non-specific" **substance** that only has the **form** of a "person". **People** should not be called "the blacks", or "the browns". A **person** should not be called "a white", or "a yellow", or "a red".

Words, and how they are used, are very important. They should be used **carefully** and **constructively.**

POLITICS

Do not call people "human beings".
Do not speak of any person as being a "human" being.

Reason(s)/Explanation(s):

For a person to be a "human" being, he or she must think, speak, **and** act "humanely" at **all** times, in **all** places, in **all** areas of activity.

In order for a person to think, speak, **and** act "humanely" at all times, in all places, in all areas of activity, he or she must think, speak, **and** act to find, reveal, and use, truth, in such manner as to promote justice and correctness, at all times, in all places, in all areas of activity. These areas of activity must include all aspects of Economics, Education, Entertainment, Labor, Law, Politics, Relgion, Sex, and War.

This means that a person, in order to be a "human" being, must not promote falsehood, injustice, or incorrectness, at any time, in any place, in any area of activity.

It also means that that person must not submit to, and/or cooperate with, any persons who do.

"Human" beings do not now exist in the known universe.

It is the duty of every person in the known universe to try to become a "human" being.

Avoid referring to Victims of Racism (non-white people) as "men" or "women". Practice referring to them, generally, as **males** or **females.**

Reason(s)/Explanation(s):

"Men" and Women" are not subject to the will of Racists (White Supremacists), at any time, in any place, in any area of activity, including economics, education, entertainment, labor, law, politics, religion, sex, and war.

Being subject to the will of Racists **is not** a characteristic of "men" or of "women". It is a characteristic of male or female "infants", and/or "children". It is the status of a "boy", or a "girl".

No non-white person is a "man", or a "woman" **during any period** when he, or she, is submitting to, and/or cooperating with, the will of any white person(s) who practice White Supremacy (Racism).

POLITICS

Ask any person classified as "white", and/or "Caucasian", one or more of the following basic questions as pertains to Racism [Note: Be courteous. It is correct to ask these questions only under circumstances where the white persons involved have agreed to openly discuss all aspects of Racism with you, including their own relationship to Racists practices]:

(1) Do you know and understand the Basic Characteristics of a Racist (White Supremacist), as regards how he or she functions in each and every area of activity, including Economics, Education, Entertainment, Labor, Law, Politics, Religion, Sex, and War?

(2) Are you now, or have you ever been a Racist?

(3) Are you now, willfully, deliberately, and by personal choice, maintaining comradeship with any person who you have reason to believe is a Racist (White Supremacist)?

(4) What are you doing now, and what have you ever done, willfully and deliberately, to eliminate Racism (White Supremacy)?

(5) What suggestions do you now offer to the Victims of Racism (non-white people) as to what they, themselves, **may, can,** and/or **must,** do to **insure** that Racism (White Supremacy) is immediately eliminated, and/or the Victims compensated?

"Praise" neither white people, nor black people for whatever they have accomplished.

Reason/Explanation:

Neither white people, nor non-white people are worthy of praise.

Neither white people, nor non-white people have produced **justice.**

Don't brag about being "Black".

Reason(s)/Explanation(s):

There is **nothing** about being "Black" that justifies bragging.

POLITICS

There is **nothing** about being "white" that justifies bragging.

There is nothing about being **anything** that justifies bragging.

Bragging cannot be justified.

Do not say that the "color", or "non-color", of any person, or thing, is "beautiful" or "ugly".

Reason(s)/Explanation(s):

"Colors" are neither "beautiful", nor "ugly".

"Colors" are.

"Colors" **exist**.

"Colors" make their own statement by the fact of their existence.

"Colors", and/or "non-colors" need not be **praised,** nor **condemned.**

"Color" — or the absence of "color" — need only be recognized.

Remarks about color should be made to describe color, and/or to describe the way that color is used, or reacted to. There are no "correct" colors.

Nor are there any "incorrect" colors.

Color, or the absence of color, can, however, be **used** for **incorrect** purposes.

"Color", or the absence of color (in people) is, most of the time, used as an excuse to treat people unjustly. A person's re-action to color, or the absence of color, may result in much speech and/or action against him or her self, and/or against other persons, against animals, things, etc. Speech and/or action against a person, animal, etc., because of "color" and/or the absence of "color" is unjust and incorrect.

Avoid making reference to any specific person as being "a Racist".

Instead, refer to a condition, and/or to an event as being Racist-dominated, and/or Racist-motivated.

When describing such a condition and/or event, always precede any major comments that you make, with the phrase:

> **"To the extent that a Racist has [or had] anything to do with it - - -".**

Reason(s)/Explanation(s):

Sometimes it is difficult for two or more Vicitms of Racism (non-white people) to agree on whether a particular white person is, or is not, a Racist. Therefore, it is best not to point to any specific white person as being "a Racist", or as **not** being, "a Racist".

To do so, may increase confusion, start non-constructive squabbles, and/or produce unnecessary division.

The following statements are examples of the correct use of the phrase:

> "To the extent that a Racist has [or had] anything to do with it - - -".

- "I don't know why the hungry people cannot be fed, but, **to the extent that a Racist has anything to do with it**, the Racists were responsible".
- **"To the extent that a Racist had anything to do with it,** the availability, and incorrect use of drugs among non-white people has been promoted and supported, rather than discouraged".
- "There may have been many causes for the [racial] riots, but **to the extent that any Racists had anything to do with it**, the Racists were responsible".

Do not accuse any "country", any "government", any "nation", any "religon", any "political body", etc., of practicing Racism, except the White Nation (White Supremacists, collectively).

Reason(s)/Explanation(s):

No "country", no "government", no "nation", no "religon", no "political body", practices Racism (White Supremacy) other than those "white" **people**, who practice Racism.

White people who practice White Supremacy are the only **functional Racists.**

White people who practice Racism are best known as "White Supremacists", and/or, collectively, as "The White Nation".

Do not speak, and/or act, as if you are exercising the "power of command" to others, when you are, in truth, only carrying messages from those who do have the "power of command".

Reason(s)/Explanation(s):

In a socio-material system dominated by Racism (White Supremacy) many non-white people like to **pretend** that they are "in charge", and/or, that it is **they** who make the **final** decisions of major matters. Since it is true that they do not, it is incorrect for them to **pretend** that they do.

Do not attempt to answer a question until you are prepared to answer it in such manner that the answer helps to not merely relate facts, but also, to reveal truth.

Reason(s)/Explanation(s):

Some "selected" facts, presented in a "special" manner, do not always reveal truth.

Facts should **always** be presented in such manner that **truth** is revealed.

Facts can, and are, ofttimes presented in such manner as to promote falsehood.

If truth is not revealed through the **correct presentation** of facts, it is impossible to promote justice and/or correctness.

Answer all questions presented to you, and at all times, answer only in a manner that will neither, directly, or indirectly, help to establish, maintain, expand, and/or

refine Racism (White Supremacy).

If you are asked a question, and you do not know the answer to that question, always say you don't know.

Reason(s)/Explanation(s):

Every remark that is made by any person, at any time, about any subject, should be made in a manner that helps to eliminate falsehood, as well as helps to produce justice and correctness.

Do not allow yourself to be rushed into answering a question when you believe that you are not prepared to answer in a manner that will reveal truth, promote justice, and promote correctness.

Reason(s)/Explanations(s):

A so-called "answer" to a question that does not reveal truth, promote justice, and/or promote correctness is **not an answer**. It is a **non-answer.**

[Note: A **non-answer** is a word, or a combination of words used to respond to a question, in such manner that facts may be presented, but truth is not revealed, nor justice or correctness, promoted].

If you are asked a question, and you are not prepared to answer the question in a manner that helps to reveal truth, and helps to promote justice and correctness, then it is correct to make the following statement to the person(s) asking the question:

> "The question you asked should be answered **correctly,** and in the **correct manner.**
>
> I am not **now** prepared to answer the question correctly and in the correct manner.
>
> With your cooperation, I will need some time, other than **this** time, to prepare the answer".

Ask questions, and if you receive "no answer" seek a [complete] knowledge and understanding of the reason(s) for your not receiving the (correct) answers.

When a person talks to you about something and you are not correctly prepared to talk about same, it is correct to make the following statement:

> "I am not prepared to talk, in a **correct** manner, about **this** particular subject, at **this** time. With your cooperation, I will talk with you at some other time, after the correct preparation".

Don't let flattery and/or so-called "gifts" blind you to Racism and other injustices.

Reason(s)/Explanation(s):

Flattery and so-called "gifts" and "favors" are some of the basic tactics and weapons used by Racists (White Supremacists) to weaken, confuse, and more easily dominate their victims [non-white people].

Do not use the term "Racial Integration" to describe any situation.
Use the term "elimination of Racism".

Reason(s)/Explanation(s):

There is no such thing as "Racial Integration". There is, and only can be, the existence of Racism, **or** the **non**-existence of Racism. Racism either **exists**, or it **does not** exist.

There is no way to "integrate" Racism.

Racism can only be **practiced**, or **not** practiced.

When Racists, and/or suspected Racists, point out your "faults", listen to them, and examine what they say.
Seek the truth, and use the truth in a manner that best promotes justice and correctness.
Do not be ashamed to call a "fault" a "fault". Also, point out the "faults" produced and/or promoted by Racism (White Supremacy) as being greater than all other "faults".

Reason(s)/Explanation(s):

Victims of Racism (non-white people) should always seek truth. The truth about all **people**, both white and non-white, is that they all have many, many, "faults".

POLITICS

The major fault of too many of the **smartest** and **most powerful** people [white people] is that they have chosen to speak, and/or act, as White Supremacists (Racists). Because of this choice, these (white) people are at "fault", on a **greater** scale, than all of the non-white people of the known uninverse, combined.

Large numbers of white people were "given" the knowledge and power to eliminate "fault" among the people of the known universe and replace it with justice and correctness. Instead, many of them have used that knowledge and power to establish Racism, and to use Racism as the **end product** of, and the reason for, the continuous promotion of falsehood, non-justice, and incorrectness.

Do not restrict yourself to the use of only those titles given to you by others, and/or to only those titles used by others to describe you.

Use any one or more titles that you choose for yourself, when you know that such titles describe you on a basis of what you are actually doing at the exact time that you are doing it.

Examples:

- "Business Person" (a person engaged in a special task).
- "Follower" (a person who follows –)
- "Foreigner" (different[?])
- "Investigator" (a person who seeks to know or understand)
- "Laborer" (a person who works — physically or mentally)
- "Merchant" (a person who buys anything, or sells anything)
- "Official" (any person who is doing his or her "duty")
- "Police Person" (a person who speaks and acts to promote justice and correctness)
- "Politician" (a person who relates to, and/or who is involved with, people)
- "Preacher" (a person who offers information and makes suggestions)

POLITICS

"Private Person" (a person who does not relate to, and/or is not involved with, any other person(s)

"Psychologist" (a person who studies how people think and act)

"Public Person" (a person who relates to, and/or who is involved with, people)

"Soldier" (a person who works for a specified cause)

"Specialist" (a person who "specializes" in a particular work or study)

"Student" (a person who studies or investigates)

"Victim" (a person who is, or has been treated unjustly)

"Writer" (a person who writes)

When people ask you about yourself, avoid telling them anything unless they are willing to answer the same type questions about themselves.

This includes any detailed questions relating to Economics, Education, Entertainment, Labor, Law, Politics, Religion, Sex, and/or War.

Reason(s)/Explanation(s):

People who ask questions of others, but who are **opposed** to **answering** the same type questions about themselves, are not justified in **asking** the same type questions of others.

Avoid persons whose conversations usually consist of "nit-picking" and belittling-type remarks about others.

When talking to such persons, concentrate on subjects that have to do with things, and/or ideas, that help to promote constructive thought, speech, or action —— not "nit-picking" remarks that only have gossip value.

When people talk to you, and make "nit-picking" and/or belittling remarks about specific people, or groups of people, make no comment, but continue to make constructive remarks about things, and/or ideas.

Do not "visit" people at their places of residence, etc., when they have proven that they like to gossip, "nit-pick",

belittle others, and/or "show-off". Also, do not encourage such persons to visit you.

Neither praise, nor vent anger against, any so-called symbol, insignia, emblem, flag, map, etc.

Reason(s)/Explanation(s):

Symbols, insignia, emblems, flags, maps, etc., **have no responsibility.**

Such things should not be "held responsible". Neither should animals, insects, rain, snow, sunshine, etc.

People, however, **are** "responsible".

In a socio-material system dominated by Racists, it is the Racists, and **only** the Racists (White Supremacists) who are "responsible" for **everything** done, or not done, by their victims (non-white people).

Speak and act to promote the Compensatory Counter-Racist "Family" as the basic functional "family" of, and by, non-white people.
Do this by speaking and/or acting to promote each person as being a part of that "family" during any period in which he or she is directly, or indirectly, speaking and/or acting to effectively counter-act and/or eliminate Racism (White Supremacy).

Reason(s)/Explanation(s):

A "family" must justify it's **reason for existence.** It must justify it's reason for existence by serving a **constructive purpose.**

Therefore, in a socio-material system dominated by Racism (White Supremacy), it is incorrect to attempt to establish any "family", "tribe", "nation", or "class", except for **one** purpose. That one purpose should be to eliminate Racism, and to do so by finding truth, and using truth in such manner as to promote justice and correctness.

As long as White Supremacy (Racism) exists, do not engage in sexual intercourse with any white person.

Reason/Explanation:

As long as White Supremacy exists, acts of sexual intercourse, or "sexual play", between white persons, and non-white persons, only help to maintain White Supremacy (Racism).

POLITICS

Do not fight, kill, argue with, and/or otherwise show hostility toward, any person, because that person calls you a name, nickname, etc., that you prefer not to be called.

Call yourself by the name, nickname, etc., that you choose for yourself.

Call others by the names, nicknames, etc., that they choose for themselves. Do not, call them by any other names, nicknames, etc.

Reason(s)/Explanation(s):

It is just and correct to call **all** persons by the names, nicknames, titles, etc., that those persons **choose** to be called.

This is basic in order to show "respect" for the **principle** of respect.

However, it is incorrect to react in a hostile manner when people do not call **you** by the names, nicknames, etc., that you choose for **yourself.**

Though it is incorrect for people to "name-call" you, it is also incorrect for you to re-act to "name-calling" in a hostile manner. If you are called a "name", it is correct for you to re-act in the following manner [Example]:

Name-caller: "You are a dirty, filthy, bastard, and so is your father".

You: [Say nothing, and do nothing].

Name-caller: "I said you are a dirty, filthy, bastard, and so is your father and your three sisters!"

You: [Say nothing, and do nothing].

Name-caller: "You don't have to answer, you stupid son-of-a-bitch.
You must be a stupid son-of-a-bitch.
Your mother was a common whore and everybody knows it!"

You: [Say nothing, and do nothing]

Etc. ----.

POLITICS

Respond to persons who speak to you in a gruff, uncouth, profane, and/or hostile manner, by doing the following:

Be Polite.

Listen carefully to each word spoken.

Do not comment on **statements.**

Do answer **questions**, and answer them **politely**, and answer in a manner that is likely to have the most constructive [just] result.

Avoid answering or asking questions in a hostile or "smart-alecky" manner.

[Repeat] **Do not** comment on **statements.**

[Repeat] **Do** answer **questions.**

Example:

White person [statement]:

"You niggers are more trouble than you are worth!"

Non-white person:

(no comment)

White person [question]:

"Why do you niggers act the way you do?"

Non-white person [answer]:

"Because of Racism".

White person [statement]:

"Don't go blaming everything on the white man. Niggers are just plain **no good**, that's all!"

Non-white person:

(No comment)

White person [statement]:

"We have done an awful lot to help you people but you don't seem to appreciate it. In fact you get worse than ever!"

POLITICS

Non-white person:

(no comment)

White person [statement]:

"It seems to me that too many of your colored are just naturally no good".

Non-white person:

(no comment)

White person [question]:

"Do you think you people will ever amount to anything worthwhile?"

Non-white person [answer]:

"No — at least I don't think we will ever be the quality of people that we should be as long as we are subject to White Supremacy".

White person [statement]:

"That's just an excuse. You people have done better under white rule than you ever could do among yourselves. You people just don't have what it takes, that's all! A nigger is a nigger and **that's** that!".

Non-white person:

(No comment)

Do not depend on, or ask others to "give you respect". Do not demand that others respect you.

If you want respect, give it to yourself. Ask, demand, or look for it from no other person.

Reason(s)/Explanation(s):

There is only one form of [true] "respect". It is **self-respect** — the respect that one "gives" to one's **self.**

There is no other form of "respect", nor no other "source" of it.

POLITICS

"Self-respect" means:

Refusing to lie to oneself, and letting **all others** know of that refusal.

As long as White Supremacy (Racism) is the dominant motivating force among the people of the known universe, always name the White Supremacists (Racists) as being the people (collectively), "most responsible" for everything that happens, and/or for everything that does not happen, in regards to the relationships of people to each other.

Reason(s)/Explanation(s):

Those white persons who practice White Supremacy (Racism) are the smartest, and most powerful people, in the known universe. Any people who, "collectively", have proven to be the smartest and most powerful people in the known universe are responsible for everything that happens in the relationships between people.

Any people who are the smartest and most powerful people in the known universe, and who have other people subject to them, are responsible for whatever those subjects do, or don't do.

Make a daily practice of observing everything that people do, and ask yourself "why are they doing what they are doing, and for what ultimate purpose?"

Reason/Explanation:

To know and understand a person's **ultimate objective**, is, to know and understand what is **most** worth knowing about that person. Such knowledge and understanding makes it easier to predict what a person will, or will not do, under most circumstances.

Study, learn, and understand what an "American" is, and what an "American" is not.
Do not call any person "American" unless he or she practices justice and correctness at all times, in all places, in all areas of activity, including Economics, Education, Entertainment, Labor, Law, Politics, Religion, Sex, and War.

Do not call any person "American" who practices White Supremacy (Racism), and/or, who, directly or indirectly,

tolerates, cooperates with, and/or submits to, the will or power of any person who practices White Supremacy, and/or who, directly or indirectly, helps to establish or maintain the practice of injustice or incorrectness.

Reason/Explanation:

An "American", is a person, who **does not**, at **any** time, in **any** place, in **any** area of activity, practice, support, or tolerate, White Supremacy (Racism), or any other form of injustice or incorrectness.

Avoid making comparisons between yourself and other Black (non-white) persons.

Avoid "measuring" yourself by watching what other Black people do.

Do not seek excuses to nit-pick, or gossip, and particularly, do not, for any reason, spend time, energy , or money, trying to "show-off".

Reason(s)/Explanation(s):

Many Black [non-white] people spend too much time comparing themselves with **each other**. They "enjoy" watching each other. They spend much time and energy gossiping about each other, and showing great interest in "nit-picking" the trivial comings and goings of each other. Many of them spend the best part of their reason for existence seeking to promote jealousy, envy, and snobbery among themselves.

However, if one understands anything about the people of the known universe, one should certainly understand that, considering all things, there is nothing involving a Black person to envy, nothing to be jealous about, and nothing to be snobbish about. There is nothing about such behavior that is constructive or complimentary. Such behavior only helps to maintain the status quo of injustice and incorrectness — particularly the injustice and incorrectness expressed in the form of White Supremacy (Racism).

It is important to remember, however, that no people in the known universe are the quality of people that **any** people **should be**. Therefore, there is absolutely nothing about **any** people that should provoke jealousy, envy, snobbery, gossip, or praise.

POLITICS

The existence of White Supremacy as the dominant motivating force among the people of the known universe, makes it correct for all non-white people, and all non-Racists white people, to watch and study those white people who practice White Supremacy in any area of activity — including Economics, Education, Entertainment, Labor, Law, Politics, Religion, Sex, and/or War.

White Supremacy (Racism) is the greatest system of injustice in the known universe. The people [white] who have chosen to practice this system do not allow any non-white people to do anything that definitely seems to lead to the establishment of justice and correctness among the people of the known universe. Under White Supremacy, Black people are, directly or indirectly, encouraged to do only those things that help to promote falsehood, non-justice, and incorrectness. They are encouraged and assisted in doing those things that help them to remain pitiful, primitive, stupid, and/or silly.

In a socio-material system dominated by White Supremacists, all major decisions involving non-white people are made by White Supremacists.

When a Black person needs serious help, he or she goes directly, or indirectly, to the White Supremacists and asks for that help.

Whatever a Black person gets, and/or is allowed to keep, is the result of decisions made by White Supremacists. This is the **functional** meaning of White Supremacy (Racism) that many people — particularly non-white people — prefer **not** to acknowledge.

Non-white people prefer not to admit to their own **lack** of mental ability, and strength of will, to **not** be dominated by Racists. They prefer not to see themselves as they truly are — pitiful, and/or comparatively primitive, stupid, or silly. They prefer to hide from the truth. They prefer to "look away" from the Racists so that they will not be forced to face the reasons for their lack of power as compared to the power of the Racists. They prefer to "look at" **each other.** They prefer to compare themselves with **each other.** This, they should not do. There is nothing to compare. Such exercises are akin to comparing one zero to another zero. Zero plus zero equals zero.

POLITICS

By watching and studying the ways of the White Supremacists, non-white people will learn more about the people, things, animals, etc., of the known universe. They will also learn very important things about **themselves**.

Victims of Racism (non-white people) should not only watch and study those white people who practice White Supremacy. They should also watch/study white people in general.

It is important to remember, however, that no people should attempt to copy **everything** that they see other people do. But **all** people should watch, study, and listen to, all other people in order to learn anything and everything that may be, or can be used for **constructive purposes**. When learning from white people and/or from White Supremacists, Black people should make a special effort to learn the **difference** between that which is constructive, and that which is not. Sometimes this is difficult to do, but, most of the time, with careful thought and attention to detail, it can be done.

The important thing is to start by having the **correct intentions** — the elimination of White Supremacy (Racism), and the establishment of justice and correctness among the people of the known universe.

Help give the word "love" it's correct meaning.
Avoid using the word "love" to describe any "feeling" or condition now in existence.

Reason(s)/Explanation(s):

"Love" is speech and/or action that produces a **result**.

"Love" is speech and/or action that **results** in the use of **truth** in a manner that **definitely** promotes the practice of **justice** and **correctness** at **all** times, in **all** places, in **all** areas of activity, including Economics, Education, Entertainment, Labor, Law, Politics, Religion, Sex, and War.

The word "love" has, incorrectly, been used to describe too many different conditions in too many different ways.

In the known universe, it is incorrect to pretend that "love" is being practiced by any person, animal, insect, place, thing, etc.

All people, animals, insects, etc., in the known universe function through the practice and support of falsehood, non-justice, and incorrectness. By so doing, it is not possible for them, at the same time, to **practice** "love".

Only by eliminating falsehood, non-justice, and incorrectness from the known universe can "love" be produced.

People have said and/or done many things in the name of, what they said was, and others accepted as being, "love". People have killed people who they said they "loved".

People have kept other persons from speaking or acting constructively in the name of "love".

Males have unjustly subjugated females in the name of "love".

People have robbed and stolen in the name of "love".

Sexual intercourse has ofttimes been referred to as "making love".

People have lied in the name of "love".

Therefore, to compensate for the confusion that has resulted from such use, it is best for each person to try to give the word a meaning that is **specific** and **constructive**.

Avoid racial "shadow boxing".

Reason(s)/Explanation(s):

When Victims of Racism (non-white people) are directly or indirectly, "assigned", bribed, coerced, and/or otherwise influenced, by the Racists (White Supremacists), to speak or act to do harm to other Victims of Racism, such speech or action can be described as "racial shadowism", and/or "racial shadow-boxing".

White Supremacists (Racists) ofttimes "hide" behind others whom they use as "shadows" of **themselves**. The intent is to cause the other Victims of Racism to believe, incorrectly, that it is the person acting in a "shadow" capacity who is the cause of the speech or action.

For that reason, it is correct to **avoid** speaking or acting against the persons who are used as "shadows" for the Racists.

POLITICS

All Victims of Racism should have knowledge and understanding of **all** of the ways that Racists use **others** to carry out their unjust acts, including the deceptive practice of "racial shadowism".

Try to minimize conflict.
When a person with whom you are conversing becomes angry and starts calling you "names", cursing you, etc., do not do the same. Instead, do the following two (2) things:

1. Say to him or her: "I will talk to you at some other time".

2. **Depart** from him or her [produce distance].

Reason/Explanation:

Where there is no **contact**, there is no **conflict.**

Do not "worship" hair.
Don't spend great time and/or effort combing it, twisting it, patting it, brushing it, pulling it, greasing it, oiling it, shaping it, or looking at it.

Don't spend so much time/effort "wondering" about it, and/or "making plans" for it.
Don't spend so much time/effort worrying about whether your hair is "right" or "wrong" or "good" or "bad". Don't worry about the hair on your head, on your chin, on your face, over your eyelids, etc.
Show more concern about the lack of constructive knowledge inside your head.

Reason/Explanation:

"Manhood", "womanhood", the elimination of Racism, nor the establishment of justice, is not a matter of giving great time and attention to hair.

Speak and/or act to promote the use of the terms "Victim", and/or Victim of Racism", to describe any person classified as, and/or who generally functions as, "Black", and/or "non-white".

Reason(s)/Explanation(s):

Since large numbers of "white" persons insist upon practicing Racism (as functionally related to "color" or "non-color" in people), and since no people called "Black" are subjugating people called "white", it is correct to promote the terms that best describe the **truth.**

The truth is that "white" people are "white" because they say that **they** are "white", and "Black" people are "Black", because "white" people who practice White Supremacy say that "Black" people are "Black".

Since people who are classified as "white" are smarter, and more powerful, collectively, than the people that they call "Black", then the people that they call "Black" are, in function, "Black". It is the smartest and most powerful people who decide the names for what is called "color" and it is they who decide which "color" or "non-color" will have which name. The smartest and most powerful people also decide what the relationships between people will be, and how these relationships will be associated with the factors of "color" and/or "non-color".

Word-terms such as "black", "brown", "colored", "minority", "mulatto", "Negro", "non-white", "red", "tan", "yellow", etc., can, and do, promote great confusion when used in a manner that is not carefully and directly employed in a fully-explained connection to White Supremacy (Racism).

This is extremely important to remember because these terms owe their **existence** to White Supremacy in the way that they are used in reference to Victims of Racism ("non-white" people).

For these reasons, when speaking of any matter involving so-called "racial" factors, it is best to use those terms which are, generally, best understood as well as accurate.

Examples of the **best** terms are as follows:

- Racists and/or White Supremacists = Any and all people who call themselves "white", and, who, **on that basis,** directly or indirectly practice subjugation of, and/or injustice against, any, and all people that they ["white" people] classify or treat as "Black" and/or "non-white".

- Victims,
  Victims of Racism, and/or
  Victims of White Supremacy = Any, and all people, who "white" people, consider to be "Black" and/or "non-white", and who are subject to socio-material conditions

dominated directly or indirectly, by White Supremacists (Racists).

Avoid being "side-tracked" into arguments about "capitalism", "communism", "fascism", "socialism", etc.
Develop the habit of not using these terms at all.

Focus your attention on Racism.
Talk about Racism in all of it's aspects, and all of it's effects.

Reason(s)/Explanation(s):

Racism, as expressed in the form of White Supremacy is the strongest and most destructive socio-material force among the people of the known universe.

Racism, as expressed in the form of White Supremacy **dominates** all other "isms". No social — material system now functioning among the people of the known universe is greater than the system of White Supremacy, and no "ism" has as great an effect on what people do, or don't do, in any one or more areas of activity.

Racism is the major functional enemy of the use of truth, to produce justice and correctness among the people of the known universe.

The words "capitalism", "communism", "socialism", etc., are functionally meaningless in a universal socio-material system directly or indirectly dominated by Racism (White Supremacy).

First things should be considered first. Fundamentals should be treated as fundamentals.

Racism (White Supremacy) is the major functional enemy of universal peace, and/or the major functional enemy of the potential for universal peace.

It is Racism that should be the focal point of all counter-action against the major functional enemy of the potential for universal peace.

The basic **element** of Racism is the Racist.

The basic "organization" of Racists is the White Nation (Collective White Supremacists).

POLITICS

The White Nation is composed exclusively of people who are classified as "white" people. Many of those white people who are members of the White Nation (Master Racist Organization) **pretend** that they are, from time to time, worried about the status of this "ism", or that "ism". They are concerned about the status of **one** "ism" only: Racism (White Supremacy).

When in doubt, it is just and correct to watch them, study what they have done, study what they are doing, then, watch them some more.

As for "capitalism" and "communism", the Collective White Supremacists (Racists) is the true "capitalist" and the true "communist" organization of the known universe. Everything that they do, is done "in common", and for a "common" purpose: White Supremacy.

The Racists (White Supremacists) sometimes call themselves "capitalists", but the **basic** things they "capitalize" on are the "strengths" and "weaknesses" of non-white people for the basic so-called "benefit" of Racists.

It does not matter if a Racists (White Supremacists) calls him or her self a "capitalist" or a "communist". Racists, collectively and individually "capitalize" on one thing in "common" — White Supremacy.

"Communism", to the extent that it exists, exists only in the form of **"Race**-Communism". The Racists (White Supremacists) of the known universe are the only **major** identifiable "group" of the people who function "in common" with each other, on a massive scale, that is both prolonged and consistently all-engrossing.

By comparison, there exists no other form of "Communism" worthy of note, either in theory or in practice.

"Capitalism", to the extent that it exists, exists only in the form of **"Race**-Capitalism". The Racists (White Supremacists) of the known universe are the only **major** identifiable "group" of people who have proven their ability to "capitalize" on the strengths and weaknesses of their subjects on a massive scale that is both prolonged and consistently all-engrossing.

By comparison, there exists no other form of "Capitalism" worthy of note, either in theory or in practice.

"Socialism", to the extent that it exists, exists only in the form of "**Race**-Socialism". The Racists (White Supremacists) of the known universe are the only **major** identifiable "group" of people who "socialize" with each other, on a massive scale, that is both prolonged and consistently all-engrossing.

By comparison, there exists no other form of "socialism" worthy of note, either in theory or in practice.

Practice thinking, speaking, and acting as if your "home" is not a particular place, but, rather, is a system of thought, speech, and action, that supports the revelation of truth in a manner that promotes the practice of justice and correctness.

Reason(s)/Explanation(s):

In a socio-material system dominated by White Supremacy (Racism), it is correct for non-white people to regard "home" as being the combined things that they say, and/or do, that help to find and reveal truth, and use truth in such manner as to promote justice and correctness.

Under White Supremacy (Racism), it is not possible for any non-white person to **correctly** regard any **geographical location** as his or her "home".

"Home", for a non-white person should be regarded as a **system of behavior.**

Example:

A Victim of Racism [non-white person] is "at home" anytime that he or she is saying or doing anything that effectively promotes the elimination of Racism (White Supremacy), and/or, effectively promotes the practice of justice or correctness.

As long as you are existing under the direct or indirect "authority" and/or power of the White Supremacists (Racists), do not claim ownership of, and/or master "authority" over, any man, woman, boy, or girl, any place in the known universe.

Reason(s)/Explanation(s):

In a "known universe" dominated by White Supremacists (Racists), **all non-white** people, of **all** ages, sexes, etc., are subject to the direct or indirect power of the White Supremacists, in **all** areas of activity, including Economics, Education, Entertainment, Labor, Law, Politics, Religion, Sex, and War.

Therefore, the White Supremacists are the direct or indirect "masters" of all non-white people, regardless of age, sex, etc.

It is the White Supremacists (Racists) who are, directly and/or indirectly, **responsible** for everything that happens, or, does not happen, as regards non-white people.

All non-white people are the "children" of the White Supremacists (Racists). The White Supremacists hope and **intend** to keep all non-white people in a "child-like" condition.

As long as any non-white person submits to, and/or co-operates with, White Supremacy (Racism), that non-white person is, for all functional purposes, a "child".

Tell, and/or admit the truth about any of your "weaknesses" in any, and all areas of activity, including Economics, Education, Entertainment, Labor, Law, Politics, Religion, Sex, and War.

Tell, and/or admit the truth about yourself to anyone who is also willing to tell, and/or admit, the truth about him or her self. This includes the truth about such "weaknesses" as envy, drunkeness, laziness, greed, incorrect sexual activity, the use of deceit, etc.

Seek to minimize the extent to which any of your weaknesses interfere with Counter-Racist speech or action.

Reason(s)/Explanation(s):

The revelation of, and the knowledge and understanding of, truth, is absolutely necessary in order to produce justice and correctness.

The knowledge and understanding of truth **plus**, the practice of justice and correctness, equals "peace".

Without knowing and understanding truth [that which is], people cannot practice justice and correctness.

Without justice and correctness there is no "peace".

POLITICS

Don't get entangled in so-called "high-priced" words. Keep all conversation simple and basic, especially when conversing with people who may be Racists (White Supremacists). Always seek truth, and always seek it through revelation and/or through detailed explanations that you can understand and utilize for constructive purposes.

Respond to criticism of your speech and/or action regarding Racism by making the following statement:

> "The Race problem has not been solved. The reason the Race problems has not been solved is because the people who have the **ability** to solve it, do not have the **will**, and the people who have the **will**, do not have the **ability**. To the extent that I am lacking in either the **will**, or the **ability**, to solve the Race problem, I apologize".

Minimize anger and/or hostility between yourself and those with whom you are exchanging views. If a person seems to be angry or hostile toward the views that you express, do the following:

(1) Ask the angered person this question:

> "Do you wish for me to be silent and not express my views to you?"

(2) If the answer is "yes", then **be silent**, and/or, do not express your views to **that** person.

(3) If the answer is "no", **continue** expressing your views, but strive to do so in such manner as to **increase understanding**, and **minimize conflict.**

Do not accuse any Victim of Racism [non-white person] of "selling out" the "rights" of non-white people to the Racists (White Supremacists).

Reason(s)/Explanation(s):

Racist Man and Racist Woman (White Supremacists) have functional power over **all** non-white people in the known universe. Therefore, no non-white person is **responsible** for "selling out" any person, animal, place, thing, idea, etc., to anybody, at any time.

POLITICS

Without the direction and/or consent of the White Supremacists, a non-white person can neither "buy", nor "sell", him or her **self**. It is incorrect, under White Supremacy, to ever accuse any non-white person of "selling out" **anyone** to the White Supremacists.

Since **all** non-white people are subject to the White Supremacists, it is the White Supremacists who are the only people in the known universe who have the **power** to "buy", "sell", or "sell out", any people, at any time. All "buying" and "selling" of people is done either directly or indirectly by Racist Man and/or Racist Woman.

Any **non**-white person who feels that he or she has been "sold-out" should accuse no one of having done so, except the Racists (White Supremacists, collectively).

Minimize conflict (between yourself and other non-white people) by minimizing contact.

Reason(s)/Explanation(s):

> **"No contact [equals]; no conflict".**

Individual non-white persons who do not "get along" with each other without fussing, fighting, name-calling, gossiping, nit-picking, cheating, etc., **should avoid all contact with each other** until such time that they **can** get along without doing such things.

This means they should stop, or avoid, any contact with each other — both direct or indirect. They should avoid **being** in the **presence** of each other. They should **avoid** talking **about** each other. They should **avoid talking to** each other.

"No contact; no conflict".

Never say that you are "proud" to be "Black".

Reason(s)/Explanation(s):

Being "Black" should have nothing to do with being proud, and being proud should have nothing to do with being "Black".

Saying that you are "proud", and/or bragging about being "Black" serves no constructive purpose.

POLITICS

A person is "Black", and/or appears to be "Black", or "dark", because he or she was produced that way. It is not necessary to be "proud" to be "Black". It is not necessary to be "proud" to be **anything**. It is necessary, however, to seek truth, and to use truth to produce justice and correctness, in order to have "peace". It is not necessary to be "proud" of producing "peace". Producing "peace" is the correct reason for the existence of people in a known universe that has no "peace".

People should produce "peace" because it is their **duty**. A person should not do his or her **duty** in order to "develop pride". A person should do his or her duty because it **needs** to be done.

Do not think, speak, and/or act as if a white person is evil, unjust, and/or Racist (White Supremacist) because he or she expresses "liking" being "white" in physical appearance.

Reason(s)/Explanation(s):

It is **incorrect** to make malicious remarks about, and/or speak or act against, **any** person because of the way that he or she "looks" to those persons who do the looking. A "white" person who speaks, and/or acts in support of White Supremacy (Racism) **is** a Racist (White Supremacist). Otherwise, a "white" person who simply "likes" being "white" in appearance, but, who does or says **nothing** that supports White Supremacy (Racism) is **not** a Racist.

AREA 7: RELIGION

▪ PREFACE ▪

The following pages present suggestions that pertain to what a Victim of Racism [non-white person] **should**, or **should not**, choose to do in the Seventh Major Area of [People] Activity: Religion.

Each person should choose to speak, and/or act, according to one or more of the suggestions presented — but only if he or she decides to do so.

No person should speak and/or act according to **any** suggestion presented herein unless he or she has judged that the suggestion chosen is of **current** and **correct** value in helping to eliminate Racism (White Supremacy), and/or, in helping to better promote justice.

It is important to know and understand that one or more suggestions selected from one Major Area of [People] Activity, should be used in constructive combination with other Major Areas of [People] Activity.

If an individual person chooses to utilize any suggestion presented herein, he or she should do so in a manner, and at a specific time, and specific place, that will produce the **most constructive results** in the revelation of truth, and/or, the production of justice or correctness.

▪ ▪ ▪ ▪ ▪ ▪

Do not "argue" about, and/or speak against any religion, except the "religion" of White Supremacy (Racism).

Be willing to explain to others everything that your religion requires you to do, and not do, or say and not say, as pertains to every area of activity — including Economics, Education, Entertainment, Labor, Law, Politics, Religion, Sex, and War.

When "religious matters" are presented to you by others, explain your religion to them, and ask them to explain their religion to you. Ask them to explain what their religion requires them to do and say, and/or not do and say, in all areas of activity — including Economics, Education, Entertainment, Labor, Law, Politics, Religion, Sex, and War.

RELIGION

Speak and act to oppose the belief that White Supremacy (Racism) is "God's Religion", or, is a part of, "God's Religion".

Reason(s)/Explanation(s):

It has been said that "God made white people for the purpose of serving God, and God made Black people for the purpose of serving white people".

This could be true. There is much to indicate that it **is** true.

If true, however, there is much to indicate that the smartest and most powerful white people have chosen **not** to "serve God". There is much to indicate that the smartest and most powerful white people [White Supremacists] have chosen to subvert, and/or replace God. They have, apparently, chosen to "make" themselves "God". It is unfortunate, non-just, and incorrect for the smartest, and most powerful of the people of the known universe to have organized themselves into a "Race".

Not all white people, presumably, are members of a Race, but, apparently, those who are smarter, and, therefore, more powerful, do function [by choice] as Race Members [Racists/White Supremacists]. They have made Racism their "religion". They have made Racism into the most powerful "religion" among the people of the known universe, and made themselves the "God" of that "religion".

To confuse their victims, they have disguised their practice of Racism by using the names and titles of many other religions and social concepts. This has helped them to refine their subjugation and abuse of their victims.

They have chosen to have non-white people "worship" them for being "white" and **supreme**. They have attempted to make God and White Supremacy one and the same. They have done all this for no ultimate purpose than to "glorify" White Supremacy (Racism), and to "glorify" themselves as "White" Supremacists (Racists).

The basic speech and action of a Racist (White Supremacist) is only for the purpose of promoting falsehood, non-justice, and incorrectness as the functional foundation for Racism (White Supremacy).

RELIGION

The Racists are masterfully skilled in the use of deceit and direct violence.

It is reasonable to believe that Racism does not serve God. Also, there is no reason to believe that a person can be a Racist, and serve God, **at the same time.**

If Racism does not serve the purpose(s) of the Creator [God], then it is the **duty** of the Victims of Racism [non-white people], as well as the duty of those white people who are **not** Racists, to speak and act to eliminate Racism. It is also the duty of those white persons who are Racists, to stop being Racists.

If these duties are performed, conditions will then be better for the Creator's [God's] purposes to be served.

The value of any "religion" should be determined by how it affects people in the way that they relate to each other, as well as all that is in the universe.

People who have great power were "given" the means and ability to develop that power. If people who have great power use that power to mistreat people, they have, by so doing, destroyed their reason for **having** that power. It is then the duty of those persons who have been mistreated to persuade those powerful persons to stop misusing that power. It is the duty of the mistreated persons to cause these powerful persons to be separated from their power. In causing this separation from power, it is correct for the mistreated to use correct social force and/or correct counter-violence.

The correct purpose for producing, receiving, or sharing knowledge, and/or power, is to reveal truth, and to use truth in a manner that produces justice and correctness — in order to produce "peace".

No people should do other than this. No people should **be allowed** to do other than this.

Remind others that you expect them to practice their religion, and that you expect them to do and say whatever their religion requires of them. Remind them, also, that they can, and should, expect the same of you, in regards to <u>your</u> religion.

Reason(s)/Explanation(s):

In matters of religion, as in all areas of activity, conflict between Victims of Racism [non-white people] should be **minimized.**

It is correct to try to talk with people and to make a maximum effort to eliminate all unnecessary conflict and violence and to try to eliminate all ill-will.

When discussing "religious matters" with those who are willing, always do the following:

1. State the name and/or title of **your** religion.

2. State and describe **everything** that **your** religion requires you to do, and not do, in each area of activity, including Economics, Education, Entertainment, Labor, Law, Politics, Religion, Sex, and War.

3. **Ask** the others to state the names and/or titles of **their** religion(s), and **ask** them to state and describe to you everything that their religion(s) require that they do, and not do, in each area of activity, including Economics, Education, Entertainment, Labor, Law, Politics, Religion, Sex, and War.

4. Remind others that **you** "expect" them to **practice** all of the requirements of **their** religion(s), and that they should "expect" **you** to **practice** all of the requirements of **your** religion.

Speak and act in such manner that there is no "conflict" between your "religion" and your "politics".

Reason(s)/Explanation(s):

To the extent that any religion is, in any way, involved with **people**, that religion is "political".

"Politics" is nothing more, nor nothing less, than "people relations".

Any relationship(s), in any area of activity, between one person, and **any other** person, is "politics".

The only way that a "religious person" can **avoid** being involved in "politics" is for that person, to **not** have anything to do with any other person, at any time, in any place, in any area of activity, including Economics, Education, Entertainment, Labor, Law, Sex, and/or War.

Do not assume that a person who says that he or she is a "Christian", a "Jew", a "Muslim", a "Buddhist", etc., is one.
Do not assume that a person who says that he or she is a "Christian", a "Jew", a "Muslim", a "Buddhist", etc., is one all of the time.

Reason(s)/Explanation(s):

A person who calls him or her self a "Christian", may, or may not, **be** a "Christian".

A person who calls him or her self a "Muslim", may, or may not, be a "Muslim" **all** of the time.

A person who calls him or her self a "Jew", may, or may not, be a "Jew" **most** of the time.

A person who calls him or her self a "Buddhist", may, or may not, be a "Buddhist" **some** of the time.

A person who calls him or her self a "Christian", may, or may not, call him or her self a "sinner". He or she may, or may not, call him or her self a "sinner" at the **same** time that he or she calls him or her self a "Christian".

A white person may, or may not, call him or her self a "Jew", while, at the **same** time, he or she may, or may not, be practicing White Supremacy (Racism).

A non-white person may, or may not, call him or her self a "Jew", while, at the **same** time, he or she **functions** as a Victim of White Supremacy.

A person — **any** person — may, or may not call him, or her self a "Christian", "Jew", "Buddhist", "Muslim", etc., and, at the same time, **be** none of them.

A person may call him or her self a "Christian" at one time, a "Jew" at another time, and a "Muslim at another time. That **same** person may, or may not, have been **any** of them, at **any** time.

A non-white person may, or may not, function as a "Pluralist" **some** of the time, and may, or may not, function as a "Jew", or a "Christian", at other times.

A non-white person may, or may not, function as a "Pluralist" at the same time that he or she is a Victim of Racism — but his or her practice of "Pluralism" **must** be in resistance to Racism, while subject to Racism (White Supremacy).

In a socio-material system dominated by White Supremacists (Racists) **all** non-white people are Victims of Racism regardless of the "religion" they say that they practice, or attempt to practice.

White Supremacy is a "religion". It is an extremely powerful and exclusive "religion". It is so powerful, and so exclusive, that any person [white] who practices White Supremacy (Racism) cannot, at the same time, practice **any** other "religion". White Supremacists do, however, use **deceit** as a basic tool of the "religion" of Racism that they practice. Within the function of White Supremacy this deceit is "religious" deception.

Thus, a white person may ofttimes **pretend** to be a "Christian", a "Jew", a "Buddhist", etc., while actually **practicing** the "religion" of White Supremacy (Racism). It is therefore difficult, and ofttimes dangerous, for any **non**-white person to **assume** that a person — particularly a white person — is a "Buddhist", a "Christian", a "Jew", a "Pluralist", etc., simply because that person **says** that he or she is.

It has been proven that many White Supremacists (Racists) can speak and/or act in a manner that leads many of their victims [non-white people] to believe whatever those White Supremacists want them to believe. The skilled use of "religious" titles is one of the most effective methods used by the Racists to deceive their victims.

AREA 8: SEX

▮ PREFACE ▮

The following pages present suggestions that pertain to what a Victim of Racism [non-white person] **should**, or **should not**, choose to do in the Eighth Major Area of [People] Activity: Sex.

Each person should choose to speak, and/or act, according to one or more of the suggestions presented — but only if he or she decides to do so. No person should speak and/or act according to **any** suggestion presented herein unless he or she has judged that the suggestion chosen is of **current** and **correct** value in helping to eliminate Racism (White Supremacy), and/or, in helping to better promote justice.

It is important to know and understand that one or more suggestions selected from one Major Area of [People] Activity, should be used in constructive combination with one or more suggestions selected from other Major Areas of [People] Activity.

If an individual person chooses to utilize any suggestion presented herein, he or she should do so in a manner, and at a specific time, and specific place, that will produce the **most constructive results** in the revelation of truth, and/or, the production of justice or correctness.

▮ ▮ ▮ ▮ ▮ ▮ ▮

As long as White Supremacy (Racism) is the dominant socio-material force among the people of the known universe, do not say that you, or any other non-white person, is "married".
Instead, use the expression: "Attempted Marriage".

Reason(s)/Explanation(s):

"Marriage" can only exist between two or more persons, **none** of whom are **dominated** by persons who practice Racism (White Supremacy).

Any person(s) who must have the direct or indirect "approval" of White Supremacists (Racists) in order to engage in sexual intercourse, "sexual play", and/or "sexual communication" **cannot** be "married".

SEX

As long as White Supremacy exists, no person, who is subject to it, is "married".

As long as White Supremacy dominates the non-white people of the known universe, consider no non-white person as "married". Practice using the expression "attempting marriage", and/or, "attempted marriage".

Reason(s)/Explanation(s):

"Marriage" is a **mutual** and **harmonious** relationship between one or more males with one or more females.

Under White Supremacy (Racism), all non-white people are forced, and/or "allowed" to make "arrangements" with each other, and/or with white people, through "mutual" **agreements.** These agreements are "mutual" because all persons involved in them, have, directly, or indirectly, "agreed" to maintain them. In this respect, the arrangments are similar to the arrangments made between the prisoner and the prison-maker, as well as between one prisoner and another.

As long as White Supremacy exists, **white** persons may, or may not, be "married" to **each other**. As long as White Supremacy exists, white people have a **choice** as to whether they will, or will not, be married to **each other.** Non-white people have no such choice. Under White Supremacy non-white persons cannot be married to **anybody** — white or non-white. Non-white persons can only "attempt" marriage, and/or, can only **pretend** to be "married".

Under White Supremacy, **all** persons are capable of conducting **mutual** relationships, but not **harmonious** ones. Under White Supremacy (Racism) no **non**-white person can have a **harmonious** relationship with **any** person — white or non-white. The very existence of White Supremacy is **intended** to establish, maintain, expand, and/or refine **dis-harmony** between non-white people, in their relationships with each other, and with all that exists in the known universe.

Without **harmony** no person can be correctly considered as "married" to any other person. Therefore, in a socio-material system dominated by White Supremacists (Racists) no non-white person is "married".

SEX

Summation:

Any persons who are subject to the power of unjust persons cannot be married.

Any persons who are **subject** to the power of **unjust** persons do not have the power to do justice (to each other, nor to others).

Any persons who do not have the power to do justice are **not** "married" and cannot be "married" — to anybody.

In a socio-material system dominated by White Supremacists (Racists), the White Supremacists **do** have the "ability" to do justice. In order to do justice however, they would have to cease being White Supremacists.

Persons who are subject to the White Supremacists are "not able" to do justice as long as they are subjects.

They can, at best, only **attempt** to promote justice. If they **attempt** to promote justice, they may be assisted in doing so by the "sum total of the powers of the known combined with the unknown [God, etc.]".

As long as White Supremacy (Racism) exists, try to discourage, disapprove of, and/or avoid all "legal" or "formal" so-called "marriages" between any persons, any place, at any time.

Reason(s)/Explanation(s):

As long as White Supremacy (Racism) exists, it is correct for males and females to be in contact with each other for the following reasons **only:**

1. To engage in **constructive labor.**

2. To **talk** with each other about ways and means of eliminating Racism (White Supremacy) and about establishing justice.

3. To engage in sexual intercourse.

As long as White Supremacy (Racism) exists, all "legal" or "formal" so-called "marriages", either directly, or indirectly, serve no major purpose except to help maintain, expand, and/or refine White Supremacy.

SEX

By avoiding "legal", and/or "formal", so-called "marriage", each person — both male and female — is forced to **relate directly, and personally,** to **all** of the major realities (and discomforts) of White Supremacy, in every major area of activity, including Economics, Education, Entertainment, Labor, Law, Politics, Religon, **Sex** and War.

If people — especially non-white people — begin to function in a manner in which **each individual person** must **relate directly** to the "realities" of White Supremacy in it's less disguised forms, the **understanding** of White Supremacy, how it works, and for what purpose, will increase.

An **understanding** of White Supremacy (Racism), by it's victims, automatically increases the desire and need to eliminate it.

Summary:

As long as White Supremacy exists, it is correct for non-white males and females to spend a very **minimum** amount of time, energy, money, etc., "entertaining" each other, and/or seeking "personal attention" from each other.

So-called "marriages", "attempted marriages", and/or "imitation marriages" require that the persons so involved must devote a substantial measure of "personal attention" and/or "material comfort" to one another.

Under socio-material conditions dominated by White Supremacy (Racism) such activity is, in effect, only a feeble attempt at **pretending** "marriage". Under White Supremacy, such activity, among it's victims, does not, and **cannot** produce or support **true** "marriage". Such activity only produces the **pretense** of "true" marriage. Such pretense of marriage only supports White Supremacy, and injustice in general.

In addition, as long as White Supremacy exists, it is correct for white people and non-white people to avoid all contact with each other that does not help to eliminate Racism (White Supremacy) and/or, does not help to produce justice. Also, until Racism is eliminated, there should be no contacts between white people and non-white people that include sexual intercourse, so-called "homosexual" [anti-sexual] intercourse, and/or "sexual play".

As long as White Supremacy exists, do not engage in a so-called "legal" marriage.

SEX

Reason(s)/Explanation(s):

It is non-just and incorrect for any person classified as "non-white" to engage in any so-called "legal" marriage as long as any non-white person in the known universe is directly, or indirectly, subject to White Supremacy (Racism) in any one or more of the following areas of activity: Economics, Education, Entertainment, Labor, Law, Politics, Religion, Sex, and/or War.

"White Supremacy (Racism)", means that **all** non-white people are directly, or indirectly, subject to the power of the White Supremacists (Racists), in **all** areas of activity. Therefore, as long as Black and/or non-white people are subject to the power of the White Supremacists, it is not possible for any Black and/or non-white person to be truly "married".

As long as the "rules" of marriage are controlled by White Supremacists, no non-white person is, or can be, the true so-called "head" of a so-called "household". Nor can any non-white person function as a member of a so-called "family" that is **not** actually subject to the dictates of White Supremacists. Non-white people are, however, encouraged to **pretend** that they function with such authority.

Under White Supremacy, the true "head" of every so-called "household" and the true "head" of every so-called "marriage", that involves a Black person, is, at all times, **each and every white person** in the known universe who practices White Supremacy.

Under White Supremacy, the effect of so-called "legal" marriage that involves Black persons is to promote the **illusion** that Black persons can depend on each other without major help from the White Supremacists. Such so-called "marriages" only serve to disguise some of the most destructive effects of White Supremacy (Racism).

It is the White Supremacists who, directly, or indirectly, dictate the functional "quality" and/or "value", of all socio-sexual relationships that involve non-white people.

Under White Supremacy, Black people do not "make policy" as to the extent and type of sexual relationships that exist between white people and Black people. Black people do not "make policy" as to the extent, and type, of sexual relationships that exist between "Black" people and "other" non-white people. Under White Supremacy, Black people are **most definitely** prevented from "making policy" involving sexual relations between **Black males** and **white females**. Only the White Supremacists make such policy, and that policy is sternly, and brutally, enforced. The White Supremacists make sure that all socio-sexual relationships between white people and non-white people are "arranged" in such manner as to best promote the maintenance, expansion, and/or refinement of the power of the White Supremacists.

In order to promote justice, it is necessary for the Victims of Racism (non-white people) to think, speak, and act in such manner as to disrupt the function and intent of the socio-sexual policy of the White Supremacists.

To avoid the so-called "legal" marriage while subject to White Supremacy is to indirectly oppose and expose the Racists in their pretense of order, stability, and justice in their regulation of the sexual activity of their victims.

As long as White Supremacy exists, it is correct for Victims of Racism to help eliminate the illusion of the existence of so-called Black "marriages" by refraining from engaging in so-called "legal" marriage and/or, "recognized" marriage.

It is correct for all persons who seek to produce justice to know and understand the **correct** purpose for so-called "legal" or "recognized" marriage. The **correct** purpose for so-called "legal" or "recognized" marriage is to help arrange a relationship between two or more persons in such manner that those persons can best help each other to produce justice. When non-white persons exist in subjugation to White Supremacy, such so-called "legal" or "recognized" marriages do not help to produce justice. They help to maintain **non**-justice.

Under White Supremacy, no non-white person is correctly "qualified", or prepared, for "marriage" to anyone, in any place, at any time.

Stop attempting marriage, and/or pretending to be married.

Reason(s)/Explanation(s):

It is not possible for any person [non-white] to be directly or indirectly subject to White Supremacy (Racism), and, at the same time, function as a "husband", or as a "wife". Therefore, no non-white persons who exists in direct or indirect subjugation to White Supremacy is, or can be, "married". Such persons are only allowed to **pretend** to be married. By **pretending** that they are, or can be, married to anyone, white or non-white, and, at the same time, be directly or indirectly, subject to the power and dictates of White Supremacists (Racists), non-white poeple only help to support, and prolong the existence of White Supremacy.

Such pretension helps to promote waste, confusion, incorrect ambition, increased conflict, and a "false sense of security" among non-white males and females, in everything that they do.

The **falsehood** that dominates such relationships helps to promote incorrect thought, speech, and/or action in every area of their existence, including, Economics, Education, Entertainment, Labor, Law, Politics, Religion, Sex, and War.

As long as White Supremacy exists, it is **correct** for all non-white people to refrain from "attempted" or "pretended" marriage. They should, instead, devote their time to those activities that will help best to eliminate Racism.

In addition, it is incorrect for any non-white person to **wish** to marry any white person who practices White Supremacy (Racism).

It is also incorrect for any non-white person to **wish** to marry any **non**-white person who is directly, or indirectly, **subject to** White Supremacy (Racism).

To express such wishes, by either word or deed, is to help to maintain, and give a more refined strength to the power of the White Supremacists (Racists).

To speak or act to make such wishes a reality will result in a continuation of the waste, deceit, confusion, and conflict that most often exists between non-white males and females. Such speech and action will also result in a greater promotion of the **trival priorities** that dominate the thinking of non-white males and females when they consider themselves to be "married".

To avoid participation in any Racist-dominated so-called "marriage" is one of the easiest, and most effective means by which those non-white persons who are dedicated to the elimination of Racism (White Supremacy) can better do so.

Note: In any socio-material system dominated by White Supremacists (Racists), the only non-white persons who are "eligible" or "qualified" for marriage are those males and females who are **not subject** to White Supremacy (Racism) in anything that they say, or do, in any area of activity.

Speak and/or act to promote the revelation that, under White Supremacy (Racism), all so-called "marriages" ["legal" or "non-legal"], that involve non-white people, are "non-marriages", and/or "play" marriages.

Reason(s)/Explanation(s):

Under White Supremacy (Racism), it is the White Supremacists (Racists) who determine directly, or indirectly, what non-white people do, or don't do, in every major part, of every major activity, including Economics, Education, Entertainment, Labor, Law, Politics, Religion, Sex, and War.

The major decisions that **most effect** the attempts at marriage that non-white people make are made by White Supremacists (Racists).

Non-white people are **not qualified** to "marry". Neither can they guarantee the protection, assistance, and/or material comfort that is necessary, and/or expected in the conduct of a "true" and/or "legal" marriage.. It is **false** for any person, or persons, to say, or pretend, that he, she, or they, are, or can be, "married", and, at the same time, be subject to White Supremacy.

Under White Supremacy, no non-white person can **protect any person** from the will and power of the White Supremacists. Therefore, under any socio-sexual-material condition dominated by White Supremacy, no non-white person can [truly] **function** as a husband, as a wife, or as a parent.

Note: The following terms and their definitions can be used to best describe so-called "marital" and/or "parental" arrangements that involve non-white persons:

Non-husband, and/or "play" husband =
Any male non-white person who exists in direct or indirect subjugation to White Supremacy (Racism),

and who attempts to constructively assist and/or protect, any female person whom he has chosen, and/or willfully accepted, as a "legal" or non-legal socio-sexual companion.

Non-wife, and/or "play" wife =
Any female non-white person who exists in direct or indirect subjugation to White Supremacy (Racism), and who attempts to constructively assist and/or protect, any male person whom she has chosen, and/or willfully accepted, as a "legal" or non-legal socio-sexual companion.

Non-marriage and/or "play" marriage =
Any "legal", or non-legal, willful socio-sexual relationship between any persons, while one or more of those persons is directly, or indirectly, subject to White Supremacy (Racism) in any area of activity.

Non-parent and/or "play" parent =
Any non-white person who exists in direct or indirect subjugation to White Supremacy (Racism), and who attempts to protect, any non-white person from the effects of White Supremacy.

[In a socio-material system dominated by White Supremacy (Racism), only white people can function as "parents"].

"Mother Superior"/"Father Superior" [Racial] =
Any white person who practices White Supremacy (Racism).

Avoid the production of off-spring:

- Until you **know,** and **understand,** what White Supremacy (Racism) is, and how it works, in **all** areas of activity, including Economics, Education, Entertainment, Labor, Law, Politics, Religion, Sex, and War.

- Until you have the **will**, and the **ability**, to adequately **feed** them, **clothe** them, and **house** them.

- Until you have the **will**, and the **ability**, to explain to them, in a manner that they will understand, what White Supremacy (Racism) is, and how it works in **all** areas of activity, including Economics, Education, Entertainment, Labor, Law, Politics, Religion, Sex, and War.

SEX

- Until you, yourself, **consistently** show, by both word and deed, that you are willing to spend **all** of your time and energy trying to speak and act **effectively** to eliminate Racism.

As long as White Supremacy (Racism) exists, do not engage in any act of sexual intercourse except for one, or both, of the following reasons:

- To help to provide **comfort for, incentive to,** and promote **constructive communication between,** those Victims of Racism [non-white people] who repeatedly strive to speak and/or act to resist or eliminate Racism (White Supremacy).

- Production of off-spring.

Reason(s)/Explanation(s):

Every person in the known universe is, at **all** times, directly or indirectly, either engaging in a "sexual" act, and/or the expression of a "sexual" act, **or**, every person is directly or indirectly **re-acting** to those who are so engaged.

Sexual motivation is second **only** to Racism (White Supremacy) as the great and domineering motivating force, by people, among the people of the known universe.

Therefore, as long as Racism (White Supremacy) is the dominant motivating force, by people, among the people of the known universe, it is correct for a person to engage in sexual intercourse **only** if such acts directly, or indirectly, help to **eliminate** Racism. All sexual intercourse that does not help to eliminate Racism is incorrect.
As long as White Supremacy exists, it is correct for non-white persons to engage in sexual intercourse only with non-white persons, and only in the manner, and/or for the reasons aforementioned.

Do not engage in sexual intercourse, and/or "sexual play" in any manner that contributes to the distress, discomfort, confusion, and/or efficiency, of any other person, while that person is, directly or indirectly, seeking to speak and/or act to resist and/or eliminate Racism (White Supremacy).

SEX

Reason(s)/Explanation(s):

As long as Racism (White Supremacy) exists, all acts of sexual intercourse and/or "sexual play" should, directly, or indirectly, contribute to the comfort, inspiration, incentive, and efficiency of those Victims of Racism [non-white persons] who **prove by their deeds** that they seek to speak, and/or act, to resist and/or eliminate Racism.

As long as Racism (White Supremacy) exists, the "pleasures" and/or "benefits" of sexual intercourse or "sexual play" should be promoted and/or "reserved" **only** for those persons who **consistently** seek to establish ways and means of eliminating Racism in everything that they say and do.

All "pleasure" that is received by a Victim of Racism [non-white person] should be a part of his or her "work".

Since all "work", by a Victim of Racism, should be for the purpose of **eliminating** Racism, then all activity that produces "pleasure" for that Victim, including sexual activity, should be a part of that "work".

Do not engage in sexual intercourse and/or "sexual play" with anyone with whom you frequently argue.

Reason/Explanation:

People who engage in frequent arguments with each other should avoid all unnecessary contacts with each other.

By avoiding all unnecessary contacts with each other, they will **minimize conflict** with each other.

As long as White Supremacy (Racism) exists, do not speak, and/or act, as if sexual intercourse and/or "sexual play" between white people and non-white people will help to eliminate Racism.

Reason(s)/Explanation(s):

Contrary to what many persons believe, **no** act of sexual intercourse, and/or "sexual play", between a white person and a non-white person, under conditions dominated by White Supremacy (Racism), contributes in any way, directly or indirectly, to the **elimination** of Racism.

Such acts, in truth, only help to **deceive** the **victims** of White Supremacy, by causing them to **think** that such sexual activity will, eventually, lead to the elimination of Racism. This is exactly what the White Supremacists intend for their victims to think.

The White Supremacists (Racists) use sexual activity with [against] their victims in a manner that causes their victims to become weaker and more confused in their efforts to resist the more "soothing" and sophisticated forms of deception and seduction as used by the White Supremacists, to **refine** the practice of White Supremacy.

Engaging in sexual intercourse, and/or "sexual play", with [against] their victims [non-white people], is one of the most effective methods used by the Racists to express, and/or refine their domination of, and/or their contempt for, all non-white persons.

Any person who willfully and deliberately "approves" of sexual intercourse and/or "sexual play" between white people and non-white people, under conditions dominated by White Supremacy (Racism), is not justified in criticizing, or complaining about, any act of sexual intercourse and/or "sexual play" between **any** two or more persons, for any "reason".

Under White Supremacy (Racism), **no act** has the **same** meaning, and/or the **same** effect, as the **same** act would have if it were committed under conditions **not** dominated by White Supremacy. If the condition is not the same, then the act is not the same in **meaning**, and/or in effect. The act is not the same in meaning, and/or in effect, because of the **reason** for the **existence** of the condition.

Sexual intercourse and/or "sexual play" between white persons and non-white persons, under conditions dominated by White Supremacy, does not help to eliminate White Supremacy. Such acts do not help to promote justice.

On the contrary, such acts, under such conditions, help, greatly, to maintain, expand, and/or refine, White Supremacy. Such acts help to maintain the practice of injustice. Such acts, themselves, are unjust. This is the effect. The acts which cause this effect is therefore, a part of the effect.

Likewise, the effect, which is a result of the act, is a part of the act. If the **effect** is unjust and incorrect, and if the **act** is unjust and incorrect, then the **effect** of the **act** is unjust and incorrect.

Racism (White Supremacy) is the "most respected" motivating force among the people of the known univese. This means that in each and every matter involving racial factors, all persons should be able to determine the **effects** of their speech and action(s) **before** they speak and/or act.

There is not now, nor has there ever been, since the establishment of White Supremacy (Racism), any greater contributing force, to the strengthening and continuation of Racism in it's most refined form, than the Racism that is practiced through sexual activity between white people and Black people — particularly between white men and Black females.

In every place in the known universe where Black people and white people are in direct contact with one another, the sexual activity between white men and Black females continues to flourish with a quiet, but devastating effect on all attempts to solve the ages-old issue of Race, and/or Racism.

The Victims of Racism — particularly "Black" males and females — generally do not know or understand the tremendous effect that such sexual activity has on the overall status of relations between people, in all areas of activity.

When known, and/or perceived, such activity is generally ignored. Such activity is usually not appreciated for it's importance, by most of the non-white people of the known universe — particularly those people classified as "Black" and/or "Negroid".

It is through the medium of sexual activity that the Racist Man [male White Supremacist(s)] uses, most effectively, the tools of flattery, bribery, pretended "love", and/or general hypocrisy and deceit.

Racist Man uses these methods to wage the most destructive aspect of his war against non-white people.

The so-called "hidden" sexual activity between white males and Black females has done more toward maintaining

confusion in the movement to eliminate Racism than any other single factor. The Black female, in particular, is the "open back door" through which the male White Supremacist (Racist) "completes" and parades his "cycle" of Racism.

When a white man [under conditions dominated by White Supremacy] has sexual intercourse with a Black female, the Black female not only becomes more confused in her thoughts about Racism, but about **all** of her values, in **all** areas of activity. Most of the time she does not see that something is not being done "for" her, but "against" her. By receiving money and/or flattery in return for being used, sexually, she likely becomes confused about her true status. She may have a vague notion that she is somehow being raped or robbed, but she usually does not associate what is being done to her as being an act of Racist Aggression. She usually prefers to "believe" that her acts of sexual intercourse with white men is a "private" and/or "personal" matter.

She seldom, if ever, understands, or prefers to believe, that such acts are the **most vicious**, and **most effective** form of White Supremacist expression and control. It is especially cruel and unjust for those white people who practice White Supremacy, (who are, collectively, the smartest and most powerful people in the known universe) to continue to take [unjust] sexual advantage of a subjugated, deprived, and comparatively ignorant, and/or silly, people.

To do so is equivalent to "grown" persons taking sexual advantage of babies.

It is, within a **racial** context, the same as child molestation, infant abuse, and/or infant murder. It is the supreme act of injustice.

To use the sexual instinct to warp and mis-direct the minds of an infantile people is to commit a **basic** crime against the fundamental law of the universe [The Law of Compensation].

Finally, it should be known and understood by all, that the **only** time that it is just and correct, for any "Black" person, and/or any non-white person, to engage in sexual intercourse, and/or "sexual play", with any white person, is **after** White Supremacy (Racism) no longer exists, in any area of activity, any place in the known universe.

SEX

Males and females [non-white]:

Do not willfully and deliberately contact each other, and/or seek each other's "company" except for the following purposes:

1. To study, plan, and/or work in a manner that directly or indirectly helps to eliminate Racism (White Supremacy), helps to produce justice, and/or helps to produce correctness.

2. To engage in sexual intercourse (but only when it helps to support activities mentioned in Item 1).

Reason(s)/Explanation(s):

As long as White Supremacy (Racism) exists, it is best and correct for all non-white persons, both male and female, to use **all** of their time and energy thinking, speaking, and/or acting to accomplish the most constructive objectives.

In a socio-material system dominated by White Supremacy, too many non-white people, both male and female, spend too much time and energy in each other's company, in a manner that, regardless of intentions and purposes, too often results in unnecessary conflict. Too many of their contacts, too often, result in too much activity, that is generally too frivolous, too wasteful of time and energy, and too wasteful of money and other materials.

Therefore, if male and female non-white persons make a maximum effort to limit **all** of their contacts with each other to no activities other than one or both of the two (2) that are aformentioned, the results should be as follows:

- **Less** physical **contact**, therefore **less** physical **conflict.**

- **Less** verbal **contact**, therefore **less** verbal **conflict**.

- **Less** non-constructive, frivolous, time-wasting, energy wasting, money wasting, material wasting, activity.

SEX

- **More** constructive physical and verbal activity between male and female non-white persons.

Females: **As long as White Supremacy exists, do not pretend that you have the same value to white men as white women have.**

Reason(s)/Explanation(s):

Under White Supremacy (Racism), **non**-white females cannot compete with white women for the true "favor" of white men.

As long as White Supremacy exists, white men cannot give non-white females the same overall consideration given to white women because Black, and/or non-white females cannot produce "white" off-spring as **reliably** as can white women.

Females: **Do not "bellywarm".**
Do not encourage the practice of Racism by serving as a "bellywarmer".

Reason(s)/Explanation(s):

"Bellywarming" is a slang term, usually meaning sexual intercourse between white men and non-white females, under conditions dominated by White Supremacy (Racism).

Under White Supremacy, many non-white females are expected to serve as "bellywarmers". Such acts of sexual intercourse, under such conditions, help make it easier for the White Supremacists (Racists) to improve their methods of mistreating non-white people, and has the effect of making non-white people weaker, sillier, and more confused.

Therefore, it is **incorrect** for any Victim of Racism (non-white person) to engage in any act of sexual intercourse, and/or "sexual play", with any person "classified" as "white", and/or "Caucasian", during any period in which any non-white persons, any place in the known universe, are directly or indirectly subject to White Supremacy (Racism).

Females: **As long as White Supremacy (Racism) exists, do not accuse any non-white male of "dominating" you.**

SEX

> **As long as White Supremacy exists, do not "depend" on, or expect, any non-white person to be able to provide you with food, clothing, shelter, or general protection from aggression or deprivation.**

Reason(s)/Explanations(s):

Racist Man and Racist Woman (White Supremacists) dominate **all** of the people on earth, either directly or indirectly, at all times, in all areas of activity. They dominate, and utilize them as **victims**, in all aspects of Economics, Education, Entertainment, Labor, Law, Politics, Religion, Sex, and War.

Most **non**-white people know or suspect this to be true. Many, however, refuse to say so openly, or directly.

Compared to white men and white women, most "black", "brown", "red", "yellow", and/or "non-white" males and females are **functionally** treated as "girls" and "boys", both by each other, and by white men and white women.

People classified as "Black" know, or suspect from experience that **anything** that they receive of major material value, other than the production of "Black" or non-white off-spring, must be obtained with the direct or indirect permission of Racists Man and/or Racist Woman.

Black females are **not subject** to Black males. The Black males can "demand" nothing of Black females that is not directly or indirectly "approved" of by the White Supremacists (Racist Man and/or Racist Woman).

Males: Do not show resentment at being "sexually rejected".
Do not express anger or contempt for a female because she lets you know that she does not want to engage in sexual intercourse with you. Be courteous to her, thank her, and if you continue to talk to her, do not pester her.

Reason(s)/Explanation(s):

Most females, most of the time, know who they desire to engage in sexual intercourse with.

SEX

It is neither correct nor justly desirable for a female to "submit" to sexual intercourse with a male simply because that is what **he** desires to do at that particular time and place.

No male should want a female to have sexual intercourse with him if she is not, by her own desire, willing to do so.

If the female changes her mind about him, she should let him know. She should be truthful about her intentions.

It is incorrect to treat the act of sexual intercourse as a "forced" social courtesy. The act should be a **mutual** and **enjoyed** form of communication.

It should not be a "quiet" form of rape. Persons who engage in sexual intercourse and/or "sexual play" with each other, should **desire** to do so, at the **same time**, for the **same reasons**. Deceit and/or coercion should have no part in the relationship.

Females: **Don't "play up" and "show-off" your "sexuality" in situations [meetings, etc.] in which it is important for male persons to keep their thoughts on matters of priority constructive value.**

In such situations, avoid placing your body, moving your body, or wearing anything on your body in a manner that tends to promote "sexual arousal" of males who are present.

Do not seek to dominate the attention of Black males in a manner that distracts them while they are trying to do something of greater constructive value.

If a Black male is trying to do something to eliminate Racism, and/or to promote justice, do not harass or berate him for not giving you "enough attention". Do not insist that he stop what he is doing and spend that time "entertaining" you.

Reason(s)/Explanation(s):

One of the major reasons for the lack of constructive thought, speech, and/or action, among many Black **males** has been the great amount of time and/or energy "artificially" directed or "programmed" toward sexual activity, and/or, toward those areas of activity that are closely associated with sexually-motivated "sport" and sexually-motivated "show-offism". Sexual activity should, at all times, support the production of justice — not hinder or distract from it.

Give most sexual attention, and all sexual "allegiance", only to those Victims of Racism [non-white persons] of opposite [complimentary] sex, who, to the best of their ability, seek, at all times, to speak and act to resist and/or eliminate Racism (White Supremacy).

Reason/Explanation:

As long as Racism (White Supremacy) exists, all sexual activity and all sexual "allegiance" should be between persons who try to spend most of the time resisting, and/or trying to eliminate, Racism.

Seek to engage in sexual intercourse, and/or "sexual play", only with those persons [non-white] who show by their deeds that they, at all times, seek to resist and/or eliminate Racism (White Supremacy). Seek to use such intimacy to improve communications with such persons, and seek to help such persons to do that which is of constructive value.

Reason/Explanation:

As long as Racism (White Supremacy) exists, it is incorrect for any person to engage in any act of sexual intercourse or "sexual play", **unless** such acts help to promote resistance to, and/or the elimination of, Racism.

As long as Racism exists, any persons who do not try to spend **most** of their time/energy speaking and/or acting to eliminate Racism, do not deserve the pleasures of sexual intercourse or "sexual play".

Seek information about all sexual activity that occurs, or has occurred, between white people and non-white people, and seek to use this information in a manner that helps to eliminate Racism (White Supremacy) and/or helps to establish justice.

SEX

Reason(s)/Explanation(s):

The extensive revelation of truth, particularly in matters pertaining to **sex**, is a **basic requirement** in the establishment of justice.

One of the greatest strengths of White Supremacy (Racism) is the deceptive, subversive, and/or "secret" **sexual** activity that occurs between white people and non-white people. This is particularly important to know and to understand, since White Supremacy is a system that **dominates all** of the non-white people of the known universe, in **all** areas of activity.

Because of the nature of this domination, all acts of sexual intercourse, "sexual play", and/or so-called "homo-sex", between white persons, and non-white persons, has the direct or indirect effect of further debasing, confusing, and weakening, all non-white people, every place in the known universe.

Therefore, it is **extremely important** that **all** sexual activity between white people and non-white people be known about, understood, and talked about openly, truthfully, and constantly.

All information pertaining to such activity should be used in a manner that best helps to promote justice. No information should be kept secret.

Do not engage in so-called "homosexual" [anti-sexual] acts, and do not, in any way, encourage others to do so. Do not speak and/or act as if such acts should be regarded as trivial, comical, or harmless.

Reason(s)/Explanation(s):

So-called "homosexuality" is **anti**-sexual.

"Anti-sexual intercourse" is incorrect. To attempt to engage in what is ofttimes called "love-making" by using the "sex organs" to penetrate the bodies of persons of the same sex is incorrect.

Such acts are incorrect in the same way that using the "sex organs" of a **person** to penetrate the body of a cat, dog, or deer, is incorrect. Such acts are incorrect in the same way that using the "sex organs" of a person to penetrate the body of the sister, brother, or mother of that person is incorrect. Such acts are incorrect in the same way that using the "sex organs" of a person to penetrate the body of a deceased person is incorrect.

"Anti-sexual intercourse" is not an expression of "love". This so-called "homosexual" act, is none other than an expression of **acute insanity** resulting from some form of acute imbalance of the mind and/or body.

In racial matters, it is the White Supremacists (Racists) who are the greatest promoters of anti-sexual intercourse among non-white people. They promote this behavior by direct participation as well as by direct and indirect example or influence.

Many non-white males function as so-called "homo-sexuals" [anti-sexuals] in an attempt to compensate for their fear of the Racist Man and Racist Woman. Many non-white males fear having to pretend "manhood" when confronted with the possibility of **opposing** Racist Man or Racist Woman for some reason or another. They sense a danger in even **acting** like "men", when in the presence of white men or white women who may be Racists. They therefore choose to escape the "test" of "manhood" in it's popular socio-material sense, and, instead, present themselves before white people as "mannish boys" or as imitation females. These non-white **males** believe that by appearing before the awesome White Nation as "females", the White Supremacists will consider them to be more of an amusement than a potential threat.

In a socio-material system dominated by White Supremacists, the supreme and only functional test of so-called "manhood" for a non-white male is the **manner** in which the non-white male conducts himself in his relationships to the White Supremacist Man (Racist Man). By speaking and/or acting as "entertainers", or as some form of sexually weak or sexually confused servant, many non-white males seek to make themselves exempt from the direct hostility of Racist Man. Many other non-white males attempt to avoid this hostility by pretending to be female. By pretending to be female, they then proceed to act as if their reason for existence is to participate in a series of trivial fads, fashions, fun, and "girlie" games, and that there is no need to be concerned about questions of non-white "man-hood" as it relates to White Supremacy and the promotion of justice or injustice.

SEX

As long as White Supremacy (Racism) exists, do not criticize, or complain about, anything, that any person does in sexual matters, if you, yourself, are engaging in any act of sexual, or so-called "homosexual", intercourse with any white person.

Reason(s)/Explanation(s):

Sexual intercourse, "sexual play", and/or so-called "homosexual" [anti-sexual] intercourse, between any white person, and any non-white person, under conditions dominated by White Supremacy (Racism), has a **worst** effect on the promotion of **justice,** than any other forms of people activity.

As long as White Supremacy exists, all such activity between white persons and non-white persons is **worse** than acts of sexual intercourse between a person and a sheep, between father and daughter, between mother and son, between sister and brother, etc.

Because sexual activity has such a strong influence on the way that people think and act in all other areas of activity, any sexual activity, and/or any attempted sexual activity [as aforementioned], between white persons and non-white persons, under conditions dominated by Racism, has the effect of doing more to help maintain Racism, than all other acts **combined.**

Such activity is also the most powerful means of maintaining and refining **injustice** of **all** kinds among the people of the known universe.

Therefore, if a person **does not express disapproval** of sexual intercourse, of "sexual play", and/or of so-called "homosexual" intercourse, between white persons and non-white persons [under conditions dominated by White Supremacy], that person **is not justified** in expressing disapproval of **anything**, that **anybody** does, that directly, or indirectly, pertains to sex.

Speak and/or act to promote sexual intercourse between white people and non-white people only after the elimination of Racism throughout the known universe, and only if such intercourse is between those white persons and non-white persons who cannot produce off-spring.

SEX

Reason(s)/Explanation(s):

It is unjust and incorrect for non-white persons to cause and/or promote the **extinction** of people who appear to be "white" (Caucasian, blond, etc.).

When White Supremacy (Racism) no longer exists, it is just and correct for **all** persons to agree that the existence of "white" people as well as "non-white" people is just and correct. Under conditions not dominated by White Supremacists, the only way to insure that "white" people will not be forced into extinction is for "white" people and non-white people to engage in sexual intercourse **only** if it is **impossible** for either of them to produce off-spring.

This practice will end the possibility of "white" people becoming extinct through sexual intercourse with non-white people. At that time, in this way, constructive communications involving sexual activity between white people and non-white people can be promoted without causing imbalances associated with genetics.

As long as White Supremacy (Racism) exists, avoid saying or doing anything that helps to promote contact between white persons and non-white persons for purposes of sexual intercourse, and/or "sexual play".
As long as White Supremacy exists, avoid being a participant in any "sexually frivolous" speech with white persons.

Reason(s)/Explanation(s):

As long as White Supremacy (Racism) exists, any act of sexual intercourse, and/or "sexual play", between a white person and a non-white person is an act that further promotes the racial subjugation of **all** non-white people. The major result of such activity is the production, on a grand scale, of the **illusion** in the thinking of many non-white people, that Racism (White Supremacy) is being **eliminated** through acts of sexual intercourse between white and non-white people.

Under White Supremacy, sexual intercourse between white and non-white people does not help eliminate Racism. Neither does frivolous talk about sexual matters. Such talk, when conducted between white people and non-white people, under conditions dominated by White Supremacy, only helps to **refine** the practice of White Supremacy, making it to seem "cute", and/or less harmless.

As long as White Supremacy (Racism) exists, do not speak or act as if any person has justifiable "authority", or justifiable dominion, over the sexual activity of any other person.

Reason//Explanation:

As long as White Supremacy (Racism) exists, it is **unjust** and **incorrect** for any person to claim, or act as if, he or she has **justifiable** "authority", or **justifiable** dominion, over the sexual activity, of any other person.

Avoid asking a person about his or her sexual activities unless you are willing to tell that person everything about your own.
Avoid telling a person about your sexual activities unless that person is willing to tell you everything about his or her own. Before engaging in an act of sexual intercourse, and/or "sexual play", with another, ask yourself this question, and answer truthfully:

> **"Would I want this person to know, everything that there is to know, about me, at all times, in all places, in all things, and, if not, why not?"**

Reason(s)/Explanation(s):

Truth, not **falsehood,** should be a **basic** part of **all** relationships.

Speech and action about sexual matters should always help to reveal **truth**, and, should always reveal it in a manner that best promotes **justice** and **correctness**.

No relationship of any kind should begin with lies, and continue to be maintained and supported by an ongoing series of lies, and/or deceptive speech and action.

Also, all talk about sex, like all other talk, should not be conducted in a manner that is likely to promote gossip, name-calling, slander, discourtesy, nit-picking remarks, or petty and unjust animosity.

SEX

Avoid promoting acts of sexual "prostitution", bribes, and/or unjust proposals of any kind.

Reason(s)/Explanations(s):

It is incorrect to use money, gifts, or any similar "material" possession, and/or "material" medium of exchange, to influence whether a person will, or will not, engage in any act of sexual intercourse, and/or "sexual play".

As long as White Supremacy exists, do not seek to depend on any non-white person for money, or for any other form of financial aid.
As long as White Supremacy exists, avoid asking for money, and avoid seeking financial aid from any non-white person, including those persons with whom you maintain a personal, social, or sexual, relationship.

Reason(s)/Explanation(s):

As long as White Supremacy (Racism) exists, it is the White Supremacists (Racists), and **only** the White Supremacists who have financial **responsibility** for non-white people. It is the White Supremacists who are the functional Masters of Finance — not their victims.

Therefore, as long as White Supremacy exists, it is **incorrect** for non-white people — including, males and females — to depend on **each other**, for money or for any other form of major financial aid.

Sexual abuse, and the **refusal** by White Supremacists to provide correct financial support to their Victims [non-white people], are two of the worst expressions of Direct Racist Aggression. It is correct for every person who believes in the elimination of injustice to consistently ask the Racists to stop their abuses and refusals, and do justice.

As long as White Supremacy (Racism) exists, non-white people have no "financial responsibility" to each other. It is correct for them to give to each other only what each of them can "afford". Under White Supremacy they can "afford" practically nothing in the form of financial aid.

SEX

Victims of Racism can best help each other by helping each other to do constructive work, by exchanging constructive information with each other, and minimizing conflict with each other by minimizing **unnecessary contact** with each other.

Avoid using the word "romance". Use the word "affection" to express the thoughts, feelings, and intentions that Victims of Racism should develop.

Reason(s)/Explanation(s):

The word "romance" is a confusing word most often directly or indirectly associated with a false, or superficial "display" of caring and/or concern, by persons, toward one another.

It is mostly associated with "acting" or **pretense** rather than a true effort toward persons caring and being truly concerned with, and constructively involved with one another.

AREA 9: WAR/COUNTER-WAR

▮ PREFACE ▮

The following pages present suggestions that pertain to what a Victim of Racism [non-white person] **should**, or **should not** choose to do in the Ninth Major Area of [People] Activity: War/Counter-War. Each person should choose to speak, and/or act, according to one or more of the suggestions presented — but only if he or she decides to do so. No person should speak and/or act according to **any** suggestion presented herein unless he or she has judged that the suggestion chosen is of **current** and **correct** value in helping to eliminate Racism (White Supremacy), and/or, in helping to better promote justice.

It is important to know and understand that one or more suggestions selected from one Major Area of [People] Activity, should be used in constructive combination with one or more suggestions selected from other Majors Areas of [People] Activity.

If an individual person chooses to utilize any suggestion presented herein, he or she should do so in a manner, and at a specific time, and specific place, that will produce the **most constructive results** in the revelation of truth, and/or, the production of justice or correctness.

▮ ▮ ▮ ▮ ▮ ▮ ▮

Avoid giving "armed" assistance to any Racist (White Supremacist), or to any armed or violent forces that are dominated and/or controlled by Racists or suspected Racists.
Avoid promoting, supporting, and/or participating in any form of violence, or counter-violence, other than Maximum Emergency Compensatory Justice.

Reason/Explanation:

It is unjust, and incorrect, to say, or do, anything, that helps Racists and/or suspected Racists, to say, or do, anything, that helps to promote Racism (White Supremacy).

Never bribe, coerce, or otherwise force any person to kill, and/or otherwise do bodily harm to, any other person.

WAR/COUNTER-WAR

If it is your will to have bodily harm done to a person, it is correct to do it yourself.

Reason/Explanation:

It is unjust and incorrect for any person to **bribe, force,** or **coerce**, a person or animal, to kill and/or otherwise do bodily harm to, any person.

Avoid doing bodily harm to any person, white or non-white.
Do bodily harm to a person for the following reasons, only:

(1) The just, correct, and direct self-defense against bodily harm.

(2) The just, correct, and direct defense and/or security of essential material possessions.

(3) The just, correct, and direct defense and/or security of persons other than self, and/or the essential material possessions of persons other than self.

(4) The enactment of Maximum-Emergency Compensatory Justice [see pages 207-233 for details].

Do not use a person as a hostage.
Do not force any person to serve as collateral in any dispute between yourself and other persons.
Do not force a person to act as an "insurance" object in any dispute between yourself and another person.

Reason(s)/Explanation(s):

A hostage is a person who is deliberately forced, by another person, to function as an "object", and/or, as a commodity for trade, barter, or sale, to one or more other persons.

A hostage is also a person who is **forced** to do **harm** to others because of fear of those persons who have power over them.

Example:

All of the **non**-white people in the known universe are functioning as **hostages** to those white people who practice White Supremacy (Racism).

WAR/COUNTER-WAR

Do not assume that those white persons who fight and/or kill one another are **not Racists (White Supremacists).**

Reason(s)/Explanation(s):

Some white people who practice White Supremacy (Racism) sometimes have **great** disagreements about **how** White Supremacy should, or should not, be practiced.

When white people who practice White Supremacy have great disagreements among themselves about **how** White Supremacy should, or should not, be practiced, they sometimes fight and/or kill each other on a massive scale.

It is, however, incorrect to think that these fights are "major" **wars**. They are, in truth, small and large "battles". "Battles" are "small wars" that are part of a major "war".

In the known universe, there is only one major "war". That war is sometimes called the "Race War".

Those white persons who practice Racism (White Supremacy) against the non-white people of the known universe sometimes fight major "battles" among themselves at the **same** time that they are conducting "The War" (Race War) against non-white people.

The **reason** that White Supremacists (Racists) sometimes fight major "battles" among themselves while fighting "The War" to maintain supremacy over non-white people, is because **some** White Supremacists seek to **gain more** "benefits" from the practice of White Supremacy than other White Supremacists.

Any "battles" that take place between White Supremacists during The War (Race War) to maintain White Supremacy are always conducted in such manner as to insure that **non**-white people remain subject to White Supremacy **before, during**, and **after** the battles.

Think, speak, and/or act to promote Maximum-Emergency Compensatory Justice as the just and correct form of willful and deliberate "counter-violence" against the "violence" that is Racism.
Think, speak, and/or act to promote the following rules that must characterize Maximum Emergency Compensatory Justice:

Don't enact Maximum-Emergency Compensatory Justice

(execute, and/or deliberately kill one or more White Supremacists) unless your **personal** suffering under White Supremacy has become so great that regardless of all that you have done to avoid it, your suffering has become **totally unbearable.**

Don't enact Maximum-Emergency Compensatory justice unless you do so in a bold and open manner that will make as clear as possible that it was **you** who acted, and that you acted **alone.**

Don't talk to **anyone** — repeat — **anyone,** about any act **of** Maximum-Emergency Compensatory Justice that you intend to commit, or that you **think** you may intend to commit.

Don't enact Maximum-Emergency Compensatory Justice unless **you** know that **you** should do so —not because someone else did so, and not because someone else did, or did not, suggest that you do so.

Dont' enact Maximum-Emergency Compensatory Justice if you, **at any time**, begin to **lose** the **desire**, or the **will**, to do so.

Be true to yourself.

Think about the total seriousness of Maximum-Emergency Compensatory Justice.

Think about the fact that the **deliberate** killing and/or execution of one or more White Supremacists (Racists), by **one** Victim of White Supremacy, acting openly and alone, is not a trivial matter. It means that at least **two** persons will cease to exist — (1) a white person who practices Racism, and, (2) a non-white person who is a Victim of Racism.

It means that the Victim of Racism will execute at least one Racist, and, afterwards, execute him or her self.

It is important to know, and to remember that Maximum-Emergency Compensatory Justice means that the person who enacts, it, **must not** surrender, **must not** conceal his or her identity, **must not** ask for "mercy", and must not "hide out" after having enacted Maximum-Emergency Compensatory Justice.

The person (Victim) who makes a plan to enact Maximum-Emergency Compensatory Justice, and who then, for any reason, begins to have doubts about enacting the plan, **should cancel both the plan and the act.**

It is unjust and incorrect to "play" with the existence of oneself, or the existence of others — even if those others are people who practice Racism (White Supremacy). One should be totally serious and extremely thoughtful.

Maximum-Emergency Compensatory Justice should not be planned or enacted "as a whim". It should not be thought of as an "adventure". It should not be thought of as a means of expressing anger. It should not be thought of as a means of testing skills, and/or, as a "game".

This serious and final decision should not be made in haste. It should not be made in anger.

One who enacts Maximum-Emergency Compensatory Justice should give him or her self lots of time to think about every aspect of the act and it's consequences. One should ask him or her self if such an enactment is absolutely necessary and that the circumstances prior to enactment **unbearably** unjust. An accurate study should be made to determine if there is a reasonable possibility that those circumstances, though painfully burdensome, will improve in time to matter to those individuals currently and grievously affected.

It should be fully understood that Maximum-Emergency Compensatory Justice is only to be considered by those non-white persons whose existence under Racism (White Supremacy) has become, for them, as individuals, **totally unbearable,** with no meaningful relief forthcoming, within a reasonable period, during their existence in the known universe.

Again, in the enactment of Maximum-Emergency Compensatory Justice, it is important to remember the following:

> **Don**'t enact Maximum-Emergency Compensatory Justice unless it is you, **yourself**, as an individual [non-white] person whose existence under Racism (White Supremacy) is **totally unbearable**.
>
> **Don't** enact Maximum-Emergency Compensatory Justice because you merely feel "bitter" or "upset" about Racism, and/or, because you feel merely "disgruntled" about the effect that Racism has had on various parts of your existence.

WAR/COUNTER-WAR

Don't enact Maximum-Emergency Compensatory Justice unless you **fully realize** that it will be the **last act of your existence in the known universe,** as well as the end of existence for one or more other persons.

Don't attempt to enact Maximum-Emergency Compensatory Justice in a "sporting" manner. Neither attempt to enact it while overcome with anger or passion to the extent that your ability to think and act **efficiently** and **constructively** is hampered.

Reason(s)/Explanation(s):

It is incorrect to destroy any person, animal, creature, etc., in a "sporty" fashion.

The destructiion of any creature should never be regarded as a trivial matter. The elimination of the existence of any person, animal, etc., in any form, and for any reason, should never be treated as a game or as a form of "exciting adventure".

It is incorrect to execute even the most non-just of persons, except when it is absolutely necessary to do so in order to promote justice, and/or to substantially help eliminate the maintenance of non-justice.

The execution of the most powerful of the deliberately non-just persons (White Supremacists), should always be because they **repeatedly refuse** to stop their practice of Maximum non-justice (White Supremacy). Therefore, when destruction of one or more of the most deliberate and most powerful of non-just persons is **necessary**, it should be done **suddenly** and without any chance being given to them to be saved, or to save themselves. To give such non-just persons "a chance" would be to make a **sport** of the act of deliberately destroying organisms whose existence and meaning you may not understand. To make **sport** of the destruction of any creature is incorrect destruction. It also encourages killing for "fun" or for other unnecessary purposes.

Maximum-Emergency Compensatory Justice is **not** a sport.

Don't enact Maximum-Emergency Compensatory Justice under any circumstance wherein a **non** white person may be killed, injured, **or** have his or her possessions destroyed or damaged as a **direct simultaneous result** of your act.

WAR/COUNTER-WAR

Avoid enacting Maximum-Emergency Compensatory Justice against any person [white] whom you have reason to believe, is doing **all** that he or she can, to stop practicing Racism, **and**, doing all that he or she can to stop **others** from doing the same.

Don't enact Maximum-Emergency Compensatory Justice under any circumstance wherein it is **known** that **white** persons whom **you** know are **not** Racists, may be killed, injured, or have their possessions destroyed or damaged as a **direct simultaneous result** of your act.

Don't plan Maximum-Emergency Compensatory justice in haste. Take plenty of time. Check, and check again every detail of the plan. **Don't** enact Maximum-Emergency Compensatory Justice when, for some reason, it cannot be enacted according to plan. Study the circumstances and make another plan.

Don't ask another person (an accomplice) to assist you in enacting Maximum-Emergency Compensatory Justice. Do **everything** yourself.

Don't tell **anyone** of any plan or intention that you have to enact Maximum-Emergency Compensatory Justice.

Don't carry any written materials on your person while enacting Maximum-Emergency Compensatory Justice except those Counter-Racist materials and/or writings which are of practical value in helping to inspire **will power**, and/or in helping to improve the efficiency of enactment.

Don't plan, or attempt to enact Maximum-Emergency Compensatory Justice if you **are not currently** existing in subjugation to White Supremacy (Racism).

Don't enact Maximum-Emergency Compensatory Justice during periods of so-called "Race Riots", and/or during periods of so-called "mob" action.

Don't enact Maximum-Emergency Compensatory Justice unless you are a victim of Racist violence, a victim of the **threat** or Racist violence, and/or a victim of non-just conditions directly or indirectly caused by, and/or promoted by Racist violence or the threat of Racist violence.

WAR/COUNTER-WAR

Don't enact Maximum-Emergency Compensatory Justice by using tools that you are not sure that you can handle and/or operate with maximum efficiency.

Don't attempt to enact Maximum-Emergency Compensatory Justice without having and knowing how to use the "tools" that are necessary for efficient accomplishment. If possible, and/or practical, use the same "tools" to terminate your own existence that you use to terminate the existence of the Racist(s).

Don't restrict the enactment of Maximum-Emergency Compensatory Justice only to those white persons that you "personally dislike". Enact Maximum-Emergency Compensatory Justice by executing any and all white persons present **who practice Racism** (White Supremacy), including those whom you "like" or "admire", as well as those whom you "dislike" or do not "admire".

Don't enact Maximum-Emergency Compensatory Justice on a basis of personal "likes" or "dislikes" of persons.

Reason:

A White Supremacists (Racist) is a White Supremacist (Racist).

A White Supremacists is a person who **willfully** and **deliberately** practices injustice against people who are classified as "non-white", and, by so doing, prevents the possibility of **justice** being established by **any** people — white or non-white — any place in the known universe.

A White Supremacist is a person who **prefers** to promote falsehood rather than truth.

A White Supremacist is a person who **prefers** injustice to justice.

A White Supremacist is a person who **prefers** war to peace.

A White Supremacist is a person who **prefers** to deceive, belittle, seduce, and exploit a non-white person rather than do all that he or she can to help mold that person into a perfect being.

WAR/COUNTER-WAR

A White Supremacist is a person who **prefers** to kill non-white persons rather than see **them** develop into people who effectively promote the revelation of truth, and the use of truth in a manner that promotes the establishment of justice and correctness.

Many White Supremacists are **extremely** intelligent. Many are very attractive and fascinating — "arresting" to the eye and pleasing to the ear. Many of them have such "likeable" personalities that it is extremely difficult to believe that such persons could be so completely dedicated to the practice of injustice. Many of them have such "likeable" personalities that it is extremely difficult to believe that they are willing to use whatever deceit and violence is necessary to maintain the ability to take unjust advantage of the primitive conditions, and/or the stupidity or silliness, of the large number of relatively pitiful non-white people of the known universe.

The Victim of White Supremacy who enacts Maximum-Emergency Compensatory Justice ceases to exist in the process. Both the Racists and the Victim of the Racists cease to exist.

In a matter so serious, the "likes" or "dislikes" of persons on the basis of "personality", though desirable, may likely hinder the promotion of justice during a time when it is the last chance for a victim of [Racist] injustice to do so.

Do not enact Maximum-Emergency Compensatory Justice in any manner, and/or during any condition, wherein it is likely that persons will be killed or injured who are senile, infantile, and/or otherwise not capable of practicing White Supremacy (Racism).

Reason(s)/Explanation(s):

In the enactment of Maximum-Emergency Compensatory Justice, **no persons** are killed except White Supremacists, **and** the Victim of White Supremacy who killed them.

These are two of the **basic requirements** of Maximum-Emergency Compensatory Justice.

If a Victim of White Supremacy, in an **attempt** to enact Maximum-Emergency Compensatory Justice, kills any person or persons, **other than** White Supremacists, **and, other than him or her self,** the act was **not** a promotion of [Maximum-Emergency Compensatory] **Justice.**

It was a promotion of **non**-justice.

Don't enact Maximum-Emergency Compensatory Justice in a manner that confuses it's enactment with some purpose other than the promotion of justice.

Reason(s)/Explanation(s):

It is **very important** that **all** of the **basic** characteristics of Maximum-Emergency Compensatory Justice be known and understood, and **never** misunderstood, by any person who undertakes to enact it, or explain it.

If such basic characteristics are **not** understood, many acts which may **appear** to be Maximum-Emergency Compensatory Justice may be **mistaken** for Maximum-Emergency Compensatory Justice.

Any act which does not conform to the specific **basic** characteristics of Maximum-Emergency Comepnsatory Justice cannot be **correctly** called, or thought of, as Maximum-Emergency Compensatory Justice.

It is important that Maximum-Emergency Compensatory Justice always retain it's special character. It should never be confused with any other form of activity, no matter how **similar** to Maximum-Emergency Compensatory Justice such activity may appear to be, either in conduct, or objective.

When enacting Maximum-Emergency Compensatory Justice, always try to execute those Racists who you have reason to believe are the smartest, the most dedicated, the most effective, and/or the most influential in the practice of Racism (White Supremacy).

Reason(s)/Explanation(s):

Though all persons who practice Racism (White Supremacy) are **equally responsible** for the **existence** of Racism, **Justice** is best promoted during an enactment of Maximum-Emergency Compensatory Justice if a special effort is made to execute those Racists (White Supremacists) who are the smartest, the most dedicated, the most effective, and/or the most influential in the practice of Racism.

WAR/COUNTER-WAR

Don't enact Maximum-Emergency Compensatory Justice unless you are:

- **Absolutely certain** that there is nothing more important than the elimination of injustice.

- **Absolutely certain** that, under the circumstances of every part of your existence, it is the just and correct thing to do.

- **Absolutely certain** that there is nothing else that you can do, during the remainder of your existence, that is likely to be **more effective** in helping to eliminate injustice.

- **Absolutely certain** that to exist without justice is worse than death [non-existence].

Don't enact Maximum-Emergency Compensatory Justice without setting a definite time limit for the completion of the enactment.

Don't enact Maximum-Emergency Compensatory Justice unless the overall conditions are supportive of an enactment that is extremely effective. Some examples of factors to be considered are as follows:

Ice	Darkness
Snow	Light
Rain	Cold Weather
Congestion	Hot Weather

Don't enact Maximum-Emergency Compensatory Justice during periods of great destruction caused by "natural" forces ["God", "The Creator", etc.].

Examples:

Disease Epidemic,	Earthquake,
Fire Storm,	Tornado,
Flood,	Hurricane,
Famine,	etc.

Reason(s):

It is unjust and incorrect for a Victim of Racism to commit any act against **any** person when that person is being injured or being killed by "natural" forces, and/or, when that person is experiencing suffering as a result of these forces.

It is just and correct for **all** persons to try to help **eliminate** suffering during periods of famine, flood, epidemic, etc.

Don't enact Maximum-Emergency Compensatory Justice until you have allowed a great period of time to pass in order for the "powers of the known and unknown" [God] to take direct action in the situation.

Reason(s)/Explanation(s):

All existence is a "gift".

The elimination of the existence of oneself, and/or of another, should not be done for any reason that is of no great constructive value.

The elimination of the "gift" of existence of any person, animal, etc., should not be done by those **subject to** the Masters of Injustice (Racists), unless there is no other known way for the subjects to effectively stop, and/or discourage the Masters of Injustice from promoting and/or maintaining the practice of injustice, within a "reasonable" period.

Those persons who are subject to these Masters should not be ashamed to ask and plead with these Masters for so valuable an act as the elimination of injustice.

The deliberate elimination of the existence of oneself along with the elimination of one, or more, of the Masters of Injustice should not be done before these Masters have been asked, repeatedly, to stop their practices.

A person who exists in subjugation to the power of the Masters of Injustice should not, however, enact Maximum Emergency Compensatory Justice unless subjugation to these Masters is **unbearable**, and, unless it is obvious that there is little chance that the Masters will cease to practice injustice, "**soon** enough", by **choice.**

Before a person decides to enact Maximum-Emergency Compensatory Justice, it is **very important** that the "Powers of the known and Unknown" ["God", etc.] be "recognized", and that the person who decides to enact Maximum-Emergency Compensatory Justice, be convinced, on the basis of reason, logic, and "faith", that the "Powers of the Known and Unknown" has clearly indicated that the enactment of Maximum-Emergency Compensatory Justice is **correct** for the time, place, and circumstances.

Do not discuss Maximum-Emergency Compensatory Justice except to describe what it is, and/or, what it is not.

Do not discuss any specific enactment of Maximum-Emergency Compensatory Justice, nor any act, by anyone, at any time, that seemed to be an enactment of Maximum-Emergency Compensatory Justice.

Reason(s)/Explanation(s):

The **only** person who is justified in calling a **specific act** of Maximum-Emergency Compensatory Justice by the title "Maximum-Emergency Compensatory Justice" is the person who enacts it.

Since the person who enacts Maximum-Emergency Compensatory Justice will have ceased to exist (as a part of the enactment), no other person is "qualified" to make **accurate** statements as to whether Maximum-Emergency (Compensatory Justice **was** enacted, or **was not** enacted.

Whereas other persons can **describe what they saw happen**, it is incorrect for them to say that they **know**, for certain, that **what** they saw was an enactment of Maximum-Emergency Compensatory Justice. In answer to a specific question as to whether a **specific act** was, or was not, Maximum-Emergency Compensatory Justice, a person's remarks should always be: "I don't know".

Important Questions and Answers Pertaining to Maximum-Emergency Compensatory Justice.

Question: What is Maximum-Emergency Compensatory Justice?

Answer: Maximum-Emergency Compensatory Justice is the willful and deliberate elimination of one or more Racists (White Supremacists), through death, **and**, the willful and deliberate elimination of **self**, through death, by a Victim of Racism (non-white person), acting alone, acting according to a detailed plan, and acting only after he or she has judged that he or she can no longer endure the effects of Racism and/or that he or she is no longer able to **effectively** promote justice, **except** by eliminating one or more Racists, and by eliminating his or her self, as a subject to the Racists.

Maximum-Emergency Compensatory Justice is the swift, efficient, unannounced execution/elimination of one or more Racists (White Supremacists) by an **individual** Vicitm of Racism (non-white person), acting **openly**, and **alone**, at a time and place of his or her **own** choosing, and, after commencing such action, **immediately** continues without respite or surrender, until he or she is forced to eliminate **self** rather than be eliminated by others, or be captured by others.

Maximum-Emergency Compensatory Justice is enacted **only** under **prolonged** conditions of **extreme** and practically hopeless deprivation caused, and/or promoted, by White Supremacists (Racists).

Maximum-Emergency Compensatory Justice is the promotion of justice through counter-violence under racial conditions of maximum emergency.

It is **not** an excuse to engage in frivolous or cowardly killing. It is not an excuse for enacting "violence" for the sake of "violence". It is the only willful deliberate, and **final** act of counter-violence that a Victim of Racism should commit against White Supremacy (Racism).

Maximum-Emergency Compensatory Justice is the promotion of justice by an individual person under racial conditions of maximum emergency. It is the only correct form of counter-violent/counter-war against **persons,** that is suitable for use by large numbers of weak and racially-subjugated people, against universally powerful Racists (White Supremacists), over a projected period of time.

Maximum-Emergency Compensatory Justice is a **just** and **correct** form of **counter**-war. It helps to promote thought, speech, and/or action in **opposition** to war.

Maximum-Emergency Compensatory Justice is **not** for the purposes of traditional "profit", or for revenge. It is not even for "traditional" purposes of direct or indirect "personal protection". The person enacting the execution of Racists also executes him, or her, **self** rather than continue to be subject to, White Supremacy.

WAR/COUNTER-WAR

Maximum-Emergency Compensatory Justice is **maximum**.

This means it is enacted **only** when the **condition** of White Supremacy causes a Victim of White Supremacy to re-act to the condition with **maximum counter-action.**

Maximum-Emergency Compensatory Justice is an **emergency** act.

This means it is enacted **only** when the **condition** of White Supremacy causes a Victim of White Supremacy to react to the condition as a life/death **emergency**, because there is, for that particular individual Victim, no other functional choices for **effectively** promoting a counter-action to White Supremacy.

Maximum-Emergency Compensatory Justice is a promotion of **compensation.**

This means it is enacted to help "make up for", and/or to help produce that which is missing. That which is missing is **justice**. Because White Supremacy promotes **injustice,** one of the basic values that is missing in the known universe, that must be promoted by the Victims of White Supremacy, is **justice.**

Justice is the only value that compensates for injustice.

Maximum-Emergency Compensatory Justice is a maximum, emergency, means of promoting compensation for the lack of justice.

This means it is enacted to help promote "balance between people" by causing the Racist to be "level" with his or her Victim through the medium of non-existence for both.

Question: What is a "Maximum-Emergency" condition?

Answer: In racial matters, a condition of maximum emergency exists whenever White Supremacy (Racism) is established, maintained, expanded, and/or refined, any place in the known universe, by the direct, or indirect, use of violence, the direct, or indirect, use of the threat of violence, and/or, as a direct, or indirect, **result** of violence (previously) used.

WAR/COUNTER-WAR

Question: **Who** is to determine **when** Maximum-Emergency Compensatory Justice is to actually be enacted?

Answer: Only the **individual** Victim of Racism can, or should, determine the **exact** condition in which he or she will, or will not, enact Maximum-Emergency Compensatory Justice.

Question: Who enacts Maximum-Emergency Compensatory Justice?

Answer: Maximum-Emergency Compensatory Justice can only be enacted by an individual person who is a Victim of Racism. It can be enacted at a time and place chosen by the Victim. It can only be enacted through the will, and **only** the will, of the **individual victim. Also, the Law of Compensation means that when one person executes another, that person must also execute him or her self.**

The enactment of Maximum-Emergency Compensatory Justice means the willful and deliberate elimination of the existence of one or more Racists (White Supremacists).

The willful and deliberate elimination of **any** existence, whether person, plant, or animal, is a **serious** act. No existence of **any** kind should ever be eliminated unnecessarily. It is never necessary to eliminate existence except when the Law of Compensation "demands" it.

To eliminate the existence of some Racists, in order to stop them from practicing Racism is ofttimes necessary. The very function of the White Supremacy system itself makes the elimination of some White Supremacists often necessary.

Question: **When** is Maximum-Emergency Compensatory Justice **necessary?**

Answer: A Victim of Racism may find it necessary to enact Maximum-Emergency Compensatory Justice only after he or she

- Has **tried,** and failed, to get the Racists to stop practicing injustice by **repeatedly asking them** for justice.

- Has **tried**, and **failed**, to remove him or her self from the direct and/or indirect power of, and dependence on, Racists in all areas of activity.

- Has spent a **substantial portion** of time and/or energy attempting to accomplish the aforementioned to the extent that he or she is reasonably certain that the Racists **do not** intend to stop the practice of Racism (White Supremacy) in time to keep the effects of such practices from becoming **totally unbearable.**

Question: As a part of Maximum-Emergency Compensatory Justice, it is **necessary** for the person enacting it to terminate his or her own existence? Why?

Answer: Any person who enacts Maximum-Emergency Compensatory Justice **should strive to survive no longer than is necessary to terminate the existence of one or more Racists (White Supremacists) whose existence has been chosen for termination.**

When the person enacting Maximum-Emergency Compensatory Justice can no longer execute more Racists, can no longer escape captivity, and/or can no longer escape being killed or maimed by others, then, **that person must terminate his or her own existence.**

A person enacting Maximum-Emergency Compensatory Justice must not "go into hiding" after terminating the existence of one or more Racists.

He or she must **directly** and **immediately** continue the execution of Racists repeatedly and without respite.

Once the enactment develops into a situation where no more Racists can be executed, the Victim of Racism enacting the executions **must** immediately terminate his or her own existence.

This is an absolute requirement of Maximum-Emergency Compensatory Justice. **The person who enacts Maximum-Emergency Compensatory Justice must terminate his or her own existence.**

To **not** do so would be to admit that there was actually no condition that the person believed to be a **maximum** emergency.

It is unjust and incorrect to **willfully** and **deliberately** seek, and enact, the elimination of others, through death, and, afterwards, seek to **maintain** one's own existence. To do so would mean that other persons — white and/or non-white — may become involved in the capture, the maiming, and/or the killing of the person who enacted the termination of the existence of others.

One of the basic principles of Maximum-Emergency Compensatory Justice is that **all** executions are enacted by the **one** person who enacts them, **including** the execution of him or her self.

An act of Maximum-Emergency Compensatory Justice is Maximum-Emergency Compensatory Justice **only** if conducted in such manner that a Victim of Racism (non-white person), acting openly, and alone, executes one or more **white** persons who practice **Racism** (White Supremacy), **and**, also, executes him or her self.

If he or she executes or maims any **other** person(s), and/or, if he or she **is executed**, or **maimed**, by any other person(s), it is **not** Maximum-Emergency Compensatory Justice.

When Maximum-Emergency Compensatory Justice is enacted, only Racists (White Supremacists) are executed, and **all** executions are enacted by **one** non-white person, who, completes the enactment by executing him or her self.

The combined acts thus produce the correct [compensatory] meaning. The completed sequence of acts is the only way for the acts to have the correct value.

Since every person's existence is a "gift" to the people of the known universe, no person should willfully and deliberately terminate the existence of another unless there is an absolute **need** to do so.

The willful and deliberate termination of any person's existence should never be regarded as an act that is less than serious to the utmost.

A person who terminates the existence of another person through the process of Maximum-Emergency Compensatory

Justice must, also, complete the process by terminating his or her own existence as a means of "proving" the absolute **need** for such final action.

The serious quality of Maximum-Emergency Compensatory Justice is particularly emphasized by the important characteristic of a person terminating his or her own existence as a necessary final part of the act itself. This characteristic best expresses the validity of the **necessity** for the act, and the importance of justice as a maximum value that is promoted through the act.

Question: What are the **specific** circumstances under which Maximum-Emergency Compensatory Justice is **justified?**

Answer:

1. When a Victim of Racism is unable to compensate for great and/or acute suffering caused, and/or promoted, by Racists, for a great period of time.

2. When a Victim of Racism is unable to experience justice, by repeatedly asking for justice, from those [Racists] who have the power to produce justice.

3. When a Victim of Racism is unable to produce justice because of the weakness, fear, and/or lack of interest, of other victims of Racist injustice.

4. When a Victim of Racism, has existed as long as he or she can bear to exist, under **most** of the conditions for existing, under Racism (White Supremacy).

Question: How does Maximum-Emergency Compensatory Justice differ from "terrorism"?

Answer: "Terrorism" is any unjust act which is basically **intended** to **frighten** people.

Maximum-Emergency Compensatory Justice is basically intended to **stop** one or more persons from practicing Racism (White Supremacy) by terminating their existence.

Maximum-Emergency Compensatory Justice is **not** enacted for the purpose of causing people to be "terrified".

A condition of Maximum-Emergency under White Supremacy (Racism) means that an individual Victim of White Supremacy [non-white person], for reasons known to his or her self, has no longer the will to submit to, and/or cooperate with, any aspect of Racist (White Supremacist) rule, at **any** time, for **any** reason, to **any** degree.

Therefore, the individual Victim of White Supremacy who enacts Maximum-Emergency Compensatory Justice does not seek to "profit" from his or her act(s) by designing to "escape" and to, **continue** to exist, under White Supremacy.

Maximum-Emergency Compensatory Justice is not for the purpose of being remembered as a "hero" or "heroine" in the Counter-War against White Supremacy. It is not for the purpose of "showing-off". It is not for the purpose of expressing hatred for the persons who practice White Supremacy. It is not for the purpose of showing how skill-ful one can be in enacting Counter-Racist counter violence.

Question: In **effect**, is not the person who enacts Maximum-Emergency Compensatory Justice committing **suicide?**

Answer: As long as White Supremacy (Racism) exists, **any** re-action to it's existence, by a non-white person, can be considered a form of "suicide".

When a non-white person submits to White Supremacy, that non-white person can be said to be submitting to a "suicidal" condition.

To submit to, and/or cooperate with, White Supremacy, can be called a prolonged "suicidal" process.

WAR/COUNTER-WAR

To submit to, and/or to cooperate with people who are extremely powerful in the practice of injustice, and, who are greatly **determined** to **continue** to practice it, can be called a commitment to the **prohibition** of **justice**. This could be called, in effect, a commitment to the **prohibition** of the "birth" of justice.

To prevent the establishment of justice, and/or to fail to resist the practice of injustice — even to the death — is to endorse the "suicide" of the basis for the **meaning** of "life" as it should exist among the people of the known universe.

Any existence that directly or indirectly supports non-justice and/or incorrectness, is, in essence, the functional equivalent of "non-life", and/or no "life" at all.

"Life", in total essence, is the sum total of truth, justice, and correctness---Peace. Those persons who "non-live" in subjection to White Supremacy, exist in support of falsehood, non-justice, and incorrectness. Therefore, they neither "live" a "life", nor support a "life", but, rather, they **exist** in "non-life", and support "non-life".

To exist in "non-life" and support "non-life", regardless of the **time** and/or **effort** spent in so doing, is to commit "suicide".

From this viewpoint, a Victim of White Supremacy who enacts Maximum-Emergency Compensatory Justice **is not** committing "suicide", but is acting as a force in support of the future establishment of "life" against the masterful force which now does the most to maintain a greatly sophisticated "non-life": White Supremacy.

Without justice, there is no "life" in people. Without justice, people do not "live". They only exist.

People who willfully and deliberately insist on practicing injustice and who do so on a **masterful scale**, over a **prolonged period,** and who show no intention of stopping the practice, do not deserve to exist.

People who submit to those who practice injustice on a masterful scale, over a prolonged period, do not do their duty to the meaning of "life" if they continue to exist in subjugation to the masterfully unjust.

To refuse to submit to such subjugation by eliminating their own existence, while eliminating the existence of one or more unjust masters, under conditions of Maximum Emergency, is to promote justice.

It is not a matter of choosing between "life" and "suicide". It is a matter of choosing between justice or non-justice.

Existence without justice is "non-life". All existence has value. But, the **value** of existence, under conditions dominated by injustice, is in the **will** to **utilize** that existence, to the utmost, to eliminate injustice, and to establish justice.

Question: What if a person, while **attempting** to enact Maximum-Emergency Compensatory Justice kills or injures a **non**-white person?

Answer: When Maximum-Emergency Compensatory Justice is enacted, no persons are executed except **white** persons who practice White Supremacy (Racism), and the **one** non-white person, who executed those white persons, then executes him or her self.

Otherwise, the combined acts **cannot** be correctly called Maximum-Emergency Compensatory Justice. Even if other persons are killed or injured by **accident**, it is **not** Maximum-Emergency Compensatory Justice.

In the enactment of Maximum-Emergency Compensatory Justice, there can be no mistakes. Mistakes destroy the purpose of the enactment.

Question: Is it correct for a non-white **female** to enact Maximum-Emergency Compensatory Justice?

Answer: Under socio-material conditions dominated by White Supremacists (Racists), it is **correct** for any **individual** non-white person, **regardless** of sex, to enact Maximum-Emergency Compensatory Justice if he or she has need of doing so.

Question: Would not the enactment of Maximum-Emergency Compensatory Justice, by any Victim of Racism who chose to employ it, cause "chaos" among **all** persons — white and non-white — Racists and non-Racists?

Answer: No Victim of Racism can, by employing Maximum-Emergency Compensatory Justice cause "chaos" among **any people** — white or non-white.

The people themselves, both white and non-white, both Racists and non-Racists determine what the relationships between people will be after any one or more enactments of Maximum-Emergency Compensatory Justice. If there is "chaos" following the enactment(s) of Maximum-Emergency Compensatory, it would be because the White Supremacists **willed** it so.

The White Supremacists (Racists) are the only people among the people of the known universe who are powerful enough to **cause** or **prevent** "chaos" among the white and non-white people of the known universe.

The Victims of White Supremacy should not concern themselves with the possibility of "chaos".

The Victims of White Supremacy should concern themselves with the promotion of justice.

In the correct measure of values, **injustice** and "chaos" are one and the same.

Question: What is the basic-functional relationship between **life** and **death?**

Answer: In the known universe:

All life is equal.

No one living thing has priority in "living", as it "lives", over any other "living" thing.

"Life" is **truth**, and **truth** is **that which is.**

All death is equal.

No one dead thing has priority in "death", as it is "dead", over any other "dead" thing.

"Death" is **truth**, and **truth** is **that which is.**

Where life and death exist, there is truth.

Where life and death **do not** exist, there is no truth.

Where there is no death, there can be no life, and where there is no life, there can be no death.

Where the "respect" for "life" in the "living" **equals** the "respect" for "death" in the "dead", and the "respect" for "death" in the "dead" **equals** the "respect" for "life" in the "living", there is **correctness.**

Where there is correctness, there will be **justice**, and where there is justice, there is peace.

Question: How should a person's existence, and/or non-existence be regarded?

Answer: "Existence" — all "existence" — should be "respected" by all correct thinking persons. Since no Victim of White Supremacy [non-white person] has absolute control over the "making" of all "existence", nor has the necessary knowledge and understanding of how all "existence" is **created**, then all Victims of White Supremacy should **avoid** causing the end of the existence of any person. This includes causing the end of the existence of a person who practices White Supremacy. A white person who practices White Supremacy is **still** a "person".

There is no person in the known universe **more unjust** than a person who practices White Supremacy (Racism).

None-the-less, each person in the known universe should be respected as an "existence" that has the potential of "living". Even though a White Supremacist exists to promote "non-life", it is possible that a White Supremacists **may** change from a Racist, into a person who produces "life" [justice and correctness]. Therefore, it is just and correct for a Victim of Racism [non-white person] to willfully and deliberately eliminate White Supremacists, **and** deliberately eliminate him or her self, only when he or she has concluded that such elimination must be done, **as a last resort**, in order to promote justice.

No person, should, at no time, have a playful or non-serious thought about death and/or killing.

Question: Would a **white** person who is opposed to White Supremacy be justified in enacting Maximum-Emergency Compensatory Justice?

Answer: No person who **is not** a Victim of White Supremacy (Racism) is justified in attempting to enact Maximum-Emergency Compensatory Justice. Under conditions dominated by White Supremacy, it is not possible for **any white person** to enact Maximum-Emergency Compensatory Justice.

No person classified as "white", and who considers him or her self as being "white", and/or "Caucasian", is, at the same time, a Victim of White Supremacy — if he or she

functions as a "white" person.

Since Maximum-Emergency Compensatory Justice is to be enacted by a Victim of White Supremacy (non-white person), against White Supremacists, it is **not possible** for a **white** person to enact Maximum-Emergency Compensatory Justice. No "white" person is a Victim of White Supremacy.

Not even a **non**-white person is justified in enacting Maximum-Emergency Compensatory Justice unless he or she, as an individual person, has suffered in subjugation to the White Supremacists to the extent that he or she judges such suffering to be completely intolerable and too prolonged.

Question: Is a Victim of Racism **justified** in acting as judge, jury, and executioner? Why? How? Does such action promote justice?

Answer: In a socio-material system dominated by White Supremacists (Racists), there are **no people** in the known universe who are justified in acting as judge, jury, and/or executioner against the White Supremacists, **except** the individual Victims of White Supremacy.

The White Supremacists function as the most powerful people in the known universe. They do not judge against themselves. They judge "in favor" of themselves by judging "in favor" of the maintenance of White Supremacy.

The White Supremacists do not accept the judgements of any person, thing, or force, that opposes the existence of White Supremacy, in any manner, that is effective.

The Victims of White Supremacy [non-white people], however, **are not,** collectively, a Counter-Racist/Counter-Force. If they were, they **would not** be Victims of White Supremacy. They would be a collective Counter-Force **against** White Supremacy.

Since White Supremacy (Racism) is all-engrossing among the people of the known universe, and since it dominates all of the so-called "groups" of non-white people of the known universe, then the only effective force, by people, against the White Supremacists must begin with, and be sustained by, **individual** Victims of White Supremacy, speaking and/or acting in a "United-Independent fashion" — like molecules or single sparks of fire.

Under White Supremacy, each Victim is "alone", in that the very conduct of White Supremacy prevents it's victims from formally organizing, as a "group", against it. This leaves only the individual Victim of White Supremacy as the only directly self-sustaining opponent of White Supremacy. This is not only functional, but just and correct. This way, no individual Victim **has** to rely on other individual Victims in order to oppose White Supremacy. In effect, this is self-reliance in it's **basic** form, and is the basic essence of Compensatory Unity for a racially subjugated classification of people.

It is not possible for one person to receive justice while any other person does not. But one person may feel the pain of injustice more than another.

Because one individual Victim of White Supremacy feels a great degree of pain due to White Supremacy, does not mean that another individual Victim feels pain to that same degree. Likewise, no Victim of White Supremacy, is capable of compensating for the pain felt by **another** Victim, while the pain, itself, is directly or indirectly being inflicted by White Supremacy. The Racists (White Supremacists) cannot, and do not, compensate their victims for the crime of Racism as long as Racism is being practiced. The only way that a Racist can **begin** to compensate the Victims of Racism is the Racist to cease being a Racist — in effect, to **eliminate** the practice of Racism (White Supremacy). The Racists have refused to do this.

Therefore, there is no person who is "qualified" to be the "judge", the "jury", and/or the "executioner" of a Racist **except** the individual person who is a Victim of Racism. This is because no one can judge **accurately** the degree of pain that the individual Victim of Racism is feeling as a **result** of Racism, at any time, in any place, in any one or more areas of activity.

Question: What is meant by the term "degree of pain"? How much pain should a Victim of Racism "feel", and/or tolerate before he or she enacts Maximum-Emergency Compensatory Justice? What is the "correct measure" of suffering for a Victim of Racism before he or she enacts Maximum-Emergency Compensatory Justice?

Answer: The "degree of pain" felt by a Victim of Racism [non-white person] as a result of White Supremacy is known to no other person than the person who feels it.

But it is correct for a Victim of Racism to enact Maximum-Emergency Compensatory Justice **only** if that "degree of pain" is "unbearable" to that person for a prolonged period.

Before any Victim of Racism enacts Maximum-Emergency Compensatory Justice, he or she should do everything that he or she can to seek justice by repeatedly requesting it, and constantly attempting to work to produce it, by all other just and correct means. He or she should attempt to do this until it is reasonably certain that the pain of injustice caused, and/or promoted, by Racism is not only too much to bear, but, that the damage to his or her ability to function effectively to promote justice by other means, is beyond repair.

Question: Is not Maximum-Emergency Compensatory Justice an **insane** means of conducting Counter-War against Racist war-makers?

WAR/COUNTER-WAR

Answer: All killing of people, by people, is the result of insane teachings and conditions.

But under current conditions [White Supremacy], Maximum Emergency Compensatory Justice is a **desparate** and **final** way that an individual Victim of Racism can oppose war, and some of the war-makers, when other means have **not** proven **effective** at the time **most needed**.

Maximum-Emergency Compensatory Justice is the most "honest" method of using **counter**-violence to express very **quickly** and **effectively**, the concept that the use of violence by one person against another for **unjust** reasons, or objectives, **must** result in "waste" for **both** rather than "profit" for either.

Maximum-Emergency Compensatory Justice is one of the most explicit-**functional** "statements" **against** war and injustice.

▪ STATEMENT OF CONCLUSION AND TRANSITION ▪

Like a crawling infant attempting to walk, all errors that are made by any person who seriously attempts to establish justice, are errors that can only be revealed through the process of the attempt.

The **will to do justice** is the first thing that must happen before justice can be produced.

The **will** to do justice, is, itself, the beginning of the end, of error.

Therefore, the **initial** purpose of this work is to help people to develop the **will** to do justice.

- SUPPLEMENTARY REFERENCE -

COMPENSATORY - FUNCTIONAL DEFINITIONS AND EXPLANATIONS OF SOME BASIC WORDS AND TERMS

■ NOTE ■

All words, and their definitions, should be designed to be used in a manner that best helps to reveal truth, produce justice, and produce correctness.

Because they are often used with **incorrect** definitions, many words do not do, what they should do.

The words presented herein, with their [compensatory] definitions, are better designed to do what words should do. Their use should help promote the **correct** reason for the existence of words and definitions.

A

Adult =

A word that generally means the same as the word "adulterer". **[Important Note:** To avoid confusion, it is best to not use the word "adult" to describe anyone **other than** a **white person** who practices White Supremacy (Racism). The better word, and the least confusing word, to describe such a person, is the word "adulterer"].

Adulterated [Racial] =

A weak or confused condition, caused or promoted by unjust and/or incorrect power(s).

Adulterated person, and/or Major Victim of Adultery =

(1) Any non-white person who engages in sexual intercourse with any white person, during any period, that any person, is directly or indirectly subject to White Supremacy (Racism), any place in the known universe.

(2) Any non-white person who came into existence as a direct, or indirect, result of sexual activity between a white person, and a non-white person, during any period in which White Supremacy existed any place in the known universe.

(3) Any non-white person who is, or has been, directly or indirectly, subject to White Supremacy in any area of activity, including Economics, Education, Entertainment, Labor, Law, Politics, Religion, Sex, and/or War.

Adulterer, and/or Adult Man/Adult Woman =

(1) White Supremacists (Racists).

(2) Those white persons, who, through the practice of Racism (White Supremacy), have succeeded in becoming "universal" **masters** in the practice of adulterating the promotion of justice and correctness among the people of the known universe, and have, instead, promoted the maintenance, expansion, and refinement of falsehood, non-justice, and incorrectness.

(3) Any white person who engages in sexual intercourse and/or "sexual play" with any non-white person during any period, in which any person, is, directly or indirectly, subject to White Supremacy (Racism), any place in the known universe.

(4) Any white person, who directly or indirectly causes, and/or helps, a non-white person to think, speak, and/or act in support of the establishment, maintenance, expansion, and/or refinement, of White Supremacy.

All Man, and/or All Woman = [Non-Existent Persons]
Any male, and/or any female person, who knows and understands truth, and, who, at **all** times, uses truth in such manner as to produce justice and correctness in all areas of activity, including Economics, Education, Entertainment, Labor, Law, Politics, Religion, Sex, and War.

America(s),
American(s),
American Citizen(s),
American Government,
American Flag(s) =

(1) Any person(s) who has (have) used truth in such manner as to have **produced** justice and correctness, at **all** times, in **all** things, in **all** areas of activity, including Economics, Education, Entertainment, Labor, Law, Politics, Religion, Sex, and War.

(2) A person who does not practice, or promote the practice of falsehood, non-justice, and/or incorrectness, at any time, in any place, in any area of activity.

(3) A person who does not practice, support, and/or promote Racism (White Supremacy).

(4) A person who does not submit to, and/or cooperate with, Racists (White Supremacists), at any time, in any place, in any area of activity, including Economics, Education, Entertainment, Labor, Law, Politics, Religion, Sex, and War.

(5) A person who speaks **and** acts to promote justice and correctness at **all** times, in **all** places, in **all** areas of activity.

(6) A non-existent person.

A

Americanism, and/or "American Way of Life" =

(1) Words and/or deeds that **have produced** justice and correctness in **all** things, at all times, in all areas of activity, including Economics, Education, Entertainment, Labor, Law, Politics, Religion, Sex, and War.

(2) The use of the truth in a manner that **has resulted** in the establishment of justice and correctness at all times, in all places, in all areas of activity.

(3) A concept and/or idea yet to be established in reality.

Anti-Racist =
Speech and/or action that is effective against Racism (White Supremacy).

Anti-Sex, and/or Anti-Sexual Behavior =

(1) Any speech and/or action by beings of the **same sex**, involving the mention of, and/or the touching of, sexual organs, in a manner that is similar to an expression of (sexual) desire between beings of the **opposite sex.**
[Note: Anti-sex, and/or anti-sexual behavior is sometimes, incorrectly called "homo-sexual" behavior**].**

(2) Any act of violence that directly involves the deliberate touching of the sexual organs of the person who is the victim of the violence [example: "rape"].

(3) Unjust and/or incorrect speech or action against a person because she is female, or because he is male.

Authority, Correct =
Any person, persons, and/or force, that produces **justice** and **correctness** in **all** areas of activity, including Economics, Education, Entertainment, Labor, Law, Politic, Religion, Sex, and War.

B

Basic "Ten Stops" for Victims of Racism [Non-White People], The =

(1) Stop **"snitching"** (volunteering information about people for purposes of gaining "personal favors" from Racists).

(2) Stop **"name-calling"**.

(3) Stop **cursing.**

(4) Stop **gossiping.**

(5) Stop **being discourteous.**

(6) Stop **stealing.**

(7) Stop **robbing.**

(8) Stop **fighting.**

(9) Stop **killing**, except under conditions of **extreme** emergency defense, and/or **maximum** emergency against Racism.

(10) Stop **squabbling** among yourselves and depending on Racists (White Supremacists) to settle the squabbles.

Being =
Any body that thinks, speaks, and/or acts.

"Bellywarming" =
Any act of sexual intercourse with/against a non-white person, by a white person, during the existence of White Supremacy in the known universe.
[Note: The non-white person, under such conditions, serves as a "belly-warmer" and/or "sexual toilet" for the white person**].**

"Better" Person =
A person who knows and understands the truth about **all** things, and who has used the truth in such manner, that he or she **has produced** justice **and** correctness, in **all** places, in **all** areas of activity, including Economics, Education, Entertainment, Labor, Law, Politics, Religion, Sex, and War.

B

"Big Business" =
White Supremacy (Racism).

"Big Government" =
White Supremacy (Racism).

"Bi-Sexual", and/or "Trans-Sexual" =
A non-existent "sex".
[**Explanation:**
(1) A person is **either** male, **or** female.

(2) Any person who is **neither** "male", nor "female", is **non-sexual.**

(3) Any male person who attempts to be a female person, or any female person who attempts to be a male person, is engaged in **anti**-sexual, and/or **counter**-sexual behavior.

(4) Any person who attempts to be both male and female — either alternatively, or simultaneously — is engaging in **anti**-sexual and/or **counter**-sexual behavior.

Such persons function directly or indirectly in such manner as to promote the destruction of sex (male-female relations).]

Black Family =
A non-existent "family". [See: "Family", and/or White Family"].

Black Fascism =
(1) The subjugation of all white people, by Black people, and/or by "non-white" people, for the basic purpose of debasing white people, and glorifying non-white people.

(2) A non-existent form of "fascism".

Black ["non-White"] Leader =
Any Black, and/or non-white person who causes the **total elimination** of the practice of White Supremacy (Racism) in **all** places, in **all** areas of activity, including Economics, Education, Entertainment, Labor, Law, Politics, Religion, Sex, and War.

B

Black Man, and/or Black Woman =
Any Black and/or non-white male or female person who is **not** subject to White Supremacy (Racism), and who does not, in any manner, directly or indirectly, do or say anything that helps to support White Supremacy in any area of activity, including Economics, Education, Entertainment, Labor, Law, Politics, Religion, Sex, or War. **[Explanation]:**

No "Black", and/or "non-white" person can be correctly called a "man" or a "woman", and, at the same time, be subject to White Supremacy (Racism).

The reason is that no "Black" and/or "non-white" person can **function** as a "man", or as a "woman", and, at the same time, submit to, or cooperate with, White Supremacists (Racists), in any manner, directly or indirectly.

That person, at the time, can only function as a **male** or **female** "child", subject, and/or victim.

Therefore, under White Supremacy, it is correct to refer to each Black, or non-white person, as a **male** or **female,** and/or, as a victim — **not** as a "man"; **not** as a "woman".

"Black" People =
Generally, any people "classified" by "white" people, as being "non-white", and/or, as being the "darker" of those people generally regarded as "non-white". The "non-white" classification generally includes persons classified as "brown", "red", "yellow", etc., and/or any "black shades", "shades" of "black", and/or "shades of shades" of "black".

Black Person =
Any person classified as, and/or, who generally functions as a "black", "brown", "red", "yellow", and/or "non-white" person.

"Black" Person =
A person whose physical structure is composed of elements which produce significant and/or pronounced skin "color" that is other than "white" in general appearance.

B

"Black" Power =

(1) Any word or deed, and/or any combination of words or deeds that prove effective against White Supremacy (Racism) when employed by the Victims of White Supremacy [non-white people].

(2) The sum total of all thought, speech, and action by Black and/or "non-white" people that helps to reveal truth, promote justice, and/or promote correctness.

Black Supremacist =
A "non-white" person who, directly, or indirectly helps to maintain the subjugation of **all** white people, for the basic purpose of "pleasing" and/or serving any, or **all** "non-white" persons, at **all** times, in **all** areas of activity, including Economics, Education, Entertainment, Labor, Law, Politics, Religion, Sex, and War.

Black Supremacy =
The subjugation of **all** white people, by Black and/or "non-white" people, for the basic purpose of "pleasing" and/or serving **any** or **all** Black or "non-white" persons, at **all** times, in **all** areas of activity, including Economics, Education, Entertainment, Labor, Law, Politics, Religion, Sex, and War.

"Boy" [Racial] =
Any male person who is racially classified as "non-white", who is directly, or indirectly subject to the power of White Supremacists (Racists) in any one or more areas of activity, including Economics, Education, Entertainment, Labor, Law, Politics, Religion, Sex, and/or War.

C

Caucasian =

A "white" person, and/or any person who generally functions as such, and/or who is generally "accepted" as such, by most of those people who, themselves, generally function as, and/or who are generally accepted as "white".

"Child" [Racial] =

Any person classified as "non-white" who submits to, and/or cooperates with, White Supremacists (Racists) at any time, in any place, in any one or more areas of activity, including Economics, Education, Entertainment, Labor, Law, Politics, Religion, Sex, and/or War.

Explanation:

A "child" is, regardless of "age" in years, any person who is "helpless" [help**less**] in thinking, speaking, and/or acting, and who must depend on a man or a woman for help in each and every area of activity, including, Economics, Education, Entertainment, Labor, Law, Politics, Religion, Sex, and War.

Since there is no non-white person in the known universe who **does not** exist in direct or indirect subjugation to Racist Man and Racist Woman, all non-white persons are the functional "children" of Racist Man and Racist Woman (White Supremacists, collectively).

As the functional "children" of Racists (White Supremacists), non-white people are only allowed to function as male and female "children".

They are not allowed to function as men and women.

Only "children" exists in subjugation to Racists. Men and women do not. Therefore, any person who is dominated by Racists is a "child".

Churchism =

The practice of worshipping and/or praising the rituals, images, ceremonies, songs, buildings, symbols, popularity, etc., of a "church", "temple", etc., **without** practicing the **religion** for which the idea of "church", "temple", etc., is intended.

Civil War =

A meaningless two-word term, with one word contradicting the other.

Explanation:

There is no such war as a "civil" and/or "civilized" war.

All "war" is "uncivil", and/or "non-civilized".

C

Civilization =
A socio-economic condition wherein truth has been used in such manner as to have **resulted in justice** and **correctness** being practiced at **all** times, in **all** areas of activity, including Economics, Education, Entertainment, Labor, Law, Politics, Religion, Sex, and War.

Civilized =
Any person, and/or persons, who have used truth in such manner as to have produced the practice of justice and correctness, at **all** times, in **all** areas of activity, including Economics, Education, Entertainment, Labor, Law, Politics, Religion, Sex, and War.

"Color", and/or "All-Color" Person =
A person who, because of elements in his or her composition, appears to be "black" in "color", and/or appears to be very dark brown, dark brown, light brown, tan, "red", "yellow", light yellow, or any "appearance", other than the **absence** of "color", and/or other than the "non-color" [white].

Common Basic Objective =
Any combination of willful thought, speech, and action, by a person or persons, that dominates all other combinations of willful thought, speech and action.
Example:
Racism is the **common basic objective** of **Racists.**

Communications, "Hard" =

(1) The practice of saying only what is **absolutely necessary,** to whom it is absolutely necessary to say it, at the time and place that it is absolutely necessary to say it, in order to reveal truth, promote justice, and/or promote correctness.

(2) One of two basic forms of [constructive] "communications".

(3) Persons talking and/or writing to each other, only when it is **absolutely necessary** to do so, in order to find, or reveal, truth, and/or, only when it is absolutely necessary, in order to promote justice or correctness.

Communications, "Soft" =
(1) The practice of saying and/or doing what may **seem** to be "trivial", "casual", and/or "frivolous", but, in effect, helps to reveal truth, promote justice, and/or promote correctness.

(2) One of the two basic forms of [constructive] "communications".

(3) Persons **mutually touching** each other, physically, and/or sexually, in order to **help** maintain the **will** to **continue** to conduct "hard" communications.
[Note: In any socio-material condition dominated by White Supremacy (Racism), "soft" communications should **only** be conducted between those Victims of Racism [non-white people] who are making a substantial effort by word and deed, to eliminate Racism (White Supremacy) in all areas of activity, including Economics, Education, Entertainment, Labor, Law, Politics, Religion, Sex, and War].

Communism [General] =
A word that is, and/or can be, used in so many ways that, used alone, it **cannot** be defined in **any** "special" way because it **can** be defined in many "special" ways.
Explanation/Example:
As a description of a "socio-material system", the word can be used to describe anything that any person says or does, that is, or seems to be, "in common" with what another person is saying or doing.

The "most common" form of "communism", and, also, the most **dominant** form, among the people of the known universe, is **"Racial** Communism" (White Supremacy).

Communism, Racial =
(1) The **sum total** of all social and material functions of the Racist Community [White Supremacists, collectively].

(2) Collective White Capitalism.

(3) The **sum total** of all White "Capitalism" combined with the **sum total** of all White "Community-ism".

(4) "Universal" White Nationalism.

(5) "Universal" Racism (White Supremacy).

(6) The **basic** "common-interest" of the Master Commune (White Supremacists, collectively).

Compensationalism =
(1) "Making" up for that which is missing.

(2) Producing that which is needed.

Explanation/Example:
Three very important things that are missing but "needed" among the people of the known universe are:

- The revelation of truth.
- [The practice of] justice.
- [The practice of] correctness.

Compensatory-Functional Definition =
(1) The "meaning" of a word or term expressed in a manner that is more useful in helping to reveal truth, and/or in helping to promote justice or correctness.

(2) The "use" of a word or term in a manner that is more effective in helping to eliminate falsehood, non-justice, and/or incorrectness.

(3) The "use" of a word or term in such manner that it helps to eliminate confusion in the thought, speech, and/or action(s) of people who are unjustly subject to other people.

Compensatory-Functional Identification =
(1) A name, title, number, etc. that a person uses to identify him or her self, that is substantially different from the name, title, number, etc., used by others to identify that same person.

(2) A name, title, number, etc., that a person uses to identify him or her self, that he or she considers to be an accurate description of what he or she **is**, and/or **does**, all, or most, of the time.

C

Compensatory-Functional Supreme Value =
The absence of falsehood, non-justice, and incorrectness.

Compensatory Law =
The Law of the Universe that eliminates imbalances.

"Conservative" [General] =
One who speaks and/or acts to save and/or protect any person, place, thing, etc.

"Conservative" [Racial] =
A white person who speaks and/or acts to maintain White Supremacy (Racsim) by **any** effective means — direct or indirect.

Constructive =
(1) Anything said or done that helps to eliminate Racism (White Supremacy), and, helps to promote justice and correctness.

(2) The use of truth in such manner that justice and/or correctness is promoted.

Constructive Study =
Looking, listening, reading, writing in a manner that helps to promote justice and correctness.

Constructive Work =
Speaking and/or acting in a manner that helps to promote justice and correctness.

Correctness =
(1) **Balance** between people, in relationship to things (etc.), **other** than people.

(2) **Balance** between action, "non-action", plants, animals, sound, silence, thought, non-thought, people, animals, heat, cold, light, darkness, insects, etc.

Correct "Privilege" =
Seeking truth, and using truth in a manner that promotes justice and correctness.

Counter-Racism =
(1) Any speech and/or action that helps to eliminate Racism (White Supremacy).

(2) Any speech and/or action that helps to promote justice and correctness.

(3) The revelation and/or use of truth in such manner that justice and correctness is promoted or produced.

[**Note:** The "authors", and/or "cause" of any Counter-Racist speech and/or action is always the Racists themselves.

The Law of Compensation [balance/justice] works in such manner that the opposition to Racism is caused by the very existence of Racism.

Counter-Racism exists because **Racism** has **no justifiable reason** to exist.

People who practice Racism are, at the same time, "sowing the seeds" of Counter-Racism, thus causing the ultimate elimination of themselves as Racists].

Counter-Racist =
(1) A person who **may**, or **may not**, be a Victim of Racism (non-white person), and who speaks, and/or acts, to eliminate Racism (White Supremacy).

(2) A person who speaks and/or acts in a manner that helps to promote justice.

Counter-Racist Discrimination =
(1) Discrimination by a Victim of Racism (non-white person) against a Racist.

(2) Counter-Racism [see: "Counter-Racism"].

(3) To speak and/or act against Racism and those who practice it.

(4) Speech and/or action against White Supremacy (Racism) by one or more Victims of White Supremacy (non-white people), and/or by others.

Counter-Racist System =
The **sum total** of all words, and all deeds, that help to eliminate Racism (White Supremacy) and/or, that help to establish justice and correctness.

Counter-Sexual Behavior =
(1) Anti-sexual speech and/or action.

(2) Any so-called "homo-sexual", and/or "bi-sexual" behavior.

(3) Any attempt by a **male person** to engage in [pretended] "sexual" intercourse with any person, or being, other than a **female person**.

(4) Any attempt by a **female person** to engage in [pretended] "sexual" intercourse with any person, or being, other than a **male person**.

(5) Pretending to be, and desiring to be, a person of a different sex.

Counter-Terrorism =
Speech and/or action that helps to produce knowledge and understanding of truth, combined with speech and/or action that helps to produce justice and correctness, in all places, in all areas of activity, including Economics, Education, Entertainment, Labor, Law, Politics, Religion, Sex, and War.

Counter-Violence =
Speech and/or action to stop a person, animal, etc. from doing unjust and/or incorrect harm.

Example:
Speech and/or action that is effective against Racism (White Supremacy) and effective in promoting justice and/or correctness.

Counter-War =
(1) Speech and/or action to stop a person, animal, etc. from doing unjust and/or incorrect harm.

(2) The **sum total** of all words and all deeds that help to eliminate Racism (White Supremacy), and help to produce the knowledge and understanding of truth, and the establishment of justice and correctness.

C

Court, Race
Court, Racist
Court, "Superior"
Court, "White" =

Any white person in the known universe who practices Racism (White Supremacy), and, who makes, and/or has made, **any** decision that directly or indirectly supports and/or promotes falsehood, non-justice, or incorrectness, among, and/or against, non-white persons.

[**Note:** The Racist Court, "White" Court, etc., **is not a** building or a geographical location. It is a **person**. It is any white person in the known universe who practices White Supremacy (Racism) in **any** place, at **any** time, in **any** area of activity.

White Supremacy (Racism) is a "Court of Law" **itself.**

Since White Supremacy is a **non**-just system, it is not possible to produce **justice** through the will of those who practice White Supremacy.]

Crime of Crimes =
Racism (White Supremacy).

Explanation:
There is no combination of speech and/or action, among the people of the known universe, that is **greater** than the crime of Racism (White Supremacy), in **promoting** falsehood, non-justice, and incorrectness.

Criminal =
(1) A person who willfully and deliberately speaks and/or acts to promote falsehood, non-justice, and/or incorrectness.

(2) A person who willfully and deliberately **avoids** speaking and/or acting to promote the revelation of truth, and the use of truth to promote justice and correctness.

(3) A White Supremacist (Racist).

C

Cult, The Master =
White Supremacy (Racism).

Culture, The White =
Direct or indirect subjugation of non-white people, by White Supremacists (Racists), in one, or more, areas of activity, particularly, Economics, Education, Entertainment, Labor, Law, Politics, Religion, Sex, and War.

"Cycle" Racism ["Closed-Circle" Racism] =
(1) Racism (White Supremacy) that is practiced in such manner that it's **existence** and/or, it's **seriousness** can only be "proven" by those who are **practicing** it, and those who are the victims of the practice.

(2) Racism (White Supremacy) as practiced so **deceptively** that it's **existence** cannot be "proven" except by those who practice it, and/or those who are the victims of it.

D

Death (1) =
The **presence** of "life".

Death (2) =
Non-justice and **incorrectness**.
[See, also, the following terms:
"Life", Living, and **non-existence]**.

Deed =
The **absence** of "time".

De-Niggerization =
(1) The process of finding truth, and using truth in a manner that promotes the elimination of White Supremacy (Racism).

(2) Speech and/or action that promotes the elimination of Racism (White Supremacy) and the establishment of justice.

Destructive =
(1) Anything said, done, written, etc., that directly or indirectly promotes falsehood, non-justice, and/or incorrectness.

(2) Anything said, done, written, etc., that directly or indirectly helps to establish, maintain, expand, and/or refine Racism (White Supremacy).

Discrimination =
Willfully and deliberately speaking and/or acting "for", or "against", persons, places, animals, things, thought, speech, etc.

Duty =
Seeking truth, and using truth, in a manner that promotes and/or produces justice and correctness at all times, in all places, in all areas of activity, including Economics, Education, Entertainment, Labor, Law, Politics, Religion, Sex, and War.

E

Eclectic-Pluralism =

(1) A compensatory-functional "religion" based on principles derived from two or more "systems" of religion.

(2) A compensatory-functional "religion" based on principles derived from two or more social and material "systems" or concepts.

(3) The concept and practice of making many principles into one, and/or one principle into many.

(4) A compensatory-functional and/or transitional "religion", which includes methods of speech and/or action, that can be used by Victims of Racism (non-white people), as a compensatory-functional means of helping to counter-act the effects of such victimization, in any one or more areas of activity.

(5) A "religion" that can be used to help a Victim of Racism (non-white person) to find the "best" religion.

(6) A "temporary" religion for Victims of Racism (non-white people) that can be used, either in part, or as a whole, to counter-act those parts of other "religions" that may, directly or indirectly, function in support of Racism (White Supremacy).

Eclectic Pluralist =

Any Victim of Racism (non-white person) who practices **one** or **more** "parts" of Electic-Pluralism, and, who identifies him or her **self** as a person who thinks speaks, and acts in support of the concept of Eclectic-Pluralism [See: Eclectic-Pluralism].

Economical =

Speech and/or action that results in justice and correctness.

Economics =

The **process** of speaking and acting in a manner that truth is revealed, and **used**, in a manner that produces justice and correctness at all times, in all places, in all areas of activity, including Education, Entertainment, Labor, Law, Politics, Religion, Sex, and War.

E

Educated Person =
A person who **knows** and **understands all** things about **all** things, and/or, a person who **knows** and **understands all** things about **one** thing.

Education =
The **process** of learning, knowing, and understanding the **truth** about **all** things.

Effective Majority, The =
(1) A term referring to the **power,** of the **total** number of those persons classified as "white", and who practice White Supremacy (Racism) in the known universe.

(2) Those white persons, collectively, who directly or indirectly dominate the non-white people of the known universe through the practice of Racism.

(3) White Supremacists (collectively).

Explanation:
The term "Effective Majority" refers to the white people of the known universe — but **only** to those white persons who practice Racism (White Supremacy).

The term **does not** refer to **all** white people. Nor does it necessarily refer to the **numerical** "majority" of white people who may be situated at a particular place in the known universe, at a particular time.

Those white persons who practice White Supremacy exercise more **power** over people than any other people in the known universe.

They do this in spite of any and all efforts made by other white persons, and by non-white persons, to stop the practice of White Supremacy. Whereas White Supremacy (Racism) may, or may not, have been established, maintained, expanded, and/or refined, by **all** white people, or, even by **most** white people, it has always been maintained by those white persons who had the will, and the ability, to **effectively** make White Supremacy the **major** force. This makes them the "effective majority" — the "majority" that is most "effective" in the exercise of power.

If this were not true, there would not have been, could not have been, nor would now be, anything in the known universe that could be correctly called "White Supremacy".

Therefore, those white people who **do not** practice Racism (White Supremacy), as well as those **non**-white people who do not want to be Victims of Racism, **are not** the "effective majority". They are the **In**effective Majority, the Power**less** Majority, and/or the "majority with minority power".

"Eight-Balling" [Racial] =
(1) A term used in a ball game called "pool".

It means, in racial terms, that a **white** person is directly, or indirectly, the cause of a **Black** and/or non-white person doing any kind of unjust harm to another Black and/or non-white person.

The purpose for this tactic is to **hide** the fact that the harm done was **caused** by the white person who was the **master** of the situation, and not the non-white person who acted as a mere ignorant, arrogant, and/or fearful, tool and servant.

(2) The practice of White Supremacists (Racists) using their power in such manner as to force, bribe, terrify, etc., some non-white persons, into acts of harm to other non-white persons.

Enemy, The Master =
(1) Any person who practices White Supremacy (Racism) at any time, in any place, in any one or more areas of activity.

(2) White Supremacists (collectively).

(3) Non-justice directly or indirectly resulting from the practice of White Supremacy.

Eternal Death =
The promotion of falsehood, and the practice of non-justice and incorrectness in **all** places, at **all** times.

E

Eternal Life =
The revelation of truth, and the practice of justice, and correctness, in **all** places, at **all** times.

Existence =
Function.

Expert =
(1) One who **never** makes a mistake.

(2) One who knows **all** things about **all** things.

(3) One who knows **all** things about "one" thing.

F

Fact(s) =

(1) Any **information** used in such manner that **truth** is revealed.

(2) Any **information** used in such manner that **falsehood** is promoted.

Failure =

(1) Any social and/or material condition that is directly or indirectly dominated by the promotion of falsehood, and the practice of non-justice and incorrectness.

(2) The **absence** of justice or correctness.

Fair =

White.

Explanation:
"Fair" means "white".
"Fair" does not mean **just**. It does not mean **justice.** It does not mean **correct** or **correctness.** It is always incorrect to use the word "fair", the word "just", the word "justice", or the word "correct", as if they all mean the same.

To do so may lead many people to believe that "fair" means "justice", and that "fair", "justice", and "white", mean the same thing.

Thus, some people may be lead to believe that "white" people are "fair" people, and that "fair" people are people who practice **justice.**

It is best, therefore, to use the word "fair" to mean "white" — and **only** to mean "white". **The word "fair" should never be used to mean justice or correctness.**

Fair Person =

White person, and/or, a person who is classifed as "white" and functions as "white".
[**Note:** See "fair", and/or "fair play"].

Fair Play =

[A meaningless term that should not be used].

Explanation:
As long as White Supremacy exists, the term "fair play" should not be used.

It is best not to use the term because the word "fair" is ofttimes associated with the word "white" as well as the word "justice".

This sometimes causes the word "white", the word "fair", **and** the word "justice" to be directly or indirectly associated with "white" people.

This direct or indirect association of these terms promote confusion and falsehood, which, in turn, promotes non-justice, incorrectness, and the refinement of White Supremacy (Racism).

Falsehood =
Non-truth, and/or that which **is not [true].**

Family =
(1) All persons, collectively, who practice White Supremacy (Racism).

(2) Any "organization" of two or more persons that exist during a period when White Supremacy (Racism) **does not** exist.

Explanation:
As long as White Supremacy (Racism) exist, there can be only one "family" of people in the known universe. That "family" is the "family" of White Supremacists (Racists).

It could be more specifically known as the "White Family", and/or, the "Racist Family".

In a social-material system dominated by White Supremacists (Racists), no "family", no "nation", no "tribe" exists, **other than** the "family", "nation", and/or "tribe" of White Supremacists (Racists).

All other so-called "families", "nations", and/or "tribes", are none other than **individual persons** who may, or may not, seem to be functioning as "independent units" of two or more persons. The truth is, they are only **individual persons.**

Persons who are **non**-white are **all subject to** the "Family"of White Supremacists.

Persons who are **white** are **not** subject to the Family of White Supremacists. Such white persons are either, themselves, White Supremacists, or, they are individual persons who, at **all** times, function against the White Supremacists.

The only other categories of white people are those who "function" neither for White Supremacy, nor against it. These white people are considered to be, and function as, "infantile" or "senile" persons.

It is not possible for any "white" person to be subject to "White" Supremacy. Each white person must function (as long as White Supremacy exists) as a White Supremacist, an anti-White Supremacists, a senile person, or an infantile person.

[**Note:** "Senile", and "infantile" persons, are persons, who, because of physical or mental limitations, are generally incapable of doing harm to others].

As long as White Supremacy exists, the word "family" **always** means, in function, the "White Family", and/or the Family of White Supremacists (White Supremacists, collectively).

Fascism =

(1) White Supremacy (Racism).

(2) White Supremacy (Racism) as it is usually practiced in its most direct, most obvious, and most violent form(s).

Fascist =

(1) A White Supremacist (Racist).

(2) A person [white] who practices White Supremacy in it's most direct, most obvious, and most violent form(s).

Fear =

The absence of knowledge and/or understanding of how to compensate for the lack of knowledge, and/or understanding.

F

Foreigner and/or Alien =

(1) To a Racist: Anyone who is a Victim of Racism.

(2) To a Victim of Racism: Anyone who is a Racist.

(3) To a Victim of White Supremacy: Anyone who practices White Supremacy.

(4) To a White Supremacist (Racist): Anyone who is classified as "non-white".

Fornication =
Any act of sexual intercourse and/or "sexual play" between persons who are deceitful, hypocritical, and/or otherwise untrustworthy, in their relationship(s) with each other.

Freedom =
The **will, plus**, the **ability**, to find truth, and to use truth in a manner that produces justice and correctness, at **all** times, in **all** places, in **all** areas of activity, including Economics, Education, Entertainment, Labor, Law, Politics, Religion, Sex, and War.

Friend =
One who has the **will**, plus, the **ability**, to find truth, and to use truth in a manner that **produces** justice and correctness, at **all** times, in **all** places, in **all** areas of activity, including Economics, Education, Entertainment, Labor, Law, Politics, Religion, Sex, and War.

[**Note:** Until such time as falsehood, non-justice, and incorrectness no longer exist in the known universe, no person, animal, etc. in the known universe, can be a "friend" to another person, animal, etc., nor can he, she, it, etc., function as a "friend" to him, her, or it **self**.

Racism (White Supremacy) prevents people from acting justly and correctly. If people do not function justly and correctly it is not possible for them to produce "friendship".

Therefore, a person can have a friend, and/or be a friend, only after **justice** and **correctness** has been established in **all** of the known universe, in **all** areas of activity**]**.

Functional = "Effective" existence.

G

Ghetto [Racial] =
Any **person [non-white]** who is directly or indirectly **restricted**, and/or **dominated**, by White Supremacists (Racists) at **any** time in **any** place, in **any** area of activity, including Economics, Education, Entertainment, Labor, Law, Politics, Religion, Sex, and/or War.

Explanation:
In racial matters, a "ghetto" is **not** a **place.**

In racial matters, a "ghetto" is any non-white **person** who is subject to White Supremacy (Racism). In any socio-material condition dominated by White Supremacy, **all** non-white people are unjustly **restricted**, and/or **dominated** [ghettoized] on the basis of "color", at **all** times, in **all** places, in all areas of activity.

Ghettoized =
The condition of a person [non-white] who is directly or indirectly restricted, dominated, and/or subject to the power of White Supremacists (Racists) in any one or more areas of activity.

"Ghetto Smart" =
(1) The ability of a non-white person to say and/or do things that may "impress" other non-white persons, but is of little or no value in the promotion of justice or correctness.

(2) The ability of a Victim of Racism [non-white person] to say, or do, many unjust, incorrect, silly, and/or stupid things, with great "style" or efficiency.

Girl [Racial] =
Any **female** person, racially classified as "non-white", who is directly, or indirectly, subject to the power of White Supremacists (Racists) in any one or more areas of activity, including Economics, Education, Entertainment, Labor, Law, Politics, Religion, Sex, and/or War.

Good =
The complete **absence** of falsehood, non-justice, and incorrectness, in the universe.

G

Good Person =

(1) A person who knows and understands **truth**, and who uses truth in such manner as to **produce** justice and correctness, at all times, in **all** places, in **all** areas of activity, throughout the known and unknown universe.

(2) A person who "knows" and understands **nothing.**

Good Speaker =

A person who has spoken **truth** in such manner that justice and correctness (in all areas of activity, throughout the universe) is the **result.**

Good White Person =

A person classified as "white" and/or Caucasian, who **does not** practice Racism at **any** time, in **any place, in any** area of activity, and, who also uses truth in such manner as to **produce** justice and correctness, at **all** times, in **all** places, in **all** areas of activity, throughout the universe.

God =

The **sum total** of the **known** and **unknown.**

Gossip =

Saying things about a person, with the intention of doing social or material harm to that person, without that person being **immediately** informed of **what** is being said, **who** is saying it, and **why** it is being said.

Government =

(1) One or more persons speaking and/or acting **effectively** to promote one or more objectives, in one or more areas of activity.

(2) A **functional** system of thought, speech, and action by persons, animals, etc.

Government, Correct =

A system of thought, speech, and action, by persons, animals, etc., that functions in such manner that it **has produced** the revelation of truth **and** the practice of justice and correctness, at **all** times, in all areas of activity, including Economics, Education, Entertainment, Labor, Law, Politics, Religion, Sex, and War.

G

Government, Incorrect =

(1) Thought, speech, and/or action, by people, that **has not produced** justice and correctness, in **all** places, in **all** areas of activity, including Economics, Education, Entertainment, Labor, Law, Politics, Religion, Sex, and War.

(2) Any person, who **dominates** another person or persons, by practicing falsehood, non-justice, and/or incorrectness in any one or more areas of activity, such as Economics, Education, Entertainment, Labor, Law, Politics, Religion, Sex, and/or War.

(3) White Supremacy (Racism).

Government Official =

(1) Any person with **maximum** power over others in any one or more areas of activity, including Economics, Education, Entertainment, Labor, Law, Politics, Religion, Sex, War, etc.

(2) Any person, while speaking, and/or acting **effectively** to promote one or more objectives in any one or more areas of activity.

Government, Racist =

(1) One or more persons classified as "white", while speaking and/or acting **effectively** to promote White Supremacy (Racism).

(2) The sum total of all thought, speech, and action by persons [white] who practice White Supremacy.

(3) White Supremacists, collectively.

Government, Subversive =

(1) The **sum total** of all thought, speech, and action by a person, or persons, that produces falsehood, non-justice, and incorrectness in any one or more areas of activity, including Economics, Education, Entertainment, Labor, Law, Politics, Religion, Sex, and/or War.

(2) The **sum total** of all thought, speech, and action, by persons [white] who practice White Supremacy (Racism).

(3) One or more persons speaking and/or acting **effectively**, to endanger the existence of any other person, while that person is speaking and/or acting to promote justice.

(4) One or more persons speaking and/or acting to prevent one or more persons from promoting justice.

(5) White Supremacy (Racism).

"Government", The =
[Note: The use of this term should be avoided because it may be too non-specific and/or confusing].

Government, The Master =
(1) The **sum total** of all thought, speech, and action by those persons [white] who practice White Supremacy (Racism).

(2) Government of, by, and for, those persons who are Racists (White Supremacists).

(3) White Supremacy, and/or, the only **functional** government among the people of the known universe.

Great Spectator =
Non-white people in general, including people sometimes referred to as "Black" — particularly people sometimes referred to as "Negro" and/or "Negroid".

Explanation:
The term Great Spectator generally means that "Black" people, and/or "Negroes", are basically "on lookers".

It means that "Black people" and/or "Negroes" generally do not do anything of great and/or significant value themselves, by their **own will**, but, for the most part, spend their time watching and waiting to "see" what **white** people will, or will not do.

The term also means, that under White Supremacy (Racism), no **non**-white person does anything of significant value that is not started, "supervised", and/or endorsed by **white** persons.

The term means that under **most** conditions Black people are "best-qualified" to **look** and maybe to copy, but not to lead or **start** any activity that is constructive.

Greater Confinement =
(1) "Jail", "Prison", etc.

(2) Generally, any "greater than usual" **restriction** of a non-white person that is directly or indirectly caused, and/or promoted, by White Supremacists (Racists).

(3) Any form of physical and/or mental confinement of non-white persons "greater" than that which is **usually** imposed on them by the very existence of White Supremacy (Racism) itself.

H

Habitat =
Any "specific" place where much time/energy is spent.

Example:
Under White Supremacy, no non-white person has a "home". He or she has only a **habitat**. White Supremacists do not permit their subjects to have, and/or to function as, a "home". In any socio-material system dominated by White Supremacists, "Homes" do not exist. [See: Home].

Handicapped and/or Retarded Person(s) [Racial] =
Any person(s) [non-white] **directly** or **indirectly** denied justice, at any time, in any place, in any area of activity, because of Racism (White Supremacy).

Happiness =
The **absence** of falsehood, non-justice, and incorrectness, at all times, in all places, in all areas of activity, including Economics, Education, Entertainment, Labor, Law, Politics, Religion, Sex, and War.

Hate =
Aggressive submission to fear.

Explanation:
One "hates" what one fears.

Holy Land =
Any "land" of the quality and/or quantity that is, or can be, used for producing justice and correctness.

"Holy War" =
(1) The **sum total** of all thought, speech, and action against falsehood, non-justice, and incorrectness.

(2) The **sum total** of all thought, speech, and action to eliminate Racism (White Supremacy).

Home =
A place and/or condition where **truth** is revealed, and **used** in such manner as to produce justice and correctness at all times, in all areas of activity, including Economics, Education, Entertainment, Labor, Law, Politics, Religion, Sex, and War.

H

Hostage =

(1) Any person who is **unjustly forced** to say, or do, anything, in any one or more areas of activity, including Economics, Education, Entertainment, Labor, Law, Politics, Religion, Sex, and War.

(2) Any person who is restricted, and/or dislocated (by other persons), **against his or her will**, and is used as an object to be offered, or received, for sale, loan, or trade.

Human Being =

Any person who **has produced** justice and correctness, in **all** areas of activity, **every** place in the known universe.

"Human Race" = [A Non-Existent "Race"]

Explanation:

(1) There is no such thing as **the**, and/or **a** "Human Race".

The word "human", and/or, the word "humane" is directly contradictory to the word "Race".

(2) It is not possible for any beings to be "human", and/or "humane", and, at the same time, be a "race", and/or practice a form of "Racism". It is not possible for any person to be a **human** person, and, at the same time, be a "Racist".

It is not possible for a person to be **humane**, and, at the same time, practice "Racism".

(3) A **human** and/or **humane** person is **not** a "Racist", and a "Racist" is **not** a **human** nor a **humane** person.

The objective of a human and/or humane person is not the same as the objective of a "Racist", nor do they practice the same things, for the same reasons.

A person who is human and/or humane knows and understands truth, and uses truth in such manner as to produce justice, and correctness, at all times, in all places, in all areas of activity.

A person who is a Racist practices falsehood, non-justice, and incorrectness, for the purpose of establishing, maintaining, expanding, and/or refining Racism (White Supremacy).

Human "Rights" =

(1) The **duty** to speak, and/or act, to find truth, and to use truth in such manner as to promote justice and correctness, at all times, in all places, in all areas of activity, including Economics, Education, Entertainment, Labor, Law, Politics, Religion, Sex, and War.

(2) The "right" [duty] to treat people humanely, and to be treated humanely.

I

Illegitimate Child/Illegitimate Person =

(1) Any person [non-white] who is directly or indirectly subject to the will, or power, of persons who practice White Supremacy (Racism).

(2) Any person that exists during the **same** time that falsehood, non-justice, and incorrectness dominates the speech, action, and/or re-action(s), of the people of the known universe.

(3) Any non-white person born as a direct or indirect result of sexual intercourse between a white person and a non-white person under social or material conditions dominated by Racism (White Supremacy).

Imbalance, The Basic Law Of =

(1) Too much on one end, side, etc., and, not enough on the other.

(2) Too much, and/or too little, of any quantity.

Immediate Emergency Compensatory Justice =
Any direct or indirect speech, and/or action used **immediately** by any Victim of Racism [non-white person], to **protect** his or her existence, person, possessions, and/or general welfare, against unjust or incorrect seizure, damage, and/or destruction by person(s), thing(s), and/or force(s).

Immediate Power =
The power to destory, eliminate, and/or kill one or more persons, animals, etc.

Immoral =
Any thought, speech, and/or action that directly or indirectly helps to establish, maintain, expand, and/or refine White Supremacy (Racism).

"Incorrect", and/or "non-Just Racism =
Any, and/or all, Racism.

Explanation:
Some persons, both white and non-white, sometimes speak, and/or act as if it is **just** and/or **correct** to permit, promote, and/or tolerate the practice

of Racism, at "certain" times in "certain" places, in "certain" forms, in one or more particular areas of activity. All such speech and/or action is incorrect. Racism is a practice that is non-just and incorrect **all** of the time, in **all** places in **all** "forms", in **all** areas of activity. There is no time, place, form, circumstance, or area for Racism to be permitted, promoted, or tolerated.

Under no circumstance can Racism be justified.

Racism is a universal crime, and is so at **all** times, in all places, in **all** forms, in **all** areas of activity.

Ineffective Minority =
All non-white persons, collectively.

Explanation:
In a socio-material system dominated by White Supremacists (Racists) those white persons (collectively) who practice White Supremacy (Racism) are, in function, the "effective majority". The White Supremacists function as the major and/or "majority" **power**. Their power is **effective**. The power of their subjects — the non-white people — is, by comparison, **ineffective.**

Non-white people function as a comparatively Ineffective Minority. They are a **minor** power. They function as "minors". They function in the manner of subject children.

By comparison with the White Supremacists [the Effective Majority], non-white people are **ineffective** in their attempts to speak and act as men and women.

Infant =
[See: **Infantile Person]**

Infantile Person =
(1) A person who is generally weak, both physically and mentally.

(2) A person who, because of physical or mental limitations, is generally incapable of doing willful and deliberate harm to others.

I

Infinite-Comparative Compensationalism =
The process of producing those things of constructive value that are missing, but **not known** to be, and/or not **understood** to be, in **existence.**

Example(s):
(1) Speaking and/or acting to produce justice without having experienced "justice".

(2) Attempting to establish a "correct" world without knowing and understanding what such a world would be.

(3) Producing "peace" without having the knowledge and/or understanding of the energy used to do so.

Information =
The revelation and/or presentation of truth, or falsehood.

Inhuman, and/or Non-Humane Being =
(1) Any person in the known universe who knows, and understands, how to produce justice and correctness, but, who deliberately, and by choice, practices non-justice, and incorrectness.

(2) Any person who deliberately, and by choice, promotes deceit.

(3) Any person who does, or says, anything that does not promote justice and correctness.

Example: A White Supremacists (Racist)

Insanity =
(1) The practice of thinking, speaking, and/or acting in support of falsehood, non-justice, and/or incorrectness.

(2) The failure, and/or refusal, to find truth, and to use truth in such manner as to produce justice and correctness.

J

Job =
Any activity that a person is required to engage in, in order to survive, and/or, in order to avoid pain or extreme discomfort. Also, any activity that a person is required to do in order to help others do the same.

"Just" War, and/or "Counter-War" =
Any thought, speech, silence, action, and/or inaction directed **against** falsehood, non-justice, and/or incorrectness.

Example:
Thought, speech, silence, action, and/or inaction that results in the elimination of White Supremacy (Racism).

Justice =
Balance between people.

Justifiable Homicide =
Killing a person for the purpose of establishing and/or maintaining justice.

Examples:

(1) The killing of a Racist (White Supremacist), by a Victim of Racism, while that Victim is directly or indirectly counter-acting one or more extremely destructive and unjust acts, caused, promoted, and/or permitted, by Racists (White Supremacists).

(2) The killing of a Victim of Racism [non-white person], by another Victim of Racism, in direct defense of the existence of the person, and/or major property, of a Victim of Racism, and/or, of the person and/or major property of a **white** person who is **not** a Racist.

(3) The Enactment of Maximum-Emergency Compensatory Justice.
[See: "Maximum-Emergency Compensatory Justice].

L

Labor, Correct =
Any thought, speech, and/or action, that helps to reveal truth, **and,** helps to use the truth in such manner as to promote and/or produce justice and correctness.

[**Note**: No form of labor is "lowly" or "degrading" if it helps to promote and/or produce justice or correctness].

Labor, Incorrect [Waste] =
(1) Any thought, speech, and/or action that helps to promote and/or produce falsehood, non-justice, or incorrectness.

(2) Any thought, speech, and/or action that helps to establish, maintain, expand, and/or refine the practice of Racism (White Supremacy).

Law =
Anything that has an effect.

Law, [Race, and/or Racist] =
(1) Anything said or done by a white person, that directly or indirectly helps to establish, maintain, expand, and/or refine White Supremacy (Racism).

(2) White Supremacy (Racism).

Lawbreaker =
Any effect that eliminates another effect.

Legal =
(1) Any law, or anything said to be a law, by those who have the **power** to make it so.

(2) Any speech or action that is **enforced** by White Supremacists (Racists).

(3) Justice and correctness, combined [inactive].

Liberal [Racial] =
(1) A White person who speaks and/or acts to maintain White Supremacy (Racism) by using a greatly refined form of deceit. The deceit that is used by such persons is so refined that it is usually very acceptable, comfortable, and satisfying, to the Victims [non-white people].

(2) Any white person who seeks to maintain White Supremacy through the use of deceit, greatly refined.

L

Explanation:
In a socio-material system dominated by White Supremacy (Racism), a "liberal" is a "refined" White Supremacists (Racist). The "liberal" Racist, both male and female, is ofttimes characterized by the following:

(1) Handling, lending, and/or granting **money** for curing "specified" physical and/or "social" ills among non-white people, while making certain that none is used effectively against White Supremacy (Racism).

(2) Moving among non-white people as teachers of subjects that are "interesting", but not effective in helping non-white people to eliminate Racism and/or in producing justice and correctness.

(3) Providing and encouraging various forms of **entertainment** that have the effect of diverting the attention of non-white people away from serious matters such as economics, education, politics, etc.

(4) Working "closely with" non-white people in a manner that he and/or she can watch and study them, and control their thinking more directly and efficiently.

(5) Making suggestions to non-white people that are "attractive", but are functionally designed to indirectly make non-white people to render better service to White Supremacy.

(6) Using **religion** as a means of **division** and **deception** and to gain greater influence over their Victims [non-white people].

(7) Using sex, an/or anti-sex, in any form that increases the influence of the White Supremacists over the sexual conduct of their Victims.

"Liberal" Racists (both male and female) promote Racism by engaging in sexual activity with non-white people and/or against non-white people.

The "liberal" Racist woman is skilled in promoting damaging influence among non-white people through the lustful presentation and use of her body.

(8) Using non-white people to fight any people, white or non-white, in such manner that White Supremacy is made stronger.

(9) Presenting themselves to non-white people as being people who are "not really white" in a racial sense, but who are "Christian", "Jew", "Moslem", "Marxist", "Aristocrat", "Liberal", etc.

They do this to confuse non-white people. They do this to eliminate the question of whether a so-called "liberal" is, or is not, a White Supremacist (Racist). They do this as a means of evading discussion of Racism as pertains to themselves. The so-called "liberal" Racist uses some **non**-white people, to do harm to some **white** people, if he or she judges it to be necessary to help maintain, expand, and/or, especially, **refine** the practice of White Supremacy.

The so-called "liberal" Racist is an "up-to-date" Racist.

"Liberal" Racists avoid "petty" and/or "nit-picking" forms of Racism.

"Liberal" Racists will kill and/or intimidate those white people who practice more direct and **obvious** forms of Racism, with the intention of getting **all** white people to practice Racism in a form that is more **refined.**

The "liberal" White Supremacist considers him or her self to be "smarter" than "other" White Supremacists.

The "liberal" White Supremacists makes plans for a world in which the **Victims** of White Supremacy (all non-white people) will come to "enjoy" White Supremacy so much that they will never wish to exist in any way **other than** as subjects to the White Supremacists (Racists).

Lie =
Speech and/or action with the intention of promoting falsehood.

Life (1) =
The **presence** of death.

Explanation:
The word "life" can be used to express the "awareness" of "death" that a being must have in order to have an "awareness" of "life". Likewise, the word "death" can be used to express the "awareness" of "life" that a being must have in order to have an "appreciation" of "death".

Therefore, the word "life", as well as the word "death" can be defined as expressions of the **same** condition in different forms.

This definition has functional value as a means of promoting thought and exploration into the "true" meaning of "life", and of "death".

When using the word "life" to mean the "presence of death", it is correct to use the word "death" to mean the "presence of life".

Life (2) =
Justice and correctness.

Explanation:
The word "life" can ofttimes be used directly, and functionally, to mean the **exact same** as the term **"justice, plus, correctness"**.

When using the word "life" to mean **justice, plus, correctness,** the word "death" should be used to mean **"non-justice plus, incorrectness"**.

[**Example**: A Victim of Racism can practice using the word "life" **only** to mean, and/or describe, a condition of **justice and correctness**, and, the word "death", **only** to mean, and/or describe, a condition of **non-justice and incorrectness]**.

The terms "life" and "death" mean more than **existence** and **non-existence**.

They can, and should, be used to also mean **justice** and **correctness**.

[See, also, the following terms: Death, Existence, Living, and Non-Existence].

"Lighter" Shades of "Black" [Color/Racial] =
A racial term referring to non-white people who, **visually**, may appear to be "brown", "beige", "red", "rust", "tan", "yellow", etc.

Examples:
Yellow = very light black.
Red = lighter black.
Brown = light black.
[Black = dark -dark].

Living =
The [complete] **absence** of falsehood, non-justice, and incorrectness, at all times, in all places, in all areas of activity.

Explanation:
A person, and/or "being", does not, and cannot, "live", and/or **is not** "making a **living"**, while dominated by, or affected by, the existence of falsehood, non-justice, and/or incorrectness, at any time, in any place, in any one or more areas of activity.

Example:
Persons who function in subjugation to White Supremacy (Racism) do not "live". Such persons only **exist.**

[See: Life, Death, Existence, and Non-Existence]

"Living" In Sin =
(1) Being hypocritical.
(2) Telling lies and/or willfully and deliberately refusing to promote truth in a manner that promotes justice and correctness.
(3) Not trying to find truth, and use truth, in a manner that promotes justice and correctness.
(4) Not trying to eliminate Racism (White Supremacy).
(5) Practicing Racism, or cooperating with those who do.

Love =
Speech and/or action, that **results** in the use of **truth**, in a manner that promotes the practice of **justice** and **correctness** at all times, in all places, in all areas of activity, including Economics, Education, Entertainment, Labor, Law, Politics, Religion, Sex, and War.

L

Lynching [Racial] =
Any act(s) of violent non-justice, and/or, any acts(s) of bodily harm, committed by one or more Racists (White Supremacists) against any one or more Victims of Racism [non-white persons].

M

Major Problem, The =
White Supremacy (Racism), and the general promotion of falsehood, non-justice, and incorrectness.

Man =
(1) Any **male** person, classified as "white", who is also treated as "white" in any socio-material system, or situation, that is directly, or indirectly, dominated by White Supremacy (Racism).

(2) Any **male** person, classified as "non-white" who is **not** directly, or indirectly dominated by, and/or subjected to, White Supremacy.

Man's Child, and/or Woman's Child =
Any **male** or **female** person classified as "Black" or "non-white", and who generally functions in direct or indirect support of White Supremacy (Racism).

Marriage =
(1) Any **mutual** and **harmonious** relationship between male and female persons who do, or do not, engage in sexual intercourse, and, who are not, in any way, **subject** to the direct or indirect **dominant will** of any person(s) who practice non-justice.

(2) Any **mutual** and **harmonious** relationship between male and female persons, **none** of whom are directly, or indirectly, subject to White Supremacy (Racism), in any one or more areas of activity, including Economics, Education, Entertainment, Labor, Law, Politics, Religion, Sex, and/or War.

[Note: Marriages must be both **mutual** and **harmonious**. Any relationship between any persons that is not **both** mutual, **and** harmonious, cannot be correctly called a "marriage".

For instance, non-white people cannot function as "married" people as long as they exist in subjugation to White Supremacy.

In a socio-material system dominated by White Supremacists (Racists), only white people **can** function in a **mutual** and **harmonious** manner, because no "white" people are subject to **White** Supremacy. Non-white people, however, cannot function in a manner that is **both** mutual **and** harmonious.

Non-white males and females, can, under White Supremacy, engage in sexual relationships that are **mutual.** They **cannot** conduct these relationships with **harmony.** The overall effect of Racism on the relationships between non-white males and females is to prevent **harmony**. The lack of harmony affects everything that they do, or try to do, in all areas of [their] activity].

Married Persons =
Any male and female persons who engage in any **mutual** and **harmonious** relationship with each other, **and**, who **are not subject** to the will of any persons who practice Racism (White Supremacy), or, non-justice, in any other form, in any area of activity, including Economics, Education, Entertainment, Labor, Law, Politics, Religion, Sex, and/or War.

Master Capitalist and/or Supreme Capitalist =
The same as a Master Communist, and/or, a Supreme Communist.

[See: Master Communist, and/or Supreme Communist].

Master Child Abuser =
A White Supremacist (Racist).

Explanation:
In a world social and material system dominated by White Supremacy (Racism), **all** non-white people, in order to survive, must function in a manner that is comparatively "child-like". They are **forced** to speak and act in a manner that is both childish, and subordinate, **all** of the time, in all areas of activity, including Economics, Education, Entertainment, Labor, Law, Politics, Religion, Sex, and War.

Since White Supremacy is the dominant form of non-justice in the known universe, those white persons who practice White Supremacy are the greatest and most masterful abusers of "children" in the known universe.

Therefore, any person who practices White Supremacy is a Master Child Abuser.

Master Communist and/or Supreme Communist =

(1) A white person who practices White Supremacy (Racism), and, who by word or deed makes "common cause" with other white persons who do the same.

(2) A Race "Capitalist".

(3) A Race "Communist".

(4) A white person who "capitalizes" on the subjugation of non-white people, by practicing White Supremacy (Racism), and who makes "common capital" with those white persons who do the same.

(5) A white person who practices Racism (White Supremacy), and, who by word and/or deed, willfully maintains membership in, and/or gives direct or indirect support to, the strongest and most effective "capital-communist", and/or "community-type" system in the known universe: the "White Nation", and/or "White Community".

(6) A person [white] who functions as a member or supporter of the strongest and most effective social and material "capital-commonwealth" in the known universe. This "capital-commonwealth" is sometimes referred to as "The White Nation", "The White Community", and/or the "Collective White Supremacists.

(7) A person [white] who is a Racist (White Supremacist), and, who maintains a "common bond" of social and/or material interests with all other Racists (White Supremacists) in the known universe.

(8) A Race Communist/Capitalist.

(9) A member of the Master Commune [White Supremacists, collectively].

(10) A person [white] who is a member of the Universal Master Community, and/or Universal Supreme Community.

(11) Any White Supremacist (Racist).

Master Criminal =
(1) A White Supremacist (Racist).

(2) Any person [white] who practices White Supremacy (Racism).

Explanation:
Those white people who practice Racism are the masters of non-white people in all areas of activity.

Since Racism (White Supremacy) is the greatest and most effective form of **injustice** among the people of the known universe, it is therefore, the greatest and most effective **crime.**

Since those white people who practice Racism are also the **masters** of **all** non-white people, in **all** areas of activity, then, **all** white people who practice **Racism**, are **Master** criminals.

Master Organization, The =
Those white people, collectively, who practice White Supremacy (Racism).

Explanation:
The white people who have chosen to practice White Supremacy (Racism) are so "organized", and so masterful, that they are, collectively, more powerful than any other category or classification of people in the known universe.

Master Parents =
In a socio-material system dominated by White Supremacy (Racism), any person [white], who practices White Supremacy.

Explanation:
In a world social and material system dominated by White Supremacists (Racists), **all** non-white persons who are directly or indirectly dominated by the effects of White Supremacy, are the "subjugated children" of **all** White Supremacists.

This means that the White Supremacists are, in effect, the functional "parents" of the non-white people of the known universe.

Since White Supremacy is a **master** social and material system, and, since it is based on the promotion of falsehood, non-justice, and incorrectness, the people [white] who practice it, are "unfit parents" of the non-white people whom they dominate.

Master Race =
(1) White Supremacists, collectively.

(2) Those white persons, collectively, who are the **masters** in the **practice** of Racism (White Supremacy).

(3) The masters of the practice of Racism (White Supremacy).

Master Security Risk =
A White Supremacist (Racist).

Explanation:
"Security" is the result of truth, that is used in a manner that produces justice and correctness.

Racism is the **greatest** threat to truth being used to produce justice and correctness. **Racism**, in the form of White Supremacy, is the **greatest** motivating force by people, among the people of the known universe.

The people [white] who practice White Supremacy are the functional **masters** of all of the people of the known universe who are classified as "non-white".

The White Supremacists (Racists) are, therefore, the Master Security Risks of the known universe.

M

Master Terrorist =
(1) A White Supremacist (Racist).

(2) Any person [white], while practicing White Supremacy (Racism) in any one, or more, areas of activity, including Economics, Education, Entertainment, Labor, Law, Politics, Religion, Sex, and/or War.

(3) Any person [white], who practices White Supremacy in such manner that one or more Victims [non-white person] are made to experience great fear, panic, dread, alarm, dismay, horror, etc.

Explanation:
White Supremacists are the **masters** of terrorism. More people [non-white] fear them, more than they fear any other force.

Master-Universal Subversive Elements =
Those people of the known universe who are the **smartest, most powerful,** and **most malicious**, and, who have, also, chosen to promote injustice by using the most destructive features of "Capitalist", "Communist", "Fascist", "Socialist" (and/or any other socio-material) concepts.

Maximum-Emergency Compensatory Justice =
(1) The willful and deliberate elimination of one or more Racists (White Supremacist), through death, **and**, the willful and deliberate elimination of self, through death, by a Victim of Racism [non-white person], acting alone, according to a detailed plan, and acting only after he or she has judged that he or she can no longer endure the effects of Racism, and/or, is no longer able to **effectively** promote justice **except** by eliminating one or more Racists, as well as eliminating him or her self, as a subject of the Racists.

(2) Swift, efficient, surprise execution of one or more Racists (White Supremacists), by an **individual** Victim of Racism, acting **openly** and **alone**, at a time and place of his or her **own choosing**, continuing to execute as

many Racists as possible, without respite or surrender, until he or she is **forced** to **eliminate self**, rather than be eliminated or captured by others.

[**Note**: Maximum-Emergency Compensatory Justice is enacted **only** under **prolonged** conditions of **extreme** and practically hopeless deprivation, and acute suffering (of injustice), caused, and/or promoted by those persons [white] who practice White Supremacy (Racism)].

Maximum Racist Aggression =

(1) Anything willfully and deliberately said or done by a **white** person, under conditions dominated by White Supremacy (Racism), that results in a **non**-white person being **deceived.**

(2) Anything willfully and deliberately said or done by a **white** person, under conditions dominated by White Supremacy, that results in a **non**-white person being deprived of something that he or she must have in order to promote justice and/or correctness.

(3) Any act of sexual intercourse, and/or "sexual play", between a **white** person and a **non**-white person, during any period in which **any** person, is subject to White Supremacy (Racism), any place in the known universe.

[**Note**: Any and all **white** persons who participate in, and/or who directly or indirectly help to promote such acts, are guilty of Maximum Racist Aggression].

Examples:

(1) A white person engaging in sexual intercourse and/or "sexual play" with a non-white person.

(2) A white person willfully and deliberately inflicting bodily harm on a non-white person.

(3) A white person speaking and/or acting in such manner as to directly or indirectly cause or promote the infliction of bodily harm by one Victim of Racism [non-white person] on another Victim of Racism.

(4) A white person giving **false** information **to** a non-white person.

(5) A white person giving false information **about** a non-white person.

(6) A white person concealing the truth, or refusing to tell the truth, to a non-white person about anything that will help to promote justice and correctness.

Maximum Racist Insult =
Any act of sexual intercourse, and/or "sexual play", between a white person, and a non-white person under any condition, directly or indirectly dominated by White Supremacy (Racism).

Member of A Nation = [See: Nation]

Militant =
A person who is willing to fight, kill, and/or die, for what he or she believes should, or should not, be done.

Minority [Racial] =
(1) In a socio-material system dominated by White Supremacists (Racists), any person who is classified as, and/or, who is treated as "Black" and/or "non-white".

(2) A "minor" person [non-white] when compared to a person with "major" and/or "master" power [a White Supremacist].

Misfitted Person [Racial] =
(1) Any Victim of Racism [non-white person].

(2) Any non-white person who is subject to White Supremacy in any one or more areas of activity.

Misfitted and/or Zeroistic Speech or Action =
Anything said or done by a non-white person, while existing in subjugation to White Supremacy, that is **not** said or done in such manner as to be **effective** in the elimination of White Supremacy.

M

Misfitted and/or Zeroistic Thinking =
Any thinking and/or thought, by a non-white person, while existing in subjugation to White Supremacy, that does not promote speech and/or action that is effective in the elimination of White Supremacy.

Money =
(1) Any person, place, animal, thing, etc. used as a tool in the accomplishment of an objective.

(2) Any person who is racially classified as "black", "brown", "red", "yellow", and/or "non-white", and who exists under socio-material conditions dominated by White Supremacists.

Morality =
The elimination of Racism (White Supremacy), and the establishment of justice and correctness in all places, in all areas of activity.

Moral Person =
A person who has eliminated Racism (White Supremacy), and, who has established justice and correctness in all places, in all areas of activity.

Motion =
The existence of more than one.

Murder =
(1) The act of killing for purposes of establishing, maintaining, expanding, and/or refining the practice of falsehood, non-justice, and/or incorrectness.

(2) The act of killing for the purpose of establishing, maintaining, expanding and/or refining, White Supremacy (Racism).

N

Nation =
Any person, or persons, who, of **their own will** establish a **common basic objective**, and, who, of their own will, successfully accomplish that **common basic objective,** and, who are **not subject to** the will of **any** person,or persons, in **any** area of activity including Economics, Education, Entertainment, Labor, Law, Politics, Religion, Sex, and War.

"Natural" War, and/or Counter-War =
(1) Effective speech and/or action against falsehood, non-justice, and/or incorrectness.

(2) Effective speech and/or action against Racism (White Supremacy).

Negress =
(1) Any female person classified as "Black", and/or "non-white", and who engages in sexual intercourse, and/or "sexual play", with a **white** person, under conditions dominated by White Supremacy (Racism).

(2) A female person classified as "Black", and/or "non-white", who is "especially chosen" for purposes of sexual intercourse with one or more white persons, in a manner that directly or indirectly helps to establish, maintain, expand, and/or refine White Supremacy.

(3) A female person classified as "Black", and/or "non-white", who is "especially chosen", and/or encouraged to speak, or act, in a manner that gives special support to the practice of White Supremacy in one or more areas of activity, such as Economics, Education, Entertainment, Labor, Law, Politics, Religion, Sex, and/or War.

[**Note**: The term "Negress" is not to be used to describe any **particular** person. Any person who uses the term in that manner is guilty of "name-calling".

"Name-calling" only serves to maximize conflict between persons who are Victims of Racism [non-white people]. Therefore, when referring to speech and/or action that is characteristic of the definition of "Negress", it is correct to use the word that describes the **speech** and/or **action**. It is better to use words that describe the **actions of those people** rather than words that can more easily be considered as "name-calling".

It is better to make statements, utilizing words in a manner similar to the following:

(1) "She, apparently, has been chosen to perform as a **Negress".**

(2) "She is, apparently, being used to function in a **Negressive** manner".

(3) "It seems that the Powers That Be, have led her into a condition of **Negression".**

(4) "She has been **Negressed".]**

Negressed =
The condition resulting from the process of Negression.
[See: Negression].

Negression =
Any thought, speech, and/or action, that results in a Black, and/or non-white, female person, being "chosen" to function as a "special servant" to White Supremacy (Racism), particularly through acts of sexual intercourse, "sexual play", and/or other forms of misuse.
[See: Negressed].

Negressive =
(1) Thought, speech, and/or action in the manner of a Negress.

(2) Thought, speech, and/or action that is designed to result in the promotion or maintenance of White Supremacy (Racism).

Negro =
A term sometimes used by White Supremacists (Racists) as a "catch-all" identification for selected "Black"

people of various shades of "color", in order to designate them as being "especially adaptable" for service to White Supremacy (Racism), in the greatest variety of ways for the longest period of time.

Explanation:
Under White Supremacy, persons called "Negro" and/or "Negroid" are generally considered to be "more primitive", and less complex, than so-called "other" non-white people.

People called "Negro" and/or "Negroid" are usually judged to be easier to confuse, deceive, flatter, bribe, and/or subjugate, by those persons generally referred to as "White" and/or "Caucasian".

The terms Negro" and/or "Negroid" have sometimes been considered non-functional, except as tools of White Supremacists.

Negro Fun, and/or Niggerized Fun =
Anything said or done, by non-white people, under White Supremacy, that is for the purpose of "showing off" to each other, mistreating each other, and/or directly or indirectly "poking fun" at each others weaknesses and/or misfortunes.

Nigger =
Any "non-white" person who, directly or indirectly tolerates, submits to, and/or cooperates with, White Supremacy (Racism), in any form, in any areas of activity, including Economics, Education, Entertainment, Labor, Law, Politics, Religion, Sex, and/or War.

Niggered =
To exist, and/or to function in a "niggerized" condition.

Niggerization =
The process through which a non-white person thinks, speaks, and/or acts in a manner that directly or indirectly helps to establish, maintain, expand, and/or refine White Supremacy (Racism), in one or more areas of activity, including Economics, Education, Entertainment, Labor, Law, Politics, Religion, Sex, and/or War.

N

Niggerized =
The social, material, physical, and/or mental condition of a non-white person, while he or she exists in subjugation to any persons [white], who practice White Supremacy (Racism), either directly or indirectly, in any one or more areas of activity, including Economics, Education, Entertainment, Labor, Law, Politics, Religion, Sex, and/or War.

Niggerized Name =
Any name, and/or title of identification, used by a **non**-white person, that was **directly** or **indirectly** given to that person by one or more white persons, during the existence of White Supremacy (Racism).

Niggerized "Power" =
Anything said or done by a non-white person, during the existence of White Supremacy (Racism) that directly or indirectly helps to maintain, expand, and/or refine White Supremacy.

Nine Major Areas of People Activity, The =
(1) Economics
(2) Education
(3) Entertainment
(4) Labor
(5) Law
(6) Politics [relations between people]
(7) Religion
(8) Sex [male/female relations]
(9) War

Non-American =
(1) Any person who **does not** speak and act as an American.

(2) Any person who **does not** speak and act **justly** and **correctly** at **all** times, in **all** places, in **all** areas of activity, including Economics, Education, Entertainment, Labor, Law, Politics, Religion, Sex, and War.

(3) Any person who practices, supports, and/or promotes White Supremacy (Racism) either **directly** or **indirectly, intentionally** or **unintentionally.**

(4) Any person who does or says anything that is false, and/or who does or says anything that directly or indirectly helps to promote **injustice** or **incorrectness** at **any** time, in **any** place, in **any** area of activity, including Economics, Education, Entertainment, Labor, Law, Politics, Religion, Sex, and/or War.

Non-Color People =
People who function as, and/or who are generally called "White" and/or "Caucasian".

Non-Existence =
Non-Function, and/or the absence of "function".

Non-Human Being =
Any person in the known universe, who for any reason, does not practice justice and correctness at **all** times, in **all** places, in **all** areas of activity, including Economics, Education, Entertainment, Labor, Law, Politics, Religion, Sex and War.

Non-Justice =
(1) Imbalance between people.

(2) The existence of White Supremacy (Racism).

Non-Justice, The Masters Of =
All persons [white], who practice White Supremacy (Racism).

Non-Just People =
(1) Any people who exist during a period when injustice exists any place in the known universe.

(2) All of the people now existing in the known universe.

Non-Just War =
(1) Any thought, speech, silence, action, and/or inaction that functions against the **use** of truth, in a manner that promotes justice and/or correctness.

(2) Any thought, speech, silence, action, and/or inaction used to promote falsehood, non-justice, and/or incorrectness.

(3) Any thought, speech, silence, action, and/or inaction, that helps to establish, maintain, expand, and/or refine, the practice of White Supremacy (Racism).

N

"Non-Organized" Unification =
Two or more persons, thinking, speaking, and/or acting, in a **prescribed** manner, to accomplish the **same basic objective,** but, with each person functioning independently of the other, as regards the time, and/or place of any particular speech, and/or action, chosen.

Example:
The United-Independent Compensatory Code/System/Concept [for Victims of White Supremacy].

Non-Poor Person =
Any person classified as "white", during any socio-material condition dominated by White Supremacy (Racism).

Explanation:
White Supremacy (Racism) is a socio-material system established for the so-called "benefit" of white people.

Therefore, as long as White Supremacy is the **dominant** motivating force, by people, among the people of the known universe, no white person can be correctly called "poor".

A white person who **appears** to be "poor" is still not "poor", in comparison to the many ways that a **non**-white person is "poor", during the existence of White Supremacy.

Non-Racists =
(1) Those persons [white], who **do not** practice White Supremacy (Racism), at **any** time, in **any** place, in **any** area of activity, including Economics, Education, Entertainment, Labor, Law, Politics, Religion, Sex, and/or War.

(2) All people [non-white] who exist in direct, or indirect, subjugation to White Supremacy (Racism).

"Non-White" People =
(1) A "catch-all" term **maliciously** used by White Supremacists (Racists) to identify **all** people who **are not** classified as "White", and/or, who are not to be permitted to generally function as "white" people function in any one, or more, areas of activity.

(2) Any people, classified [by white people] as "black", "brown", "red", "yellow", "tan", and/or "non-white", and/or, who are regarded as such, or treated as such, and/or, subjugated because of factors associated with such classification.

(3) Any people, who are generally, or specifically considered to be "not white" by those people who consider **themselves** to be "white", and who practice White Supremacy (Racism) on the basis of that consideration.

Explanation:
The people of the known universe who call themselves "white people", call all other people "**non**-white".

Since the classification term "non-white people" **is not** the **opposite** of the classification term "white people", the two terms are, therefore, **not of equal value.**

The classification term that is the **opposite** of the classification term "white people", is the classification term "Black people".

"Black" people are "black" people.

"White" people are "white" people.

"White" people are also people who are "non-black".

"Black" people are also people who are "non-white".

"Brown", "Red", "Tan", and "Yellow" people are "shades" of "Black" people.

Non-Truth =
(1) That which **is not**.

(2) That which does not exist.

"Number One" [Racial] =
Any white person who practices White Supremacy (Racism).

Explanation:
The white people who practice White Supremacy (Racism) are the **smartest** and **most powerful**

people in the known universe. They are "first" [number one] in knowledge, and "first" in **direct** power by people, over **all** people classified as "non-white", in **all** areas of activity by people, including Economics, Education, Entertainment, Labor, Law, Politics, Religion, Sex, and War.

O

Official and/or Master Lynch Force =
Any one or more **white** persons who speak and/or act in any manner that directly or indirectly helps to establish, maintain, expand, and/or refine White Supremacy (Racism).

"Old" Person =
(1) Any person who **loses** the **will** to think, speak, and/or act, to find truth, and to use truth to produce justice and correctness.

(2) Any person who **loses** the **will** to think, speak, and/or act to eliminate Racism (White Supremacy).

"Open-Airism", and/or "Universalism" =
A method of thinking, speaking, and acting, according to a "code" that includes **all** areas of activity — Economics, Education, Entertainment, Labor, Law, Politics, Religion, Sex, and War.

This "code" is made to function by an individual person who chooses to use one or more parts of the "code", at a time, place, and under those specific conditions that he or she thinks best.

"Open-Airism", and/or "Universalism", means that each person functions as an "organization" unto him or her self. "Open-Airism", and/or "Universalism" means that each person is his or her own "leader", as well as his or her own "follower", in the use of what he or she chooses to select from a "code" of behavior that he or she uses as a basic guide. He or she, through that "code", seeks to function as an "organized" and/or "unified" body.

Example:
The United-Independent Compensatory Code/System/Concept.

This "code" is used by some persons as a means of attempting to compensate for the lack of ease, and/or ability, in "organizing" and/or maintaining a "formal group" that is **consistently** and **continuously** effective against the activities of the Racists (White Supremacists), and, is, at the same time, greatly resistant to those things said or done by Racists to resist the effects of the "code".

O

Oral Sex =
Any use of the lips or mouth, between **male** and **female**, as a means of expressing **affection**, or, as a means of expressing **contempt**.

"Organization" [The] =
(1) White Supremacists (Racists), collectively.

(2) The **sum total** of all **speech,** and all **action**, of all persons [white] in the known universe who practice White Supremacy (Racism).

Organized Crime =
White Supremacy (Racism).

Ownership =
Possession that is acquired by just and correct means.

P

Peace =

(1) **Truth**, plus **justice**, plus **correctness.**

(2) The universal non-existence of falsehood, non-justice, and incorrectness.

Pitful People, The =

(1) Any and all non-white people, during any period in which White Supremacy exists.

(2) Any and all people [non-white] who exist in direct or indirect subjugation to White Supremacy, in any area of activity.

Police Officer =

Any person who, speaks and acts to promote **justice** and **correctness** among **all** people, at **all** times, in **all** places, in **all** areas of activity, including Economics, Education, Entertainment, Labor, Law, Politics, Religion, Sex, and War.

Political =

Any relationship **between two or more persons,** at any time, in any place, in any one or more areas of activity, including Economics, Education, Entertainment, Labor, Law, Religion, Sex, and/or War.

Political Prisoner =

(1) Any person who is unjustly restricted.

(2) Any person who is **willfully and deliberately prevented**, by other persons, or by another person, from speaking and/or acting to promote **justice** and/or **correctness**, at any time, in any place, in any area of activity.

(3) Any person classified as "non-white" during the existence of White Supremacy (Racism).

Politics =

(1) **Any** and/or **all** relationships between people.

(2) Any relationship, in any area of activity, that one person has with another.

(3) Any thing that one person says or does, that affects what another person says or does.

P

Poor People =
Any and/or **all** non-white persons who, directly, or indirectly, exist in subjugation to White Supremacy (Racism) in any one, or more, areas of activity, including Economics, Education, Entertainment, Labor, Law, Politics, Religion, Sex, and/or War.

Pornography and/or Obscenity =
(1) Anything said or done that directly or indirectly helps to promote falsehood, non-justice, and/or incorrectness.

(2) Anything said or done that helps to establish, maintain, expand, and/or refine the practice of White Supremacy (Racism).

Possession =
Anything acquired, and/or retained by any means, and/or for any purpose, whether **just** or **non-just.**

Prejudice =
(1) To judge, before knowing and/or understanding the truth.

(2) To judge, without knowing and/or understanding the difference between **what is [true]**, and, **what is not [non-true].**

Primitive =
Knowing and/or understanding **comparatively** little about **all**, or **most**, of the major areas of activity, including the areas of Economics, Education, Entertainment, Labor, Law, Politics, Religion, Sex, and/or War.

Example:
In any socio-material system dominated by White Supremacists (Racists), Black people are "primitive" when compared to the White Supremacists who dominate them.

Primitive People [Racial] =
Non-white people [collectively], when compared to those white people [collectively], who practice White Supremacy (Racism).

P

Prisoner Of The War [Race Prisoner] =
Any non-white person while existing in direct, or indirect, subjugation to White Supremacy (Racism) in any one or more areas of activity.

Privilege, Correct =
The **will**, plus the **ability**, to seek truth, **and**, to use truth in such manner as to promote justice and correctness.

Property =
Those things that are acquired, and/or retained, only by **just** and **correct** means, and used only for just and correct **purposes**.

Prostitution =
(1) Use of a person's mind or body for purposes **other than** promotion of justice and correctness.

(2) Sexual intercourse, and/or "sexual play" between a white person, and a non-white person, under social and/or material conditions directly or indirectly dominated by White Supremacists (Racists).

(3) Submission to, and/or cooperation with, White Supremacy (Racism), in any one, or more, areas of activity.

R

Race, and/or Racism =

(1) A system of thought, speech, and action, operated by people who classify themselves as "white", and who use deceit, violence, and/or the threat of violence, to subjugate, use, and/or abuse people classified as "non-white", under conditions that promote the practice of falsehood, non-justice, and incorrectness, in one or more areas of activity, for the **ultimate purpose** of maintaining, expanding, and/or refining the practice of White Supremacy (Racism).

(2) Unjust speech, action, and/or inaction, based on the color, and/or non-color, of persons, and/or factors associated with, the color, and/or non-color, of persons.

(3) White Supremacy.

Race Possession =

Any person [non-white] who exists in direct, or in-direct, subjugation to Racism (White Supremacy), in any one or more areas of activity, including Economics, Education, Entertainment, Labor, Law, Politics, Religion, Sex, and/or War.

Race Tax =

A term referring to the condition under White Supremacy (Racism), that means that anything in the "possession" of **non**-white persons, is "worth" **less** than the **same** thing, when possessed by white persons.

Examples:

Houses, land, money, knowledge, ability, etc.

Race War =

Any speech and/or action, by any white person, that is **willful** and **deliberate**, and that **directly**, or **indirectly**, helps to establish, maintain, expand, and/or refine White Supremacy (Racism).

Racial =

(1) Anything said or done that involves **white** people, with **non-white** people, in social and/or material activities that are directly or indirectly dominated by White Supremacy (Racism).

(2) Anything said or done, by any person, in any place, in any area of activity, during any time that White Supremacy (Racism) exists.

(3) Any circumstance and/or event, that directly, or indirectly, is caused, or affected by the practice of Racism in any one or more areas of activity, including Economics, Education, Entertainment, Labor, Law, Politics, Religion, Sex, and/or War.

Racial Compensation =
The act, or acts, of using specific forms of thought, speech, and/or action, to make up for the practice of falsehood, non-justice, and/or incorrectness, directly or indirectly caused by, and/or promoted as, a result of, the establishment, maintenance, expansion, and/or refinement of White Supremacy (Racism).

Racial Compensationalism =
The **sum total** of all thought, speech, and/or action by the Victims of Racism (non-white people), that helps to use truth in such manner as to promote justice and correctness, and/or, that helps to promote thought, speech, and/or action to eliminate Racism (White Supremacy).
[Note: Also use "Racial Compensation"].

Racial Discrimination =
(1) Discrimination by a Racist against a Victim of Racism.

(2) Discrimination by a Victim of Racism against a Racist. **Counter-racial** discrimination.

Racial "Exhibits" =
Any and all non-white persons who are "selected", and/or greatly publicized, [usually by Racists], as "examples" of the way non-white persons should, or should not speak and/or act, while existing in subjugation to White Supremacy (Racism).

Racial Expert =
A person who **has proven** to all, that he or she knows **everything** about "Race" and/or "Racism", including how to practice it, and how to stop it from being practiced.

Racial Incident =
Any conflict between any **white** person, and any **non**-white person, in any situation that is directly or indirectly dominated by White Supremacy (Racism).

Racial Integration =
A very confusing term that consists of two words that contradict each other in meaning, and that is used to describe a "racial" practice that does not exist, and could not be described, recognized, and/or defined if it did exist.

Explanation:

(1) A "Race" is one or more persons who practice "Racism" — domination of others on the basis of "color".

(2) Any person who is a member of a "Race" practices "Racism".

(3) Any person who practices "Racism" is a **Racist.**

(4) A "Race" **cannot** "integrate".

(5) A "Racist" **cannot** "integrate" with a Victim of Racism.

(6) A person who practices Racial Subjugation **cannot** "integrate" with a person who is a Victim of Racial Subjugation.

(7) There is no such things as "Racial Integration". There is only **Racial Subjugation**, or, the **absence** of Racial Subjugation.

There is only Racism, **or**, the **absence** of Racism.

(8) To use the term "Racial Integration" is like using the terms "false truth", or "justifiable injustice", or "correct incorrectness", or "non-racial Racism, based on Race".

(9) **People** cannot "integrate". People can practice **justice** and **correctness**, or, they can practice **non-justice** and **incorrectness.**

R

Racial Mathematics =
The sum total of the direct and indirect effects of Racism on what people think, do, and say, at any time, in any place, in any one or more areas of activity.

Racial Name =
A name given to, and/or used by, a Victim of Racism (non-white person) that was directly or indirectly given to that Victim by a White Supremacist (Racist) for the purpose of helping to promote White Supremacy (Racism).

Racial Overtone, and/or Racial Undertone =
[A false and/or incorrect term].

Explanation:
There is no such thing as a racial "overtone" or a racial "undertone".

Example:
If an incident or situation is, in any way, directly or indirectly associated with, and/or affected by, the practice of Racism (White Supremacy), it is a **racial incident**.

Racial Plantationalism [Racism] =
The practice of White Supremacy, and the direct and indirect effects of the practice, on any one or more non-white persons, in any one or more areas of activity, including, Economics, Education, Entertainment, Labor, Law, Politics, Religion, Sex, and/or War.

Racial Prejudice =
[An incorrect term that should not be used to describe any condition].

Explanation:
To say that a person practices "racial **prejudice**" is confusing.

It is best, and correct, to say that a person practices **Racism.**

To exercise **prejudice** is to "judge" **before** knowing and/or understanding the **truth** about something or someone.

A Racist is **not** a person who is "prejudiced" against another person.

A Racist is **not**, necessarily, a person who doesn't know, and/or understand, the **truth** about their victims.

A Racist is a person who simply **intends** to subjugate, restrict, and/or mistreat, another person, on the basis of color and/or factors "associated with" color.

White Supremacists do not mistreat non-white people because they **lack** knowledge and/or understanding of them.

White Supremacists mistreat non-white people because they know and understand that they **want** to mistreat them. It is their **reason for existence.**

Racial Segregation =
[An incorrect term that should not be used to describe any condition. See: "Racial Subjugation", and/or "Racism"].

Racial Show-Offism =
(1) Saying or doing anything that helps a non-white person to **pretend** that he or she is no longer subject to the will of, White Supremacists (Racists), in any one, or more, areas of activity.

(2) Non-white people **bragging** about themselves, to each other, while existing in subjugation to White Supremacists.

(3) Non-white people **belitting** each other while existing in subjugation to White Supremacists.

Racial Subjugation =
(1) White Supremacy (Racism).

(2) Treating a person unjustly and/or incorrectly because of factors associated with the "color", and/or the "shade" of "color" of that person.

[**Note:** The term "racial subjugation" is sometimes **incorrectly** called, "racial **segregation"].**

Racial Subjugationist =
(1) A White Supremacist.

(2) A person who practices Racism (White Supremacy).

Racial Zeroism =
A term used in "Racist Mathematics", that means non-white persons, generally, are "worth" nothing (zero) of social or material value, **except** as subjects of, and servants to, the system of White Supremacy (Racism).

Racism =
(1) The scientific practice of unjust subjugation, misuse, and/or abuse of persons classified as "non-white", by persons classified as "white", on the basis of color or non-color, and/or, on the basis of factors "associated with" color or non-color.

(2) White Supremacy.

[**Note:** It is incorrect to use the term "White Racism". To use this term is to imply that Racism exists in a form **other than** White Supremacy].

Racist =
(1) A white person who, directly or indirectly, speaks and/or acts, in a manner that helps to establish, maintain, expand, and/or refine, the practice of White Supremacy (Racism), at any time, in any place, in any one or more areas of activity, including Economics, Education, Entertainment, Labor, Law, Politics, Religion, Sex, and/or War.

(2) A White Supremacist.

(3) A person [white] who practices White Supremacy (Racism).

(4) Any white person, who is mentally or physically **able** to speak, and/or act, to eliminate White Supremacy, but who does not do so.

R

Racist Family, The [and/or Racist Tribe, The] = White Supremacists, collectively.

Racist Law =
(1) Anything said or done by a Racist.

(2) Anything said or done that results in the establishment, maintenance, expansion, and/or refinement of Racism (White Supremacy) in any one or more areas of activity, including Economics, Education, Entertainment, Labor, Law, Politics, Religion, Sex and/or War.

Racist Organization, The =
(1) The sum total of all speech and action by all persons [white] who practice White Supremacy (Racism).

(2) White Supremacists, collectively.

Racist Suspect, and/or Suspected Racist =
(1) Any person classified as "white", and/or "Caucasian", who exists any place in the known universe, at the **same** time that any person classified as "non-white" exists, and functions, in direct or indirect subjugation to persons who practice White Supremacy (Racism).

(2) Any person classified as "white", and/or "Caucasian", who exists, and/or who **had existed**, during a time when White Supremacy (Racism) is, and/or was, practiced among the people of the known universe.

(3) Any person classified as "white", and/or "Caucasian", who, during any socio-material condition dominated by White Supremacists (Racists), **has not proven**, by both word, and deed, to the Victims of White Supremacy (non-white people), that he, or she, **is not** a White Supremacists.

(4) Any person classified as, and/or generally functioning as, "white", and/or "Caucasian", who is suspected of practicing Racism (White Supremacy), by any person who is "non-white".

(5) Any white person who receives social and/or material "benefits" as a direct or indirect result of White Supremacy (Racism), but, who does not utilize **all** of those social and/or material "benefits" to help to eliminate White Supremacy.

(6) Any person classified as "white" and/or "Caucasian", who, during any socio-material condition dominated by White Supremacy (Racism), **attempts** to engage in any form of sexual intercourse, and/or "sexual play", with any non-white person.

Rape =

(1) Robbing or despoiling a person.

(2) Causing a person to dislocate by using unjust force, and/or threats of death, discomfort, or deprivation.

(3) Sexual intercourse "with" (against) a person through the use of deceit, violence, and/or the threat of violence.

(4) Sexual intercourse "with" (against) a person through the use of false promises.

(5) Sexual intercourse "with" (against) a person by deliberately taking advantage of his or her lack of knowledge and understanding of truth, justice, and/or incorrectness.

(6) Sexual intercourse "with" (against) a person by offering "material benefits" to that person.

(7) Sexual intercourse "with" (against) a person for purposes of gaining "material benefits" from that person.

(8) Sexual intercourse as a result of bribery.

(9) **Anti**-sexual acts, by a person "with" (against) a person of the **same** sex, and/or "with" (against) a dog, cow, horse, sheep, etc.

(10) Sexual intercourse between a white person, and a non-white person, under social and/or material conditions dominated by White Supremacy (Racism).*

[***Note**: A **white** person who willfully and deliberately engages in sexual intercourse, with a **non**-white person, under conditions dominated by White Supremacy (Racism), is guilty of doing **violence** to both the mind and the body of that person.

A **non**-white person who willfully and deliberately engages in sexual intercourse with a white person, under conditions dominated by White Supremacy (Racism) is **acutely insane** and his or her condition of insanity is being **racially** exploited].

Refined Racism
Racism (White Supremacy) that is practiced in a manner that is so **deceptive**, and/or so "appealing", that it is generally acceptable, and/or very pleasing to the victims of it [non-white people].

Refined Racist =
A person [white], who practices Racism (White Supremacy) in a manner that is so **deceptive**, and/or so "appealing", that it is generally acceptable, and/or very pleasing to the victims of it.

Religion =
(1) The **sum total** of **everything** that a person **thinks**, plus, everything that he or she **says**, plus, everything that he or she **does**.

(2) Believing that everything that is done, should be done to accomplish **one basic purpose**, plus, at all times openly letting others know that everything should be done to accomplish that **one basic purpose**, plus at all times, speaking and acting to accomplish that **one basic purpose**.

Religious Person =
A person who thinks, speaks, and acts according to the "requirements" of a particular religion, and who does so, at all times, in all places, in all areas of activity, including Economics, Education, Entertainment, Labor, Law, Politics, Sex, and War, as well as in relationship to religion as practiced by others.

Respect =
The **process** of **seeking** to know and understand **all** that is not known and understood.

Explanation:
Respect is not something that one "has", as much as it is something that one **does**. Respect is something that one **participates** in.

Reverse Racial Discrimination =
(1) A meaningless, and/or confusing term ofttimes used by White Supremacists (Racists) to **pretend** that white people are the victims of Black Supremacy. Such pretending is, in turn, used as an excuse to refuse to compensate for the practice of White Supremacy (Racism) in one, or all areas of activity, including Economics, Education, Entertainment, Labor, Law, Politics, Religion, Sex, and/or War.

(2) A **non-existent** form of racial discrimination.

Explanation:
There exist only **two** forms of racial discrimination [Racism/anti-Racism] among the people of the known universe:

(1) White Supremacy (Racism) over, and/or against, non-white people, and/or

(2) Counter-action [compensatory action] against White Supremacy by the **Victims of White Supremacy** [non-white people].

Rich Person =
Any person who knows and understands **truth**, and, who **has used** his or her knowledge and understanding in a manner that **has produced** justice and correctness at **all** times, in **all** places, in **all** areas of activity.

[**Note**: There is no "rich person" in the known universe].

S

Sane Person =

A person who has found truth, who knows and understands truth, and who uses truth in such manner as to **produce** justice, and correctness, at **all** times, in **all** places, in **all** areas of activity, including Economics, Education, Entertainment, Labor, Law, Politics, Religion, Sex, and War.

Note: It is not possible for a **sane** person to exist in the known universe, and at the same time, **practice**, or **tolerate** the **existence** of falsehood, non-justice, or incorrectness in **any** area of activity.

Self-Respect =

Refusing to **lie** to oneself, and, letting **all** others know of that refusal.

Savage =

Any person who speaks and/or acts to promote falsehood, injustice, and/or incorrectness, in any area of activity, including Economics, Education, Entertainment, Labor, Law, Politics, Religion, Sex, and/or War.

Secret =

Information known only to **one** person.

Self Defense, and/or Self Preservation =

(1) To seek and find truth, and to use truth in such manner as to promote justice, and correctness, at **all** times in **all** places, in all areas of activity.

(2) To think, speak, and act to oppose falsehood, non-justice, and incorrectness, at **all** times, in **all** places, in **all** areas of activity.

Senile Person =

(1) A person who is extremely weak in effective activity.

(2) Any person who has little or no ability to cause, or assist in promoting significant **deliberate** harm to any other person.

S

Sexual Abuse =
Any relationship between a male and female in which any part of the body of either is used for an unjust and/or incorrect purpose that is **directly related to the sexual classification** of the male and/or female so used.

Sexual Communication =
Any speech and/or action between **male** and **female** based on the needs, and/or attraction, directly or indirectly motivated by the physical and/or mental qualities or differences between male and female.

Sexual Expression =
Any speech and/or action between male and female, that directly or indirectly involves the mention of, or the touching of the sex organs.

Sex (and/or Sexual Relations) =
Any direct relationship between **male** and **female**, usually, but not necessarily, including willful and deliberate physical contact, for purposes of comfort, communications, production of off-spring, etc.

Sexual Intercourse =
The insertion of the male penis into the female vagina.

Sexual Perversion =
(1) Any speech and/or action that causes, or promotes, **non**-constructive speech or action between male and female.

(2) Anything willfully and deliberately said or done by a male and female, in their relationship(s) with each other, that does not promote justice and/or correctness.

Sexual Play =
(1) Male and female speaking to, acting toward, and/or touching, one another, in such manner as to promote thoughts of sexual intercourse.

(2) Any contact between male and female that includes deliberately playful, and/or aggressive, touching of any part of the body of one by the other — particularly the touching of the vagina, penis, buttocks, mouth, breasts, hair, etc.

Sexual Politics =
Any deliberate relationship between male and female persons, based primarily on consideration of sexual differences, and which does, or does not, include sexual intercourse and/or "sexual play".

School =
(1) Any and/or all parts of the entire universe (and/or "university").

(2) The **sum total** of all that exists, and/or all that can exist.

(3) Any situation in which something can be learned.

Explanation:
Every person, animal, insect, etc., is in "school" **all** of the time.

Every situation, is a learning situation, as long as **everything** is not known or understood.

"Shadow" Fighting [Racial] =
Non-white people fighting **each other,** and/or blaming **each other** for the existence of White Supremacy (Racism), rather than speaking and/or acting to eliminate it.

Sin =
(1) Hypocrisy.

(2) **Pretending** to **believe** one thing while, in truth, believing another.

(3) **Pretending** to **say** or **do** one thing while, in truth, "saying" or **doing** something very different and/or contradictory.

Slave =
(1) A person who is dominated by any unjust and/or incorrect force.

(2) A person who lacks **both** the **will**, and the **ability**, to find truth, **and** to use truth in such manner as to produce justice and correctness, at **all** times, in **all** places, in **all** areas of activity, including Economics, Education, Entertainment, Labor, Law, Politics, Sex, and War.

Example:
All people who exist in subjugation to Racism [White Supremacy].

Slavery =
(1) Domination by any unjust, and/or incorrect force.

(2) The lack of **both** the **will**, and the **ability**, to find truth, and to use truth in such manner as to produce justice and correctness, at **all** times, in **all** places, in **all** areas of activity, including Economics, Education, Entertainment, Labor, Law, Politics, Religion, Sex, and War.

Explanation:
Every person in the known universe is a "slave" — at least to his or her own ignorance and/or weaknesses.

The slavery of Racism, however, is the most damaging **form** of injustice and incorrectness, that, also **could** be most easily avoided and/or eliminated.

It is a form of slavery in which **truth** is **deliberately** prevented from being used in a manner that would best promote justice and correctness among the people of the known universe in a relatively short span of time.

Smart People =
People who know how to do many things, with **great effect,** in **most,** or **all**, areas of activity, including Economics, Education, Entertainment, Labor, Law, Politics, Relgion, Sex, and/or War.

Smartest People [Collectively] =
White Supremacists (Racists).

Explanation:
Of all the people in the known universe, those people [white] who practice White Supremacy (Racism) are the **smartest.** They are the people who say and do the things that directly or indirectly have the **greatest effect** on what **all** people say, or do, in **all** areas of activity,

including Economics, Education, Entertainment, Labor, Law, Politics, Religion, Sex, and War.

Smartless People [Collectively] =
(1) Non-white people, generally, and/or collectively.

(2) All people [non-white] who exists in direct or indirect subjugation to Racists (White Supremacists).

(3) The people of the known universe who are classified as "non-white", when they are compared, both collectively and functionally, with the people of the known universe who are classified as "white".

(4) People who are **less** "smart" than people who are "smart", and/or people who are **less** smart than people who are the **smartest.**

[See: "Smart People", and "Smartest People**].**

Socio-Economic =
A term generally referring to any speech, action, and/or inaction that affects any or all parts of any persons existence.

[Note: A **better** term than "socio-economic" is the term "socio-material".

The word "economics" should be used to express only that speech or action that is just and correct in any one or more areas of activity].

Sophisticated =
Speaking, and/or acting, with greater **effect**, because of greater knowledge and understanding of what **is**, and what **is not.**

Soul =
(1) The **will**, plus, the **ability**, to think, speak, and act, to use truth in such manner as to produce justice and correctness.

(2) The **will**, plus, the ability of a Victim of Racism [non-white person] to eliminate Racism.

Soul Art =
Any speech, action, thing, etc. that helps to develop the **will**, plus the **ability**, to find truth, and to use truth in a manner that promotes justice and correctness.

S

Soul Food =

(1) Anything put into the body that **best** helps one to think, speak, and act in a manner that produces **justice** and **correctness.**

(2) Any **information** that **best** helps one to think, speak, and act in a manner that produces **justice** and **correctness.**

(3) Any food, drink, or information that **best** helps one to develop the **will** and the ability to eliminate Racism (White Supremacy).

Soul Music =

(1) Any words and/or sounds that **best** helps one to think, speak, and act in such manner as to produce **justice** and **correctness.**

(2) Any words and/or sounds that **best** helps one to think, speak, and act to eliminate Racism (White Supremacy).

Soweto =

Any place, and/or condition, where non-white persons are subject to White Supremacists (Racists).

Sowetoism =

Restriction and/or subjugation of non-white persons, by White Supremacists (Racists) for the purpose of establishing, maintaining, expanding, and/or refining White Supremacy (Racism).

Sowetoized =

A term used to describe the restricted, and/or subjugated condition of a non-white person, who is required to speak and/or act according to the will of White Supremacists (Racists), in any one or more areas of activity, including Economics, Education, Entertainment, Labor, Law, Politics, Religion, Sex, and/or War.

Space =

The **absence** of **time** and **deed.**

Standard-Universal War =

The basic-functional relationship between those who practice White Supremacy (Racism), and those who are the **victims** of the practice [non-white people].

S

State =
(1) A person.
(2) A basic condition.
(3) The status-quo.

Status-Quo =
White Supremacy (Racism), and/or injustice in general.

Student =
One who seeks to know, and/or understand.

Subversive Activity =
(1) Masterful, willful, and deliberate promotion of falsehood, non-justice, and/or incorrectness.

(2) Masterful, willful, and deliberate speech, action, and/or inaction in support of the establishment of, maintenance of, expansion of, and/or the refinement of, White Supremacy (Racism).

(3) White Supremacy (Racism).

Success =
The end of Racism (White Supremacy), and the use of truth, in such manner that justice and correctness is produced in all places, at all times, in all areas of activity, including, Economics, Education, Entertainment, Labor, Law, Politics, Religion, Sex, and War.

Superior Capitalists =
The White Supremacists (Racists), of the known universe, collectively.

Superior Communists =
The White Supremacists (Racists), of the known universe, collectively.

Superior Race =
(1) White Supremacists, collectively.

(2) The only "Race" of people in the known universe.

Supporter of the United-Independent Compensatory System =
(1) Any person, thing, etc., while speaking and/or acting to use truth in such manner as to promote justice and correctness.

(2) Any person, force, etc., **while** speaking and/or acting to promote the elimination of Racism (White Supremacy).

Suspected Racists =
[See: Racist Suspect].

System, The =
The sum total of all speech, and all action, by White Supremacists (Racists), that directly or indirectly dominates non-white people in any one or more areas of activity, including Economics, Education, Entertainment, Labor, Law, Politics, Religion, Sex, and/or War.

T

Terrorism =
(1) Causing extreme fear.

(2) One of the major products of the practice of White Supremacy (Racism).

The Crime of Crimes =
Racism (White Supremacy).

The People =
(1) Any people who **do not** practice Racism (White Supremacy).

(2) All people **other than** Racists (White Supremacists).

The Powers That Be =
The Collective power of the White Supremacists (Racists).

The Problem =
White Supremacy (Racism).

Time =
The absence of deed.

Tragic necessity =
The absolute **need** to kill and/or eliminate a person, animal, plant, insect, etc., in order to establish and/or maintain justice and/or correctness.

Truth =
That which is.

U

Un-American, and/or Non-American =

(1) Any person, during any period, that he or she is **not** speaking, and/or acting, in a manner that **produced** justice.

(2) Any speech, action, and/or inaction that directly or indirectly promotes non-justice.

(3) Any speech, action, and/or inaction that helps to establish, maintain, expand, and/or refine White Supremacy.

Uncle Tom =
Any non-white person, who directly or indirectly cooperates with White Supremacy, and/or with White Supremacists, at any time, in any place, in any area of activity, including Economics, Education, Entertainment, Labor, Law, Politics, Religion, Sex, and/or War.

[**Note:** It is unjust and incorrect to **ever** call **any** person an Uncle Tom if it is **not** a name that that person uses to identify himself. To do so constitutes "name-calling" and serves no constructive purpose].

Unimportant, and/or Wasted Time =

(1) Anything said or done that does not, directly, or indirectly, help to eliminate the practice of Racism (White Supremacy).

(2) Anything said or done that does not directly, or indirectly, help to promote justice, and/or correctness.

United-Independent Compensatory Code/System/Concept =
A term that means, when expressed in practice, the **sum total** of everything that is thought, said, or done, by one individual person [non-white], who is a Victim of Racism [Victim of White Supremacy] that is effective in helping to eliminate Racism (White Supremacy), and/or in helping to "make up" for the lack of justice and correctness, in any one or more areas of activity, including Economics, Education, Entertainment, Labor, Law, Politics, Religion, Sex, and/or War.

U

United States =
Any two or more persons who **willfully** and **deliberately** think, speak, and act to accomplish the **same basic purpose,** in **all** areas of activity, including Economics, Education, Entertainment, Labor, Law, Politics, Religion, Sex, and War.

United States [of/for] America/American(s) =
Any two or more persons who **have produced** justice, **and** correctness, **and**, who have eliminated falsehood non-justice, and incorrectness, in all that is said, and in all that is done, in all areas of activity, including Economics, Education, Entertainment, Labor, Law, Politics, Religion, Sex, and War.

[Note: The aforementioned is a **non**-existent person, people, condition, and/or practice].

United States [of/for] White Supremacy (Racism) =
(1) Any two or more white persons who think, speak any/or act in such manner that White Supremacy (Racism) is established, maintained, expanded, and/or refined in any one or more areas of activity, including Economics, Education, Entertainment, Labor, Law, Politics, Religion, Sex, and/or War.

(2) White Supremacists, collectively.

Universal Alien =
A White Supremacists (Racists).

Universal Color Conspiracy, and/or Universal Racist Conspiracy =
The **sum total** of **all** aspects of Racism, both known and unknown, both direct and indirect, as practiced against the non-white people of the known universe, by the White Supremacists (Racists) of the known universe.

Universal Color Conspirator =
(1) A White Supremacist (Racist).

(2) Any person [white] who practices Racism (White Supremacy) at any time, in any place, in any one or more areas of activity, including Economics, Education, Entertainment, Labor, Law, Politics Religion, Sex, and/or War.

U

Universal Language =
Death or suffering, and/or the ability to inflict death and/or suffering.

Universal Man, and/or Universal Woman =
Any male, and/or any female, person, who knows and understands **truth**, and, who has used that knowledge and understanding in a manner that **has produced** justice and correctness, in **all** places, in **all** areas of activity, including Economics, Education, Entertainment, Labor, Law, Politics, Religion, Sex, and War.

[**Synonyms:**
All/Man/All Woman
Correct Man/Correct Woman
Good Man/Good Woman
Holy Man/Holy Woman
Just Man/Just Woman
Life Man/Life Woman
Maximum Man/Maximum Woman
Peace Man/Peace Woman
Perfect Man/Perfect Woman
Total Man/Total Woman
Ultimate Man/Ultimate Woman
Whole Man/Whole Woman].

Universal Religion =
(1) The sum total of **truth, justice,** and **correctness.**

(2) Peace.

(3) The religion of religions.

(4) Ultimate religion.

(5) The religion of Universal Woman and Universal Man.

(6) The "unknown" and/or **non-practiced** religion.

Universal Subversive =
A White Supremacists (Racists).

"Universal" White Community =
(1) White Supremacists (Racists) collectively, plus, the sum total of all their speech and action that directly, or indirectly, helps to maintain, expand, and/or refine their "common" objective of promoting White Supremacy (Racism).

U

"Unreal" Realities =
A condition that seems to exist only in relationship to another condition, and/or, at the same time, seems to not exist at all.

Examples:

Death	Fear	Space
Deed	Hate	Time
Eternal Death	Life	Truth
Eternal Life	Love	
Existence	Motion	

V

Victim of Racism =
Any person who is racially classified as, and/or, who is generally considered to be, "black", "brown", "red", "yellow", and/or "non-white", and, who is, and/or has been, directly or indirectly dominated by White Supremacists (Racists).

Violence =
Any **unjust** and/or **incorrect harm** to a person, animal, thing, etc.

[**Note:** **Counter**-violence is any speech, and/or action used to **stop** a person, animal, etc. from doing unjust and/or incorrect harm].

W

War, Universal (and/or The War) =

(1) The **sum total** of all thought, speech, and action by those persons [white] in the known universe who practice White Supremacy (Racism).

(2) The practice of Racism (White Supremacy), and the **sum total** of it's effects in helping to promote falsehood, non-justice, and/or incorrectness.

Welfare Recipient [Racial] =

(1) Any non-white person, who, directly or indirectly, depends on Racists (White Supremacists) for anything received, in any one or more areas of activity, including Economics, Education, Entertainment, Labor, Law, Politics, Religion, Sex, and/or War.

(2) Any non-white person who is a Victim of White Supremacy, and who, at the same time, depends on the White Supremacists to provide him or her with social and/or material guidance or support.

Western Civilization =

[Note: It is best not to use this term because it is generally used in a manner that promotes more confusion than understanding.

There is no such condition as a "civilization", now in existence, any place in the known universe**]**.

Western World =

[Same as "Western Civilization" — is best not used because of it's unclear meaning].

White Authority =

White Supremacists (Racists), individually and/or collectively.

White Conservative =

A White person who says or does **anything** to establish, maintain, expand, and/or refine White Supremacy (Racism).

White Cult =

(1) The combination of all speech, and all action by those white persons who practice White Supremacy (Racism), in any one or more areas of activity.

(2) White culture.

White Culture =
White Supremacy.

"White" Family, The =
Two or more white people who practice White Supremacy (Racism).

Explanation:
As long as White Supremacy exists, it will, by the definition of it's existence, be the dominant motivating force among the people of the known universe.

This means that no other "family", of people, can exist, at the **same** time, that the "White Family" exists. The existence of the "White Family" cancels, and/or nullifies, the existence and/or function of all other so-called "families", "tribes", "political groups", etc.

The term "White Family" **always** refers to a **racial** purpose. The term always means, in function, two or more **white** persons who directly, or indirectly, speak, and/or act, in a manner that helps to maintain, expand, and/or refine the existence of White Supremacy (Racism).

As longs as White Supremacy (Racism) exists, the use of the term "family" can, truthfully, refer **only** to persons who practice White Supremacy (Racism). Any other so-called "families" of people do not exist, and, are in function, simply two or more persons who associate with each other on the basis of limited social and/or material interests.

Those white persons who **do not** practice White Supremacy **are not** members of the White Family, nor do they function as a "family" of any kind. They function as **infantile persons** — persons who, because of physical or mental limitations, are generally **incapable** of doing **deliberate** harm to others, on a significant scale.

White people can **choose** to be members of the White Family. An effective number of them **have chosen** to do so.

All other white persons have either chosen to function **against** the White Family (White Supremacists, collectively), **or**, they have been so infantile or senile that they were not physically or mentally able to make a choice.

As long as White Supremacy exists, **all** non-white people are subject to White Supremacy. Since all non-white people are subject to the White Supremacists (White Family), no non-white person can function as a member of **any** "family".

The existence of the superior power and purpose of the White Family automatically prohibits any non-white people from functioning as a "family". Two or more non-white people may **appear** to function as a family, but they cannot function as such as long as they are directly or indirectly subject to the White Family (White Supremacists, collectively).

No people can correctly call themselves "family", and, at the same time, be **subject** to a "family". Such persons, are **subjects** — not, "family".

[See: Family].

White "Land" Base, and/or Racist "Headquarters" =
The mind/brain/thought process/of each individual [white] person who practices White Supremacy (Racism).

White Liberal =
(1) A White person who speaks and/or acts to maintain, expand, and/or refine the practice of White Supremacy (Racism) by very skillfully **pretending not** to do so.

(2) A White Supremacists (Racist) greatly skilled in the use of deceit.

(3) A Racist (White Supremacists) who does not seek to eliminate Racism (White Supremacy), but, who only seeks to change it's form, in order to make it **more acceptable** to it's Victims.

White Man and/or White Woman =
When used with the **first letters capitalized**, the terms refer **only** to those white males and/or females

who practice White Supremacy (Racism).

[**Note:** It is best and less confusing to use the terms "Racist Man", "Racist Woman", and/or "White Supremacist(s)".

These terms are more descriptive than the broader terms "White Man", and/or "White Woman". The terms "Racist Man", "Racist Woman", and "White Supremacists" refer **exclusively** to those white people who practice Racism. The terms "White Man" or "White Woman" **may**, or **may not**. To avoid confusion, it is best not to use the terms "White Man" or "White Woman" to describe people who practice Racism. A person is **not necessarily** a Racist because he or she is "white"].

White Nation =
(1) Any one or more persons [white] who practice White Supremacy (Racism).

(2) The sum total of all speech and action by those persons [white] who practice White Supremacy, in any one or more areas of activity.

(3) White Supremacists, collectively.

"White Person" =
(1) Any person who considers him or her self as "white", **and,** who is considered as "white" by a substantial number of **other** persons who consider **themselves** as "white", and who generally function as "white" in all areas of activity.

(2) Any person "classified" as "white", and/or "Caucasian", and, who generally functions as a "white" person in his or her relationships with other "white" persons, and/or in his or her relationships with "non-white" persons.

(3) Any person **not** classified as "non-white", who **does not** consider him or her self as "non-white", and who generally does not "function" as a person who is considered to be, and/or who has been "classified" as "**non**-white".

(4) Any person who is "classified" as, and/or who is generally "accepted" as a "white" person by other people who are also classified as, and/or generally "accepted" as "white".

White Race (and/or, Racist Organization) =
(1) The only "Race" (Racists) in the known universe.

(2) White Supremacists (Racists), collectively.

[**Note:** To avoid, and/or minimize confusion, this term should **not** be used. The **best** terms to use are as follows:

Race Nation
Racists
Racist Nation
White Nation
White Supremacists].

"White" Racism =
The **only** "Racism" in existence.

[**Explanation:** White Supremacists (Racists) are the only people in the known universe who actually **practice** "effective" RAcism. As long as White Supremacy exists, no other "Racism" **can** exists. The term **"White" Racism** should not be used as long as White Supremacy is the dominant socio-material force among the people of the known universe. The term **"White" Racism** implies that there exist some other form of Racism. For that reason, **the term should not be used.**

"Racism", functionally, **is** White Supremacy, and White Supremacy is Racism. A Racist is a White Supremacist, and a White Supremacist is a Racist.

As long as White Supremacy exists, **all** Racists are "white" people, but, all "white" people may, or may not, be Racists.

As long as White Supremacy exists, no non-white person can function as a Racist. No non-white person can be a Racist while existing in subjugation to White Supremacy. It is not possible for a person to be a Victim of Racism, and be a Racist, at the same time. One who is a prisoner is not the same as one who is a Prison Master.

Non-white Supremacy does not exist.
White Supremacy does exist.

White Supremacist =
A White person who directly, or indirectly, helps to establish, maintain, expand, and/or refine the subjugation of one or more "non-white" persons, on the basis of "color", and/or factors "associated with" color, for the basic purpose of "pleasing" and/or serving any, or **all** "white" persons, at **all** times, in **all** areas of activity, including Economics, Education, Entertainment, Labor, Law, Politics, Religion, Sex, and War.

White Supremacy =
(1) The direct or indirect subjugation of **all** "non-white" people by white people, for the basic purpose of "pleasing" and/or serving any or all "white" persons, at **all** times, in **all** places, in **all** areas of activity, including Economics, Education, Entertainment, Labor, Law, Politics, Religion, Sex, and War.

(2) The only functional Racism, in existence, among the people of the known universe, that is based on "color" and/or "anti-color" in the physical make-up or physical appearance of persons.

(3) Racism "for the sake of" Racism.

Wise =
Knowing and understanding truth, and using truth, at all times, in a manner that produces justice, and correctness, in **all** areas of activity, including Economics, Education, Entertainment, Labor, Law, Politics, Religion, Sex, and War.

Wise Person =
(1) A person who knows and understands **all** that needs to be known and understood, and who **has produced** justice and correctness in **all** places, in **all** areas of activity.

(2) A person who has used **truth** in a manner that **has produced** justice and correctness in **all** places, in **all** areas of activity, including Economics, Education, Entertainment, Labor, Law, Politics, Religion, Sex, and War.

W

Woman =

(1) Any **female** person who is classified as "white", who is generally "accepted" as "white", and who generally functions as a "white" person in her relationships with other persons.

[**Explanation**:
In a socio-material system dominated by White Supremacy (Racism), no female person who is not classified and accepted as "White" is allowed to function as a **woman**.

Under this condition, only "white" **females** are allowed to function as **women**, and only "white" males are allowed to function as **men**. Since White Supremacists (Racists) do not relate to non-white people as men and women, but as racial subjects and possessions, non-white males and females may **pretend** to be "men" and "women", but they are not allowed to **function** as men and women.

While subject to White Supremacy, non-white persons can only function as **male** or **female** subject persons — not **men**, and not **women**].

(2) Any **female** person classified as "non-white", who is **not** directly, or indirectly, dominated by, and/or subjected to, White Supremacy (Racism).

Worthless People, The =
Non-white people.

[**Explanation**:
All non-white people in the known universe exist in subjugation to the White Supremacists of the known universe. It is the White Supremacists who determine the "worth" of non-white people in comparison to the "worth" of white people.

Under White Supremacy, it is not possible for any non-white person to be equal to and/or, to be "worth more", than any white person, at the **same time** that that non-white person is subject to **White** Supremacy.

Therefore, if a non-white person cannot be equal to, and/or "worth more", than a white person, in a socio- material system dominated by White Supremacy (Racism), then it is **impossible** for that non-white person to be "worth" **other than** "less".

W

The fact that non-white people do exist in subjugation to White Supremacy makes them "worth" **less** to themselves than they are "worth" to the White Supremacists (Racists).

Their worthlessness is evident in all areas of activity, including Economics, Education, Entertainment, Labor, Law, Politics, Religion, Sex, and War.

Z

Zeroized, and/or Zeroistic, Behavior [Racial] = Anything said or done, and/or, anything not said or done, by a Victim of White Supremacy [non-white person], that directly or indirectly helps to maintain, expand, and/or refine the practice of White Supremacy (Racism), and/or, that directly or indirectly helps to promote falsehood, non-justice, and/or incorrectness.

Quotations For Thought, Speech, &/or Action

"Everything that a Racist (White Supremacist) says, and everything that he, or she, does, is intended to help establish, maintain, expand, and/or refine, the practice of Racism (White Supremacy)."

- 1971

"There are many problems in the known universe. But no major problem, in the relationships between the people of the known universe, can be eliminated; until Racism (White Supremacy) is eliminated."

- 1970

"Many 'white' people 'hate' 'black' people. Those 'white' people who 'hate' 'black' people do not 'hate' 'black' people because 'black' people are 'black'. They 'hate' 'black' people because 'white' people are not 'black'."

- 1964

"In racial matters, many 'look' but few 'see'. 'See' what? 'See' what they are 'looking' at."

- 1967

"Nothing has 'meaning', unless it has 'meaning' - if you get what I 'mean'."

- 1967

"The seeds of the destruction of Racism (White Supremacy) are implanted in the very existence of Racism itself."

- 1978

"As long as Racism (White Supremacy) exists, the only people in the known universe who are 'experts' on the practice of Racism are the Racists (White Supremacists) themselves."

- 1979

"The most important question in all 'racial matters' is 'Why?'-One should always ask it."

- 1962

Neely Fuller Jr.

▮ ABOUT THE WRITER/AUTHOR OF THIS BOOK ▮

I, Neely Fuller Jr. (1/0), the writer/author of this book, have been, like millions of others, a long-time Victim Of and Servant To, Racism (White Supremacy) in all areas of activity. My experiences, observations, and/or studies, have led me to believe the following:

▮ **Racism**, has done more to promote **non**-justice, than any other socio-material system known to have been produced, or supported, by the people of the known universe.

▮ **No major problem**, that exists **between the people** of the known universe, can be eliminated **until** Racism is eliminated.

▮ The fear, frustration, malice, and confusion, that is caused by Racism, retards or prevents all **constructive** activity between the people of the known universe.

▮ The **only** form of **functional** Racism that exists among the people of the known universe is "White Supremacy".

▮ The people who have the **ability** to eliminate Racism do not have the **will** to do so, and, the people who have the **will** to do so, do not have the **ability.**

▮ Regardless of all that has been said or done, the **quality** of the relationship(s) between white people and black people is, and has been, a **total disaster.**

▮ **Justice** is **better** than **Racism.**

▮ As long as Racism exists, anything said, or done, by people, that is **not intended** to help **eliminate Racism**, and to help **produce justice**, is a waste of time/energy.

▮ Each and every Victim of Racism should **minimize** the time and effort spent doing **anything** other than, thinking, speaking, and acting, in a manner that helps to eliminate Racism, and helps to establish justice. Each and every **person** should seek to do this, **every** day, in **every** area of activity, including, Economics, Education, Entertainment, Labor, Law, Politics, Religion, Sex, and War.